THE SOCIAL COST OF CHEAP FOOD

The Social Cost of Cheap Food

Labour and the Political Economy of Food Distribution in Britain, 1830–1914

SÉBASTIEN RIOUX

McGill-Queen's University Press
Montreal & Kingston · London · Chicago

ISBN 978-0-7735-5899-1 (cloth)
ISBN 978-0-7735-5900-4 (paper)
ISBN 978-0-7735-5957-8 (ePDF)
ISBN 978-0-7735-5958-5 (ePUB)

Legal deposit third quarter 2019
Bibliothèque nationale du Québec

Printed in Canada on acid-free paper that is 100% ancient forest free
(100% post-consumer recycled), processed chlorine free

This book has been published with the help of a grant from the
Canadian Federation for the Humanities and Social Sciences, through
the Awards to Scholarly Publications Program, using funds provided
by the Social Sciences and Humanities Research Council of Canada.

Funded by the   Financé par le
Government   gouvernement
of Canada   du Canada

Canada Council   Conseil des arts
for the Arts   du Canada

We acknowledge the support of the Canada Council for the Arts.

Nous remercions le Conseil des arts du Canada de son soutien.

Library and Archives Canada Cataloguing in Publication

Title: The social cost of cheap food : labour and the political economy
   of food distribution in Britain, 1830–1914 / Sébastien Rioux.
Names: Rioux, Sébastien, 1980– author.
Description: Includes bibliographical references and index.
Identifiers: Canadiana (print) 2019011536x | Canadiana (ebook) 201901
   15394 | ISBN 9780773558991 (hardcover) | ISBN 9780773559004
   (softcover) | ISBN 9780773559578 (ePDF) | ISBN 9780773559585 (ePUB)
Subjects: LCSH: Food industry and trade—Great Britain—History—
   19th century. | LCSH: Food industry and trade—Great Britain—
   History—20th century. | LCSH: Labor—Great Britain—History—19th
   century. | LCSH: Labor—Great Britain—History—20th century.
Classification: LCC HD9011.5 .R56 2019 | DDC 338.1/941—dc23

This book was typeset by True to Type in 10.5/13 Sabon

À mes parents,
Louise et Daniel

Contents

Tables

Acknowledgments

For their ongoing help and support, I owe a great debt of gratitude to Isabella Bakker, Jennifer Clapp, Stephen Gill, Genevieve LeBaron, Philip McMichael, and David McNally. I also benefitted immensely from conversations with Ian Bruff, Jamie Peck, Kendra Strauss, Cemal Burak Tansel, and Marcus Taylor. I am most grateful to the unwavering friendship of Maxime Bélanger, Thierry Drapeau, Frantz Gheller, Xavier Lafrance, Jonathan Martineau, Rémi St-Maur, and Michel Tétreault. I also want to thank James MacNevin and Kyla Madden, my editors at McGill-Queen's University Press, for their sound advice and steadfast commitment to this project. Special thanks to two outstanding reviewers for their help; they know who they are. This book would not have been possible without the intellectual contribution, dedication, and editorial skills of Sibel Ataoğul, whose love and patience made even the most difficult moments bearable. Finally, I want to thank my parents, Louise Tétreault and Daniel Rioux, and my sister, Élizabeth Rioux, for their encouragement throughout those years. For all their love and support, I dedicate this book to my parents.

THE SOCIAL COST OF CHEAP FOOD

Introduction

When the *Quarterly Review* published its volume of June to September 1854, it estimated the number of food distributors in London alone at over 100,000 persons. "The smooth working of this great distributive machine," it concluded, "is due to the principle of competition – that spring which so nicely adjusts all the varying conditions of life, and which, in serving itself, does the best possible service to the community at large."[1] Arguably, "this great distributive machine" must not have been so well adjusted if we consider the extent to which the rising political importance of the Fabian Society and the idea of municipal socialism were in large part founded upon the movement's continuous attack on the insufficiencies in food distribution infrastructures in the metropolis.[2] The journal's blind faith in the precepts of bourgeois political economy was just that, impervious to the reality of poverty, hunger, and precariousness within which were caught many actors in the food distribution sector. Yet, while the journal's ideological glasses masked the harsh economic reality of those toiling daily to provide the metropolis its food, it was right in recognizing their vital importance in giving "the best possible service to the community at large." Contemporaries were all too aware that food distribution was central to a market-dependent population.

In its classical formulation, political economy is the study of production and trade, and the ways in which they interact with government, law, and custom. Its focus on production and the commodification of land, labour, and money, while essential to understanding the ways in which societies produce and reproduce themselves across time and space, has nonetheless tended to obscure or downplay other spheres of economic activities or moments in the circuit of capital.

Political economists working on food have tended to derive the source of social change and transformation from dynamics pertaining to food production, including labour and agrarian relations, food sovereignty and the politics of food, land and resource dispossession, and the financialization of food and agriculture. Whereas political economy tends to problematize distribution as being the distribution of wealth among classes and social groups, the political economy of food in general and agrarian political economy in particular have tended to downplay the conceptual and historical importance of distribution in the food chain economy by overwhelmingly focusing on relations of production and, to a lesser extent, consumption patterns.

To the extent that transformations in the sphere of distribution are problematized and their consequences assessed for production and consumption, they tend to be portrayed as a new phenomenon following neoliberal restructuring.[3] While I fully agree that the rise of a corporate food regime registers a dramatic shift in world-scale agrifood relations, too narrow a focus on contemporary developments runs the risk of reproducing the unacknowledged historical importance of distribution within the food system, therefore suggesting that political economy's overemphasis on production was justified, at least until the neoliberal restructuring of the food system. The lack of theoretical and conceptual reflection on the role of distribution within political economy is puzzling given its historical importance in Britain, the cradle of the Industrial Revolution. As we shall see, distribution was not only a key dimension of the Victorian and Edwardian social, political, cultural, legal, and economic history; it was also central to debates, conversations, and concerns at the time.

By the 1830s Britain was rapidly transitioning from an agricultural society to an urban, industrial one. Improvements in communications, especially railways, accelerated the pace and scale of change, and contributed further to increasing the space between food production and consumption. Although greatly impressed by the changes in methods of production and the associated shifts in consumption, contemporaries were also fascinated and preoccupied by questions pertaining to the sphere of distribution. People's growing dependence on the market for their food supplies demanded an appropriate, thoroughly modern distributive system capable of ensuring the efficient circulation of goods in time and space. *The Social Cost of Cheap Food* is concerned with food distribution in modern Britain. Although many of the elements of modern distribution already existed by 1830, the year my study starts, it was after, between 1830 and 1914, that food distribution, in the context of rapid urbanization and industrialization and heightened retail competition, acquired its main characteristics: the development of labour- and capital-intensive methods of accumulation; the progressive flexibilization of labour; the rise of precarious employment and low wages; the growth of fraudulent practices; and the heightened dependence on self-exploitation and family labour. Most, if not all, of these characteristics continue to inform twenty-first-century food distribution dynamics. Understanding the political economy of food distribution in Britain between 1830 and 1914 is therefore key to teasing out the historical importance of distribution under capitalism as well as the elements of continuity and change characterizing the sector.

DISTRIBUTION: THE MISSING LINK

The period between 1830 and 1914 was characterized by a general shift away from producer-retailers and towards specialized distributive functions, notably through a more comprehensive division of labour. The emergence of a capitalist system of food distribution was premised upon the growing distance between farm and fork, which entailed the growing importance of the intermediary, the distinction of market functions between retailing and wholesaling, an expanded division of labour and deskilling, and the slow but constant transition towards a capital-intensive retail environment. To be sure, not all of these aspects were fully developed by 1914. The evolution of the food distribution system in Britain was anything but smooth: piecemeal in nature and regionally uneven, transformation in the distributive system entailed a dramatic reorganization of the space and interface between consumers and producers. But while food distribution remained firmly based on labour-intensive methods, the trend towards a more capital-intensive retail environment was clearly visible and accelerating. The result was the ongoing production of a social and economic environment increasingly characterized by the presence of retailers operating at radically different scales and commanding vastly different means. The changing reality of the food distribution system must therefore be analyzed through the dialectics between capital's search for distributive infrastructures that reduce distribution time and the complex social reality animating competing retail interests and labour-intensive methods.

Scholars and historians of nineteenth-century Britain have demonstrated that a substantial and sustained rise in the conditions of life of the British working class occurred after 1870. As historian Eric Hobsbawm puts it, the growth of the home market after 1870 was "due largely to a rise in the standard of living [owing] to cheaper food import."[4] Historian Roderick Floud also stresses the close connection between falling prices of food and rising imports, and Robert C. Allen shows that the stagnation in food supplies between 1770 and 1850 was not relieved until the 1870s, with the rise of international trade in food commodities.[5] For his part, economic historian Charles Feinstein demonstrates the impact of falling food prices after 1870 on rising real wages, thus confirming with greater details his contemporaries' understanding of the relationship between mass food imports, growing per capita food supplies, lower food prices, and rising real wages and standards of living.[6] For an undernourished nation who saw the opening of the reign of Queen Victoria marked by the "discovery" of the grim reality of deaths by starvation, and in a kingdom united by poverty and hunger and hardship, falling food prices from 1870 onwards constituted nothing short of a dietary revolution in working-class people's lives.

Of course, questions pertaining to well-being, standards of living, and social, material, and health improvements were not reducible to income structure and the proportion of the household budget dedicated to food. Major works and improvements in sanitation, clean water supply, working conditions, urban planning, political participation, and combinations thereof positively influenced rising standards in the second half of the nineteenth century.[7] Despite these important environmental changes in people's life experiences, however, there is no denying that underpinning major improvements in people's health were not only their ability to command a greater quantity of food commodities and a more varied diet from the 1870s onwards but also the dramatic changes in the quality of food itself, as shown by the decline of food adulteration. To be sure, the overall quantity of food consumed throughout the period under review remained insufficient, and there was still a substantial proportion of the population living a hand-to-mouth existence of chronic poverty and systemic undernourishment on the eve of the First World War. However, compared to the grim reality and intense sufferings that were commonplace during the middle decades of the nineteenth century, the British working class was healthier and much better fed by the early twentieth century.

Scholars have rightly stressed the importance of cheap food imports for rising real wages and working-class improvement. Yet their emphasis on real incomes and prices has tended to exclude from the analysis a critical investigation of the conditions that made cheap food possible in the context of rapid social and economic change and development. While I agree that cheap food imports was the main factor influencing rising real wages during the last quarter of the nineteenth century, it also feeds the tendency to equate the cheapening of food with something *external* to Britain. This tendency reduces the British food distribution system to a passive national container, that is, a mere transmission belt between the dynamic development of international food markets and the growing expansion of consumption demand, notably through the creation of new needs. It is the purpose of this book to demonstrate that the food distribution system was an active component of the political economy of food, channelling food commodities in time and space, mediating people's experience of food consumption, and reconciling the gap between production and social reproduction.

The main argument of *The Social Cost of Cheap Food* is that the production of cheap food was very much dependent upon specific social relations of distribution *internal* to Britain, which were essential to the realization of the potential for the mass of cheap food reaching its shores. In a capitalist society in which the vast majority of the population depends on the market to secure its reproduction, cheap food depends on a complex and comprehensive distributive system capable of moving great quantities of food commodities quickly and effectively across time, space, and scale. Food distribution must therefore be understood as part of a larger process of capital reproduction, which is premised upon the opening up of distributive activities to capital accumulation, both as a sphere of investment in its own right and through distributive technologies, institutional practices, and labour regimes dedicated to the acceleration of the turnover time of capital as a whole. This entails a distributive environment geared towards efficiency and velocity through retailing and wholesaling infrastructures as well as organizational methods and labour practices to enable food distribution on a mass scale. Systems of food distribution are essential to capitalist development and accumulation, and therefore vital for the emergence of a consumer society. The book does not undermine previous works on the history of retailing and the importance of cheap food imports; rather, it adds a new dimension by linking the two, arguing that the British distribution system was key to cheap food production.

By providing a comprehensive understanding of the pivotal importance of food distribution in Britain between 1830 and 1914, *The Social Cost of Cheap Food* makes two central claims. First, that economic development during this period was premised upon locking food distribution actors into growing insecurity and chronic poverty. As we shall see, cheap food production was achieved through the constitution of a food-related underclass in the distributive sector capable of delivering the means of subsistence cheaply. Second, and related to this, food distribution transformed the political economy of food in enabling rising real wages and working-class living standards. The socio-economic evolution of the main actors composing the distributive class in relation to each other, as well as the tensions and contradictions arising from the different yet overlapping political and economic geographies of distribution claimed by its different members, is key to an understanding of both the strategic role played by these actors and spaces in mediating British society's daily access to food and their changing social and economic status according to the working classes' shifting strategies of reproduction. I am therefore particularly – although not exclusively – interested in unearthing the social cost of cheap food in Britain. This can be done by emphasizing the living and working conditions of key actors in the food distribution sector, and by showing how rising living standards for the majority of working-class families were in part secured through the economic marginalization of those toiling daily to provide this market-dependent population its sustenance.

While the capacity to offer low prices was increasingly dependent upon the constitution of a capital-intensive environment based on the mass distribution of food, especially after 1880, one of the main purposes of this book is to demonstrate the extent to which labour-intensive methods remained the principal form of economic reproduction throughout the period under review. Cheap food production and rising real wages were thus based on retailers' chronic insecurity and precariousness. *The Social Cost of Cheap Food* is therefore an attempt to contribute to a new and more holistic understanding of the social, economic, and political role of food between 1830 and 1914. In analyzing the social relations of distribution in the period under review, I argue that these relations of distribution were essential to the realization of the potential for the mass of cheap food reaching its shores after 1870. The book highlights the commonality and diversity of experiences among different members of the distributive sector, problematizes how their social and political statuses were intimately linked to their economic condition as provider of food goods, and sheds light on the varied implications of different strategies of reproduction for national food security, socio-economic development, and labour practices. Finally, the book raises awareness of the vital importance of distribution as a sphere of economic activity for political economy analysis. In this respect, it aims to provide a rich case study demonstrating the mediating effects and wider implications of distribution for our understandings of capitalist developmental patterns and dynamics. By showing how the problematization of distribution modifies and enhances conceptualizations of change and economic development, my aim is to highlight what I consider to be a largely neglected sphere of political economy inquiry.

As we shall see, the close connection between food distribution and cheap food production was itself segmented into a series of specific dynamics related to actors and institutions. This book explores the uneven yet unified dynamics of the distribution sector in relation to broader social and economic developments. More specifically, it shows how the scalar transformation and spatial reorganization associated with cheaper food imports in the 1870s was followed by major changes in the dynamics of food distribution, including: (1) the transition from retail to wholesale public markets; (2) the growing number of street sellers and the consolidation of the sector as an economic refuge; (3) the shift in the economics of shopkeeping towards labour-intensive methods based on extended hours of work, unpaid overtime, the introduction of cheap labour, and unpaid family labour; and (4) the rise of capital-intensive ventures based on international sourcing, economies of scale, high turnovers, and low prices. Each contributed in unique ways to the production of cheap food, as they responded differently to economic competition.

THE POLITICAL ECONOMY OF FOOD DISTRIBUTION: LIMITS AND PROMISES

Social and economic historians have been particularly productive in contributing to our knowledge of food distribution. Food historians have shown the social and economic dimensions underlying the food sector. They have also emphasized cultural and structural changes in the perception of food commodities as well as the access to and the diversity thereof, thus problematizing the changing quality of food and highlighting structural transformations in the food industry.[8] Similarly, historians interested in living standards, as we shall see in the next chapter, have contributed greatly to our knowledge about food availability and variety, dietary changes, and people's ability to command greater or lesser quantities of food. While these two bodies of literature have analyzed food distribution only indirectly, a third one has studied it systematically by focusing on retailing organization infrastructures and innovations,[9] the development of specific consumption patterns in relation to the evolution and trajectory of the distributive environment,[10] and the spatial dynamics of food retailing within the rapidly changing urban environment of nineteenth-century industrial towns.[11] This literature has paid special attention to the inherently dynamic and changing nature of the distribution system, providing us with a rich corpus of historical research on the social, cultural, and economic dimension of food distribution in the wake of the Industrial Revolution.

Despite its key contributions and important insights for our understanding of the evolution of food retailing, however, the literature on British food distribution suffers from a certain number of shortcomings. First, it fails to highlight the importance of distribution as a sector of economic activity with broader implications for social change and economic development, and therefore does not appear to develop its historical insights into a broader theoretical and conceptual intervention about the political economy of distribution. The emphasis here is clearly on documenting the evolution of the food distribution sector, the result of which is a historically rich body of work that unfortunately has made little or no attempt to comprehend how it relates to wider dynamics of production and social reproduction. Second, the literature tends to focus almost exclusively on specific actors or spaces of distribution, studying either the evolution of shopkeepers,[12] or itinerant and street sellers,[13] or the marketplace,[14] or large-scale retailers in silos.[15] The outcome is a series of extremely well researched, yet disconnected vignettes speaking to the lack of an integrated, comparative approach capable of retrieving the broader dynamics underpinning their common evolution and specific developmental patterns.

Third, apart from rare exceptions, labour relations and working conditions in the distributive sector are virtually absent from this literature.[16] This, as we shall see at great length, is problematic not only because working conditions in food distribution remained precarious and highly exploitative throughout the period under review but also because it speaks to a certain tendency within the literature to equate capital's expansion with human progress and development. This explains why the literature has so far been comparatively biased towards the study of the political and organizational dimensions pertaining to the formal character of the distributive system. As Deborah Hodson notes: "the preoccupation of business historians and economists with innovation, growth and scale has focused work on the more obviously dynamic aspects of the retail sector: the multiplication of fixed shops and the rise of the department store."[17] One of the main goals of this book is to rescue the millions of street sellers, child labourers, shop assistants, blind-alley workers, and shopkeepers' relatives from what British historian Edward P. Thompson aptly calls "the enormous condescension of posterity."[18] Despite these different shortcomings, however, my debt to the numerous scholars and historians who have contributed to the literature on food distribution – be it directly or indirectly – will be evident throughout.

The Social Cost of Cheap Food is a historically and geographically informed argument about the importance of taking the political economy of food distribution seriously. It aims to contribute to our common knowledge by shedding new light on understudied aspects of the food distributive system. It offers a study of the evolution and dynamics of the British food distributive system and its impacts on the conditions of life of the working class through its ability to produce cheap food. Given the current state of scholarship on retailing and distribution, however, there are some significant gaps in our knowledge of the economics of food distribution, including the working conditions and living standards of those employed and self-employed in the sector. As a result, a comprehensive history of the close relationship between cheap food and spaces of distribution in the context of an emerging, British-centred international food regime has yet to be written. This book is a first step in this direction. My main concern is to provide a coherent framework and illuminating account of the centrality of food and its distribution for the British working class between 1830 and 1914, and to show the extent to which the production of cheap food, especially after 1870, rested on the constitution of a highly exploitative distributive environment geared towards the mass circulation of commodities in space.

STRCTURE OF THE BOOK

Chapter 1 provides a general overview of the period with the express purpose of situating food distribution within its proper social, historical, and political-economic context. It paints a broad canvas of the period's food relations and provides the necessary tools and historical context to situate the emergence of cheap food as a core economic, political, and social concern under capitalism. Situated within the longer crisis of agriculture that began ca.1760, the chapter provides a social and economic history of market dependency between 1830 and 1914, and problematizes the effects of the rescaling of the value of labour-power through the repeal of the Corn Laws in 1846. In this respect, it demonstrates not only the morbid effects of an expanding capitalist universe based on the increased distance between farm and fork but also the growing importance of food distribution as a dynamic, mediating interface between production and consumption. Cheaper food imports from the 1870s onwards reversed previous trends and contributed to rising living standards for the working class, notably by offering a greater quantity, quality, and variety of food. As we shall see, the shift from national to world agriculture did not address the fundamental contradiction between capital and labour so much as it displaced it spatially through policies oriented towards cheap food imports.

Chapter 2 analyzes the evolution of public markets and argues that the reorganization of the medieval marketplace along capitalist lines was one of the most important social, economic, and architectural transformations of Britain's urban environment during the nineteenth century. It shows that the constitution of the bourgeois urban hegemony was rooted in its capacity to gain political and economic control over the town's food supply in order to impose its spatial order over the flow of food commodities. I trace the origin of these changes over the control and organization of the urban environment in the evolution of the traditional marketplace and its redirection towards capitalist motives. The provisioning of sufficient market accommodations was key to the cheapening of food, and the ability of local authorities to link the provisioning of the marketplace with technologies of mass food circulation such as the railway became vital to supplying the town with the cheapest and most varied food commodities. The transformation of the marketplace into a rationally organized site geared towards the more efficient movement of food commodities in the distributive space was central to rearticulating food distribution in the context of growing urbanization. The ultimate evolutionary form of this transformation was the gradual alteration, particularly salient in larger towns from the 1870s onwards, of the social function of the marketplace from retailing to wholesaling.

Chapter 3 analyzes the role of costermongers, hawkers, and other street sellers in providing the working class with cheap food, the possibility of which I trace back to their chronic marginalization and precariousness. The ability of this class of retailers to sell cheaply the means of life and therefore to transfer the full benefits of cheap food directly to the working class was very much rooted in its own poverty and destitution. Street sellers were "walking contradictions" within the bourgeois distributive order. Indeed, they represented the most extreme exploitative form of capital's need to subject the distributive sphere to the dictates of accumulation. Their growing presence in the streets of Britain continuously undermined the idea of linear progress, and their portrayal by the elite as a threat to the social order remained a thin ideological veneer against the strong solvent that was their vital role in the daily functioning of capitalist social relations. Their economic importance was linked to their economic hardship and the ambiguity of their position within the urban environment. Low food prices after 1870 lowered barriers to entry, which was visible not only in the growing number of costermongers but also in the transformation of the trade from a largely hereditary occupation in the mid-1850s to an economic refuge by 1914.

Chapter 4 explores the contradiction wherein middle-class aspirations of independence from wage labour were perennially frustrated by the dynamics of capital itself, as embodied in the shopkeepers. It investigates the erosion of the shopkeeper's economic base and social status, further documenting how, following the flooding of the food markets with cheap imported goods in the 1870s, shopkeepers' strategies of social and economic reproduction in the context of cutthroat competition shifted from fraudulent practices (e.g., food adulteration, false weights and measures) to the extensive use of, and dependence upon, cheap and coercive forms of labour. While employers of labour increasingly survived by degrading labour conditions through long hours of work, unpaid overtime, the imposition of the living-in system, and the introduction of cheap juvenile and female labour, the economic redemption of domestic shops became ever more dependent on unpaid family labour and very long hours of work. For these proud members of the lower- and middle-class orders of society, the maintenance of their social status increasingly came to depend upon heightened exploitation and self-exploitation. Shopkeepers were often powerful members of their respective boroughs, and they sometimes used their influence to push local policies that would shield them from the worst effects of competition. Despite their political reach, however, shopkeepers proved unable to control the competitive environment after the 1870s, as mass imports of cheap food created new possibilities for the growth of large-scale retailers.

Chapter 5 documents the growing importance of large-scale retailers after 1860 through a study of the ascent of both the co-operative movement and multiple shops. It also demonstrates that their ability to offer cheap food was based on capital-intensive strategies of growth and labour-intensive methods of exploitation based on the flexibilization and overall degradation of the terms of employment. One important feature of these large-scale retailers was their active development towards vertical integration, which allowed for further economies of scale by the cutting out of the intermediaries. The increased capitalization of the distributive chain was nowhere better illustrated than in the mushrooming of small retail empires such as Lipton or Home and Colonial. Most important, this chapter highlights the extent to which the rise of large-scale retailers, although indicative of the vital role that the distribution system came to play in the politics of consumption, was premised upon regressive forms of employment. Although co-operative retail stores tended to offer comparatively better working conditions than did multiple shops, both remained dependent on cheap labour to the extent that labour relations in large-scale retailers before 1914 were not substantially better than they were in the rest of the food distribution sector.

Finally, the concluding chapter reflects on comparative lessons in light of my overarching arguments regarding the central role of food distribution in social change and development, and attempts to shed new light onto the historical subordination of the food distributive sector in the capitalist economy. It also reflects on the implications of the analysis for processes of capital accumulation, taking advantage of the opportunity to expand on the contemporary form and limits of these processes in light of my historical analysis. In so doing, I try to tease out insights and potential avenues for the constitution of a wider research agenda.

1

From National to
World Food Production

The first half of the 1830–1914 period was characterized by the
uninviting reality of dire poverty, uncontrolled urbanization, dilapidated dwellings, overcrowding, and endemic and epidemic diseases
secured by the lack of resistance of an underfed working-class population. Although there are very few signs that social inequalities
diminished between 1830 and 1914,[1] the second half of the period
was characterized by substantially higher living standards as working-
class people were increasingly capable of commanding access to a
greater quantity of goods. The rise of a genuine mass market in consumer goods and services for the working class, the consolidation of
a national market and the associated culture of consumerism that supported it, as well as the growing number of families who could afford
vacations and mass cultural events such as the music halls, cinemas,
and professional sports were signs of the profound social changes that
accompanied higher living standards.[2] By 1911, 55 percent of the English people could afford to visit the seaside on holidays.[3] Increasingly,
then, millions of working-class people were capable of pulling together two fundamental aspects of the consumerist culture typical of
advanced capitalist societies: time and money.

Food distribution does not happen in a vacuum. It is a key dimension in a chain linking food production, transportation, and consumption. The political economy of food distribution must therefore
be seen holistically, that is, in relation to other spheres or moments in
the space between farm and fork. While it is not the purpose of this
book to offer a thorough historical account of the production, transportation, and consumption of food in Britain ca.1830–1914, this
chapter provides a general overview situating the dynamics of food

distribution within their larger socio-spatial context. It delineates broader trends attached to, and problematizes key dimensions of, food relations in Britain. More generally, it seeks to recover the shifting spatial and scalar relations underpinning mass food distribution, notably through the gradual repositioning of food relations from the national to the international level.[4]

AGRARIAN CHANGE IN HISTORICAL PERSPECTIVE

Starting in the seventeenth century, England's first agricultural revolution was the result of profound societal transformations commonly associated with the enclosure movement. Changing agrarian class structures and new property relations led to profound transformations in land tenure and husbandry. Crop rotations, seed selection, livestock improvement, drainage, and the intensification of cultivation through the adoption of best practices of farm management and land use and organization also became part of an increasingly rationalized, market-oriented agrarian capitalist landscape. Mixed farming, which was at the core of this agrarian revolution, embodied this constant search for well-organized, integrated farming activities. The main goal of this closed circuit was to increase capital and labour productivity through enhanced management practices. Despite these achievements, however, these new techniques proved incapable of assuaging the hunger of a growing landless proletariat with nothing to sell but its capacity to work. It was in this context that the Corn Laws, which had regulated the import and export of grains for centuries, became politically important. Food prices, it was discovered, not only played an active role in the social and political life of Britain but also influenced the price of labour in fundamental ways. In this respect, the repeal of the Corn Laws in 1846 represented nothing short of the rescaling of the value of labour power at the international level.[5]

As Jason Moore explains, one of the key foundations of seventeenth- and eighteenth-century agrarian relations was its "'inner' conversion of nitrogen-rich pasture into arable land, opening a nitrogen frontier internal to England."[6] Evidence suggests that this inner frontier of agricultural productivity reached its peak in the middle decades of the eighteenth century, with stagnating crop yields growth per acre. Output per worker in agriculture and agricultural output per capita declined between 1750 and 1800, and daily calorie production per person decreased from 3,909 in 1750 to 1,970 in 1850, thus suggesting an agricultural sector unable to provide for the needs of a rapidly growing urban-based working class.[7] In the context of a declining rural population, capitalist farmers tended to adopt labour-intensive methods, with the result that annual working hours in agriculture increased dramatically between 1760 and 1830.[8] The willingness to enforce profit maximization through longer hours of work in the context of a declining agricultural labour force is indicative of British capitalism's opposition to moving "labor back into agriculture at the moment such labor supplies were most needed, to propel both the industrialization drive and to meet the manpower demands of the war."[9]

While Moore is certainly right to point out that North America would come to play a key role in presiding over the restoration of cheap food after 1815, as the breadbasket of capitalism slowly moved from Europe to North America, it was not until the 1870s that Britain started capturing the fruits of this expansive capitalist world-ecology. Meanwhile, the search for productivity growth and profit maximization in British agriculture led to what historian Francis M.L. Thompson calls the "second agricultural revolution," which took place from 1815 to 1880. Accentuating earlier trends, its essence lies in the fact "that it broke the closed-circuit system [of mixed farming] and made the operations of the farmer much more like those of the factory owner. In fact, farming moved from being an extractive industry … into being a manufacturing industry."[10] To a certain extent, stagnating per-acre-yield growth after 1750 already betrayed the limits and contradictions of the first agricultural revolution. Against Malthus's understanding of the gradual exhaustion of soil fertility as a natural, absolute limit to agricultural productivity, Scottish political economist James Anderson had argued that soil fertility was better understood as a socio-ecological process whose relative productivity varied according to the history of land use as well as farming practices and knowledge. In his opinion, soil exhaustion and declining soil fertility ca.1800 were the result of the growing division between town and country, which constituted a rupture in this closed system as natural sources of fertilizers escaped agricultural production.[11] As John Bellamy Foster explains, Anderson's views proved to be central to Karl Marx's concept of the "metabolic rift" as a rupture in nutrient cycling between town and country, with towns and cities becoming sinks for soil nutrients.[12]

According to Thompson, the importance of manures in the course of the second agricultural revolution has therefore less to do with the novelty of its use than with its reconstitution as a commodity. Rather than a recycled outcome internal to an ecologically integrated farming system, manures, especially after 1815, became an externally produced input in an agricultural production process geared towards profit maximization. Beyond the limits imposed by climate, managerial skills, and soil structure and nutrient composition, larger yields could be obtained through input-intensive farming practices, including the purchase of off-farm, nitrogen-, phosphate- and potassium-rich sources of fertilizers. For example, imports of bones rose from 4,400 tons in the first half of the 1820s to 86,690 tons in 1872–76, before declining to 66,830 in 1887–91. Similarly, net imports of guano, mostly from Peru, increased from 119,940 tons in 1843–46 to 209,460 tons in 1868–71.[13] What really changed the face of agriculture, however, were significant advances in chemistry, first through the production of phosphate-based fertilizer around 1850, and second with the development of synthetic nitrogen fertilizer at the beginning of the twentieth century.

Despite these efforts to conjure the centrifugal forces of the metabolic rift on the system of mixed farming, the main problem plaguing Britain after 1815 remained essentially the same as before, that is, the inability of British agriculture to meet the demands of a growing, market-dependent urban population. The widening gap between cheap labour and cheap food after 1750 was evidenced by stagnating and even declining real wages, rampant food adulteration, the employment of children, social and political unrests, and the filth and squalor and diseases associated with a rapidly expanding unplanned urban universe. Cheap labour in the absence of cheap food was therefore largely maintained by curtailing improvements in the condition of the working class. The growing divide between cheap labour and cheap food after 1750 showed capitalism's inability to secure cheap labour by driving down "the *system-wide* costs of reproducing labor-power."[14] Estimates suggest stagnating or declining per capita food supplies between 1770 and 1850, even after adding imports.[15] For a large segment of the population, then, daily calorie consumption declined steadily between 1750 and 1850.

The immiseration of the working class was such that the Speenhamland System of relief emerged in 1795 to grant assistance to the poor, especially in the south of England. According to Karl Polanyi, the system "introduced no less a social and economic innovation than the 'right to live,' and until abolished in 1834, it effectively prevented the establishment of a competitive labor market."[16] With the Representation of the People Act, 1832, granting seats to large cities that had mushroomed during the Industrial Revolution, the bourgeoisie's economic interests moved into Parliament with the act broadening the franchise's property qualification to include small landowners, tenant farmers, and shopkeepers. Within two years the Poor Law Amendment Act, 1834, was enacted, effectively enforcing the "liberty to die" over the "right to live" institutionalized under Speenhamland. In addition to imposing labour as the foundation of social reproduction, the 1834 reform elevated pauperism as the new social question of industrial capitalism.[17] As a mechanism to legally impose cheap labour in spite of the lack of cheap food, the 1834 reform reinforced the destructive tendency to pay labour power below its value.

The grim reality of industrial capitalism was visible in the mounting political tensions and social unrest plaguing Britain before 1850. The Captain Swing protests, food riots, the radicalism of Luddism, and the emergence of the Anti-Corn Law League and Chartism were some of the many political responses to the British working class's horrific living conditions. Their economic misery and social despair were extensively documented in Blue Books and countless other official and unofficial reports and statistical surveys decrying unsanitary urban environments and widespread poverty. The middle decades of the nineteenth century were also characterized by a dramatic rise in food adulteration and a growing number of cases of deaths by starvation and rickets.[18] Contemporary political economists Thomas R. Malthus, David Ricardo, Friedrich Engels, and Karl Marx, as well as novelists and social commentators Thomas Carlyle, Charles Dickens, Benjamin Disraeli, and Elizabeth Gaskell, entertained no doubt that underpinning the rise of industrial capitalism was the widespread pauperization of the masses. Living standards stagnated – and in many cases declined – between 1770 and 1850.[19]

Given that family budgets were often misleading and consumption statistics scarce, soon anthropometric historians realized that adult height, as a measure of completed growth, could be a replacement for nutritional status. Using military recruiting data, Roderick Floud, Kenneth Wachter, and Annabel Gregory's pioneering study reported a decline in the average height of successive birth cohorts of British army recruits between 1820 and 1840.[20] Paul Riggs upheld this conclusion in the case of Scottish men and women, and a study of English convict women transported to Australia between 1826 and 1840 revealed that average height and literacy rates fell for those who grew up as children or adolescents or both between 1795 and 1820.[21] Similarly, Paul Johnson and Stephen Nicholas concluded from criminal height records in England and Wales that a generalized decline in nutritional status took place in the 1840s and 1850s.[22] Overall, there is a broad agreement among anthropometric historians that the period from the early 1820s to the mid-1850s saw a net decline in the average height of the British population.

Mortality rate is another important biological indicator that can be used as an index of living standards. Edward A. Wrigley and Roger Schofield estimated that life expectancy at birth in England, which was about 36.1 years between 1757 and 1801, had increased to about 40 years in the mid-1820s, before stagnating until the 1870s.[23] Simon Szreter and Graham Mooney's most recent estimations of life expectancy at birth suggest a sharp deterioration during the second quarter of the nineteenth century, a prolonged period of stagnation during the 1850s and 1860s, and the beginning of improvement only in the 1870s.[24] Their findings are in line with local and regional studies.[25] Because it tends to capture environmental factors, wealth distribution between social classes, and the social impacts of urban disamenities on public health, infant mortality has also come to be considered a valuable biological indicator that can serve as an index of living standards.[26] For example, Paul Huck's study of nine parishes situated in the heartland of the industrial revolution – Handsworth, Walsall, West Bromwich, and Sedgeley in Staffordshire; Armley on the outskirts of Leeds in the West Riding; and Wigan, Great Harwood, Denton, and Ashton-under-Lyne in Lancashire – shows that infant mortality rose by 14 percent between 1813 and 1846.[27]

An assessment of these biological indicators confirms the low nutritional achievement of the British population in the first half of the nineteenth century, especially but not exclusively in the "cotton" northwest of England.[28] This is consistent with estimates that per capita consumption of tea, sugar, and tobacco more or less stagnated during the first half of the nineteenth century,[29] while beer and wine consumption per capita declined by 33 and 41 percent, respectively, during the same period.[30] While a turning point in living standards ca.1850 is more consistent with the social reality of capitalist devel-

Table 1.1
Life expectancy at birth and childhood mortality rate in England and Wales

	Life expectancy at birth				Childhood mortality rate (per 1,000 births)			
Decade	London	Large towns	Small towns	Rural	London	Large towns	Small towns	Rural
1841–50	36.7	32.0	36.0	44.0	317	341	310	252
1851–60	38.0	32.3	37.2	45.5	320	358	320	255
1861–70	37.7	33.0	38.0	46.5	323	355	310	248
1871–80	40.4	36.6	41.4	47.7	282	295	277	235
1881–90	42.6	39.0	44.0	51.0	265	269	249	205
1891–00	43.7	39.6	44.8	53.5	261	282	257	196
1901–10	49.4	46.3	50.5	56.5	201	219	198	173

Source: Woods, *Demography of Victorian England and Wales*, 369.

opment in Britain,[31] it was only with mass food imports after 1870 that real wages rose decisively and not until the 1890s – when the generation born in the 1870s came to adulthood – that rising standards of living materialized in a healthier and better-fed population (table 1.1).

DIETARY CHANGES AND THE BETTERMENT OF THE WORKING CLASS

Working class structure played a key role in dietary habits and changes. Representing about 80 percent of the population, the working class was hardly homogeneous, segmented as it was by incomes, social status, and culture. Before the Industrial Revolution, work traditionally fell into two basic categories: (1) skilled craftspeople who had learned a specialized craft through a long period of apprenticeship, and (2) unskilled labourers without formal training who had nothing to sell but their muscular strength. The arrival of the factory system created a new class of semi-skilled or less skilled workers for whom only a short period of training was necessary.[32] While skilled craftspeople, who represented from 10 to 15 percent of the working class, stood out with incomes of up to 50 shillings per week, semi-skilled workers generally earned between 25 and 35 shillings per week. Unskilled workers such as general labourers, navvies, domestic servants, and agricultural labourers formed a third segment of the working class, earning less than 25 shillings per week.[33] Although manual work from the late 1830s was often divided between skilled, semi-skilled, and unskilled labourers, with each group having its own internal hierarchy of incomes and social status, William Booth identified a fourth group – "the submerged tenth" – comprised of the unemployables, tramps, and the destitute.[34]

The restructuring of working-class occupations after 1850 – following the Second Industrial Revolution and the development of capital-intensive forms of production based on technological progress, improved manufacturing and production methods, and rising labour productivity – transformed semi-skilled workers into the largest single group. Its significance rested in the proportion of industrial workers such as machine operators engaged in better-paid jobs. Between 1881 and 1911, mining and quarrying grew from 4.6 percent to 7.2 percent of total wage earners, while employment in transport (e.g., railways, road, ships, canals, docks, messengers) increased from 7.6 percent to 10.1 percent during the same period. Profound mutations were developing in the manufacturing sector as well, which comprised about one-third of wage earners. Sectors like engineering, shipbuilding, pig iron, and manufactured iron and steel grew from about one-fourth to one-third of those employed in manufacturing, while the opposite trend occurred with regard to employment in textile industries. The number of workers in these new sectors doubled during the same period, while those employed in the old industries of textiles, clothing, and footwear remained roughly the same.[35]

Despite rising nominal wages in these more prosperous sectors during the 1860s and early 1870s, higher rents and food prices hindered these advances, preventing them from materializing into real gains. The cattle plague of 1865 further pressured an already inadequate food system, forcing up the prices of meat and milk.[36] When prices started to fall in 1873 following massive imports of cheap food, those who benefitted the most were precisely the skilled craftspeople, semiskilled operators, and those situated at the higher end of the unskilled occupations, all of whom experienced the benefits of rising real wages, the security and comfort of better nourishment, and growing purchasing power. "Meals are more regular. For dinner, meat and vegetables are demanded every day. Bacon, eggs and fish find their place at other times. Puddings and tarts are not uncommon, and bread ceases to be the staff of life … In this class no one goes short of food."[37]

For a hungry nation, the first outcome of rising real wages has always been the increased consumption of food.

Robert Giffen calculated that, between January 1873 and January 1879, the overall index of prices fell by 24 percent, with wheat and flour falling by up to 35 percent and 51 percent, respectively; beef of inferior quality by 26 percent, and sugar by 26 percent as well.[38] The reduction of the food bill would eventually reach 30 percent, as the index of food prices (1867–77 = 100) declined from 107 in 1873 to 94 in 1880 to 72 in 1888 to 62 in 1896, before settling at 77 in 1913.[39] It is hard to overestimate the importance of these changes on a population spending up to 70 percent of its total income on food. Perhaps one of the main indicators that growing segments of the working class were on the road to prosperity was the shrinking proportion of the food budget spent on bread. Bread, which took one-third of total expenditure on food in 1841, represented one-sixth in 1881 and continued to decline thereafter. The average price of the four-pound loaf of bread in London dropped from 10.75 pence in 1855 to 8 pence in 1870 to 5.08 pence in 1895.[40] "The important point is that while bread consumption had continued to rise to an estimated average of 270 lbs per year, it had, because of reduced cost, already ceased to be the article of primary food expenditure."[41] The increased consumption of bread and its declining share of the food budget tended to create new consumption capacities for "luxuries" such as cheese, butter, milk, and meat, thus marking the beginning of a process through which the luxuries of the previous generation became the food staples of the new one. For more and more people, then, bread had stopped being the meal itself.

With the price of bread declining, meat rapidly came to replace it as the main food expenditure. Sparked by the cattle plague of 1865, tinned meat from Australia soon reached the shores of England. Cheaper than butcher's meat, many still looked at it with suspicion, except the very poor who could not afford to be disdainful.[42] With developments in the means of transportation as well as the technologies of preservation, more meat at a better price became available to the working hands. Livestock and chilled beef imports from North America grew significantly from 1875 onwards, and from the early 1880s, with the development of refrigeration, imports of frozen beef and mutton from Argentina, Australia, and New Zealand rose sharply, pushing prices further down. Although bacon remained an important source of protein, other types of meat became accessible to all but the lowest-paid working classes. Even prime English beef and mutton fell respectively by 31 percent and 27 percent between 1873 and 1893.[43] One can appreciate the importance of falling meat prices through the parallel decline in poaching and game. In 1851, Mayhew estimated that, among others, 145,000 partridges, 107,000 snipes, 46,000 plovers, 313,000 larks, 33,000 widgeons, 102,000 hares, 860,000 rabbits, and 1,002,000 geese were sold annually in the streets of London.[44] His findings "implied that large-scale poaching was not merely a means of assuaging the hunger pangs of the rural poor but was organized on a commercial basis for the urban market."[45] The mass arrival of cheap food on the market seriously undermined the economic basis of poaching as well as other illicit practices such as food adulteration.[46]

Massive imports of meat in the 1870s dramatically transformed people's consumption. "Where one man ate meat 20 years ago," said Septimus Lambert Jr in 1877, a cattle salesman in Manchester, "I think 10 eat it now in Lancashire."[47] Average per capita consumption of meat per annum in the United Kingdom remained relatively stable between 1831 and 1870. From 86.8 pounds in the 1830s, it dropped to 82.5 pounds in the 1840s, before resuming its course at 87.3 and 90.0 pounds in the following two decades. It was not until the 1870s, when it reached about 110 pounds, that the consumption level finally departed from previous trends. Peaking at 132 pounds during the first half of the 1900s, meat consumption slightly declined to about 127 pounds during the decade preceding the First World War.[48] Meat consumption was heavily determined by class. For instance, artisans, mechanics, and labourers ate on average 107 pounds of meat per annum in 1903, compared with 122 pounds for the lower middle class, 182 pounds for the middle class, and 300 pounds for the upper middle class and upper class.[49] Similar trends were discernible for other food commodities as well, the upper class consuming on average three times more milk and butter than urban workers.[50] Moreover, food goods were unevenly distributed among the members of the household, with men obtaining almost systematically a greater quantity and variety of food of superior quality, often to the detriment of their wives and children.[51]

The high prices of milk, cheese, and meat in the 1860s had made it "a matter of certainty that only in homoeopathic doses can any of these luxuries reach the stomach of the father or mother of a family of the labouring class."[52] From the mid-1870s onwards, however, a whole series of previous luxuries become accessible. The consumption of milk, butter, and cocoa per person doubled, and eggs, fish, and fruit and vegetables also made important inroads. Historically, only skilled workers, artisans, and lower-middle-class people could afford to eat their midday meal at the tavern or at a cheap eating-house. Sign of the new prosperity, a growing number of workers were now relying on pubs, taverns, and food shops for their meals.[53] As new standards were slowly being established, others were firmly consolidated. Per capita consumption of tea more than tripled between 1850 and 1914, the consumption of tea per person per year rising from two to seven pounds.[54] Eggs, rarely eaten in the 1850s and 1860s, were obtained at the rate of forty-five per person per year in 1880 and 100 in 1913, and a trade in cracked eggs often flourished in poorer districts.[55] Fuelled by developments in trawling and transport technologies, the consumption of fish rose substantially, as demonstrated by the meteoric rise of the fish and chip shops.[56] For the majority of the working class earning between twenty-one and thirty shillings per week, declining food prices represented profound and positive dietary changes.

Stable at about eighteen pounds between 1820 and 1846, the consumption of sugar per person per year more than quadrupled over the next decades, peaking at ninety-one pounds in 1901 before settling down at eighty pounds in 1914.[57] The increasingly low cost of sugar was instrumental to the creation of a whole new variety of products. Sweetmeats, an obvious favourite of the children, was not an uncommon treat in working-class families. Ice cream, another sweet delicacy, found many obedient customers. Writing about the "street rarity of ice creams," which left the buyer confused as to "how the ice was to be swallowed," Mayhew noted that most customers in the mid-nineteenth century were gentlemen's servants, doctors' boys, women of the town, and what seemed like schoolboys. For one pence they could buy the famous "penny lick," a serving of ice cream in a small glass. New inroads in refrigeration pushed the trade to new heights after 1880 as ice cream became more easily transportable and storable.[58] Much more important to people's diets were two new products that appeared in the 1870s – condensed milk and jam. Condensed milk was comparatively cheap and its sweetness inhibited bacterial growth, a serious advantage given the lack of refrigeration in the home. Jam, which contained between 50 percent and 65 percent of its weight in sugar, was accessible to every pocketbook.[59] It was an instant success, leading many mothers to complain of their children's greater appetite for bread.

Jam quickly became "the backbone of the fruit industry," with the production of domestic fruits like cherries, plums, strawberries, and raspberries finding a ready market in the jam factories. For most urban dwellers, jam was the medium through which they ate their fruit.[60] While the popular belief that fruits were injurious to children's health often proved to be a cultural barrier to fruit consumption, the popularity of jam helped to develop a readier acceptance, as demonstrated in the increased consumption of grapes, oranges, bananas, gooseberries, currants, and prunes. Lower prices for fruit also triggered growing consumption as the vast majority of working-class people would have been unable to afford them before the 1870s. Oranges, still a novelty in the middle decades of the nineteenth century, were imported at the rate of 5 million hundredweight in 1900, averaging 14.7 pounds per person per year. Bananas, virtually unknown to the working classes at the last decades of the nineteenth century, were consumed at approximately nine per person per year in 1900–04 and twenty in 1909–13. Despite these changes, however, tasty novelties like melons, pineapples, pomegranates, and mangoes remained inaccessible.

In the middle decades of the nineteenth century, the diet of working-class families was starchy and monotonous in the extreme, made up almost entirely of bread, potatoes, butter, and bacon. As George Dodd wrote in the 1850s, fruit and vegetables were "secondary on the tables of the metropolis."[61] Overall, diets were short on vitamins A, C, and D; deficient in protein, fat, and energy; and low in calcium but high in carbohydrates and dietary fibre.[62] By 1914, however, the great majority of working-class dinner tables exposed a greater quantity, variety, and quality of foods. Diets were still stodgy, dull, and starchy, but there could be no comparison with the middle decades of the nineteenth century. This was all the more impressive given that the population of Britain almost doubled between 1851 and 1911, rising from about 18 million to over 36 million in England and Wales, and from 2.89 million to 4.75 million in Scotland.[63]

Based on the different household budgets of working-class families, some have concluded that, at the dawn of the twentieth century, widespread malnutrition and chronic undernourishment remained a reality for the majority.[64] While there is no doubt that hunger and starvation still existed in the early 1910s and that people living in chronic poverty constituted an important part of the population, there is also a risk in elevating these sociological surveys to the status of objective truth on dietary realities. To begin with, household budgets rarely "record[ed] consumption of alcoholic beverages and sweets, foods purchased and eaten away from home, foods eaten by visitors, nor the amount of food wasted."[65] Temperance propaganda and reformist attitudes did not invite confidence over drink expenditures and treats, and working-class families that meticulously kept track of their spending were rare. Because the vast majority of these surveys were based on oral interrogations, most were informed approximations over what housewives were ready to share. Conflicting class cultures also existed between social reformers and working-class people, such that suspicion existed on a large scale.[66] Household budgets were subject to be filled out with "selective omission of foods and practices that were likely to generate disapproval, especially alcohol of all kinds (after all, beer does have food value), and tasty treats cooked outside the home, such as fish and chips."[67] Too literal an interpretation would indeed make it difficult to explain the growth and strength of the food industry, including grocery stores and butchers, fishmongers, greengrocers, and confectioners shops.

THE RESCALING OF FOOD RELATIONS

The great "middle class agitation" of the late 1830s and early 1840s for the repeal of the protectionist Corn Laws did not have its promises immediately fulfilled. It took at least another thirty years for living standards to show any signs of improvement. After all, free trade policies could only do so much, and the diminution of tariffs on imported foodstuffs was no substitute for the productive and technological capacities needed to supply the needs of an increasingly urban population. In this respect, the repeal of the Corn Laws in 1846 had had no direct effects on the prices of wheat, and though greater quantities of it reached British ports, supply continued to run behind demand. Transportation technologies that would permit the vast movement of food commodities across oceans and continents were still in their infancy. Sustained capital investment in the built environment (e.g., roads, railways, canals, ports, steamships), both at home and abroad, prepared the groundwork for the development of international food markets. In was not until the 1870s, with the establishment of a comprehensive network of transport infrastructures, that the benefits of free trade policies, combined with imperial and colonial domination, were able to force the world to feed the British working class.

The British-centred international food regime was premised upon an increasingly sophisticated and spatially expansive international division of labour in the provisioning of key food commodities such as grains, meat, cheese, sugar, tea, oilseeds, and butter. As sociologist Philip McMichael notes, this period of food relations "combined colonial tropical imports to Europe with basic grains and livestock imports from settler colonies, provisioning emerging European industrial classes, and underwriting the British 'workshop of the world.'"[68] The rescaling of food relations at the international level is indeed a crucial aspect of the period's political geography as well as a key moment in the expansion and consolidation of capitalist social relations.[69] Notwithstanding the political and juridical importance of the 1846 repeal, key to the ability of the British government to assuage its hungry nation was the development of a vast, international network of infrastructures capable of transporting great quantities of food quickly and efficiently. The ability to connect foreign producers with national consumers required colossal investments in the built environment as well as the development of new technologies of transportation and communication.[70] While steamships, railways, telegraphs, the submarine cable, and the Suez Canal were many tools underpinning British imperial and colonial conquests,[71] they also served as the instruments through which the granaries of the world were transported to Britain.

By opening vast international and colonial spaces for capital accumulation through free trade policies, the imperial government gave the signal to an "investment rush" that was about to lastingly transform the capitalist space economy. British investments abroad rose from £195–230 million in 1855 to £700 million in 1870, before reaching £2,000 million in 1900 and about £3,750 million in 1913. Although there was some overlap, the geography of investments shifted from Europe and the Middle East before 1870 to Asia, Australasia, and North and South America after 1870. "By 1913, 65 percent of British investments were in newly settled countries, including the white settled colonies, but ranging far beyond them: over the period 1865–1914, roughly three-fifths of all the money raised in London went to foreign countries and two-fifths to the empire, with the centre of gravity in the latter area shifting steadily from India to the white colonies."[72] Not surprisingly in the context of an international economy based on free trade, railways were often the first choice of British investors, who understood all too well their vital importance in underpinning the international shipping industry by linking inland areas with ports.[73] Total railway mileage open in North America rose from 9,100 miles in 1850 to 100,600 miles in 1880,[74] and £404.5 million of the £1,179.9 million (34.3 percent) of British investment in Latin America were destined to railways, Argentina and Brazil capturing 62.2 percent of total investments.[75]

These investments were not only the necessary foundation upon which the mass import of cheap food that started in the 1870s would proceed but also the medium by which the world was gradually unified through a geographically uneven capitalist economy. The colonial excitement of *The Economist* in 1857 that British colonial railways in India would bring "English arts, English men and English opinions" no doubt was true, although it conveniently omitted to say that railways were also the vectors through which India's agricultural economy would be plundered, the sub-continent militarized, and capital investments secured.[76] As Indian historian Irfan Habib puts it, the development of railway systems during the second half of the nineteenth century "completed the 'colonization' of the Indian economy, pulling all its erstwhile isolated segments inside the net of British Free Trade."[77] From a geographical point of view, railways represented nothing short of a dramatic compression of space by time as resources from distant lands and regions, once difficult to access, became available to international capitalist markets.[78] The opening of the Suez Canal in November 1869 for international navigation further accelerated this process, bringing India even closer to imperial Britain.

Few technologies did more to organize the commercialization of agriculture than the railway as it introduced cash crops at the same time that it subjected farmers to "the expansive rhythms of the world reproduction-process of capital."[79] By 1910, £136.5 million had been invested in railways in India and Ceylon.[80] "All the money," one British official wrote, "came from the English capitalist and, so long as he was guaranteed five per cent on the revenues of India, it was immaterial to him whether the funds which he lent were thrown into the Hooghly [River] or converted into bricks and mortar."[81] Between 1849 and 1900, Rs.568 million were paid out to British investors from the Indian treasury.[82] The Government of India was in fact nothing but a gigantic wealth-sucking machine organized as an appendage to the British Treasury and actively working against the development of any industrial and commercial capacities on the sub-continent. Whether in the form of guaranteed returns on capital investments or by bleeding the country dry of its food for international markets, railways were the prime movers of this organized drain on India's wealth.[83]

At the end of these iron lines were ports, the immensity of the oceans lying in between them giving all its meaning to the word *trans*port. Ports were crucial nodal points in the global circulation of food commodities, connecting as they did the industrial efficiency of the railway with powerful merchant navies carrying the fruit of distant lands, including the colonial empire, back home.[84] The sailing ship, which was key to Britain's commercial, colonial, and imperial expansion from the sixteenth to the nineteenth century, simply could not bear the pace of industrial capitalism, although the transition "to the iron and steel cargo streamer was not completed for another three decades or more after 1850."[85] Cheaper freight rates, the completion of the Suez Canal in the late 1860s, and developments in refrigeration in the 1870s underpinned the dominance of the sailing ship until 1880 as it was able to increase its spatial reach while cutting navigation time. However, the mass production of goods and growing working-class consumption increased the need for faster and bigger ships. By the 1870s, it was obvious that the rapid expansion of world trade required a revolution in waterborne transportation. The steamship was the industrial response to an industrial problem: it was at once bigger and quicker than the sailing ship, and its self-propelling capacity made it more reliable as well. While the superiority of the steamship in the last quarter of the nineteenth century did not eliminate the sailing ship, it greatly marginalized its economic importance.

Sailing ships in the meat trade probably reached the limits of their technological development in the mid-1880s. The inability of British agriculture to match demand, largely the consequence of cattle disease, was visible in the decline of the number of United Kingdom food animals from 46.7 million in 1867 to 42.9 million in 1880.[86] The initial response was to import live cattle from Canada and the United States, the result of which was to start a regional shift in the structure of meat marketing. Up to the early 1870s, the Continent held a monopoly over the supply of foreign cattle, which reinforced the importance of Norfolk and Suffolk in the dead meat industry. By 1880, with the development of shipping technologies and the opening of new sources of supply, it was the ports of the west coast – principally those of Liverpool, Birkenhead, Holyhead, and Bristol – that received the bulk of the foreign meat.[87] New developments in chilling and freezing techniques further reinforced this spatial shift through large-scale imports of meat from Australia, New Zealand, and South America, principally from Argentina.

Most refrigerated steamers and sailing ships at the time carried from 10,000 to 15,000 carcasses, with a few mastodons embarking up to 25,000 carcasses. By 1910, steamers with carrying capacity exceeding 100,000 carcasses were common, and there existed an impressive fleet of steamers capable to transport from 75,000 to 85,000 carcasses. Competition in tonnage, which was quickly increasing, meant that further reductions in the rates were achieved. While the number of ships in the frozen meat trade increased from 57 to 251 between 1888 and 1911, total capacity (in carcasses of sheep) rose from 955,000 to 16 million during the same period.[88] The steamer was also quicker, a key variable for time-sensitive food commodities such as meat. There was indeed no comparison between the sailing ship, which took from 90 to 110 days to reach Britain from New Zealand, and the mail steamers' 40 days.[89] The combination of refrigerated technologies and steam was instrumental in the transition from live cattle to chilled and frozen meat as well as in the growing import of other perishable foods such as butter, eggs, cheese, and fruit.

With refrigerated steamers transporting increasing quantities of dead meat, the problem of handling growing volumes of perishable commodities became ever more acute. In this respect, one of the most important developments in port technologies during those years was the introduction and rapid expansion of cold stores. These storage facilities thoroughly changed the dynamic of meat imports by delaying the need to "showcase" right away, notably by giving importers and wholesalers alike the ability to control the decaying time of imported goods. As more and more firms and market and port authorities recognized that the expansion of the dead meat trade was dependent on capital investments in cold stores, their number and capacity increased greatly.[90] Companies such as the Union Cold Stores were established in virtually all the great ports of Britain, and many multiple stores conducting business in the dead meat trade (such as Eastman, James Nelson and Sons, the River Plate Fresh Meat Company, and Sansinena) owned their own cold stores. The number and capacity of cold stores were heavily concentrated: whereas London and Liverpool had a total of forty-eight cold stores that could store up to 5.2 million fifty-six-pound carcasses of sheep, the combined capacities of the ports of Glasgow, Southampton, Manchester, Cardiff, Hull, Newcastle, and Briston represented thirty cold stores and capacity for 2.8 million carcasses.[91] Public and private cold stores were usually situated alongside principal railways so as to facilitate the loading of wagons for distribution either to wholesale public markets or to private multiple stores scattered across Britain.

The impact of the steam revolution was also visible in the fish industry, which was dominated by sailing smacks until the 1880s. Despite their early importance, sailing vessels were rapidly reaching their limits, as suggested by the intensification of the practice of fleeting in the late 1870s and early 1880s. "Fleets of sailing trawlers worked on the fishing grounds for up to eight weeks at a time and were serviced by fast steam cutters which took their catches to the port on a daily basis. The smacks could therefore maximise their fishing effort by reducing the number of individual voyages to and from the port."[92] Combined with growing demand, their limited spatial range condemned them to overexploiting the North Sea fish stocks, which, in turn, lowered profit rates as more labour was needed to catch the same quantities of fish stocks. In this context, the stream trawler brought key advantages. First, it was more profitable as it allowed a greater quantity of fish to be caught, notably through the introduction of the otter trawl, which was much more efficient than the old beam trawl. Second, it gave access to a much greater range of fishing grounds, pushing fishing activities out of the depleted North Sea towards the northerly fishing grounds off the Faroe Islands and Iceland. Soon thereafter the Grand Banks of Newfoundland and the Greenland coast came into the orbit of this expansive fishing universe. Finally, the steam trawler could work in weather impracticable to the smacks. As Walter Wood remarked in 1911, the shift to an industrial age in waterborne transportation was also visible in the names chosen for the smacks, substituting for the romantic, sentimental names of the old trawling days such as the *Gleaner* or the *Breadwinner* the industrial, unbending arithmetic of consequently numbered vessels from *One* to *Two* and so on.[93]

As wood and canvas were quickly abandoned for steel and steam, however, those who had invested up to £1,600 in the 1880s on modern and well-equipped sailing trawlers were the biggest losers as their investment was worth no more than £60 a decade later.[94] "By the early twentieth century the ports of Hull and Grimsby had sold off all of their sailing smacks while the 'newer' trawling ports of North Shields and Aberdeen, which had grown to prominence in the 1880s, based their expansion almost completely on steam vessels."[95] For instance, the number of steam trawlers in Aberdeen rose from 59 to 217 between 1891 and 1910, and by then 500 were active in Hull.[96] Given that the steam trawler was a capital-intensive technology beyond the means of individual fishers or small owners, and given the growing importance of ports as an interface to mass imports of cheap food, railway companies soon developed enormous interests in these sites, particularly the largest fishing ports of Grimsby, Hull, and Aberdeen.[97] For example, Grimsby, "an obscure town with little or no fish traffic" in the 1850s, possessed seven hundred steam fishing-vessels worth £3.5 million in the early 1910s and employed close to six thousand fishers. Owing much of its importance to the Great Central Railway (formerly the Manchester, Sheffield, and Lincolnshire Railway), which owned all of the market and fish wharves and where over five hundred merchants attended to their business, no less than fifteen express fish trains with an average load of 150 tons per fish train were dispatched from the port every day by 1911.[98] The quantity of fish carried by railway from the ports of Britain increased from 377,415 tons in 1890 to 704,270 tons in 1914, supplying as it did wholesale and retail fish markets all over Britain.[99]

Amidst colonial expansion, imperial ambitions, international free trade policies, and massive capital investments in transportation and communication technologies, one of the major consequences of the opening up of new sources of supply for primary products was the growth of food imports. These changes in the sourcing of food were characterized by three general trends. The first one was linked to the growing dependence of Britain on international food markets (Table 1.2). For instance, meat imports increased from 13.6 percent of total meat consumption in 1872 to 42.3 percent in 1912, and wheat imports from 48.3 percent in 1872 to 80.8 percent in 1913.[100] On the eve of the First World War, it was estimated that about 25 percent of Britain's total imports measured by weight were food.[101] Some 80 percent of wheat, 40 percent of meat, 75 percent of butter and margarine, 80 percent of cheese and almost all sugar came from abroad. Although home production of milk, vegetables, poultry, eggs, and meat remained important until 1914, there is no doubt that Britain's food security had become highly dependent on international food markets for key temperate foodstuffs such as butter, wheat, meat, and cheese. This needs some qualifications in the case

Table 1.2
Imports and home production, 1910–14

	Home production (percent)	Imports (percent)		
	United Kingdom	British Empire overseas	Foreign countries	Total imports
Wheat	19.0	39.3	41.7	81.0
Meat	57.9	10.7	31.4	42.1
Poultry	82.7	0.2	17.1	17.3
Eggs	67.6	0.1	32.3	32.4
Butter (including margarine)	25.1	13.3	61.6	74.9
Cheese	19.5	65.4	15.1	80.5
Milk (including cream)	95.4	0.0	4.6	4.6
Fruit	36.3	8.3	55.4	63.7
Vegetables	91.8	1.1	7.1	8.2

Source: Hall, Agriculture after the War, 12.

of tropical food goods like coffee, tea, palm-oil, bananas, and oranges, which Britain could not produce. Apart from tea, tropical food goods were marginal in working-class diet, which continued to rely heavily on meat, bread, butter, cheese, margarine, and vegetables, especially potatoes.

The second important trend is the substantial share of British imports in food taken by foreign countries. Emerging as major suppliers of wheat in the 1860s and 1870s, Russia and the United States remained key exporters until 1914, with Argentina joining them in the mid-1880s. Benefitting from cheap grains that it used as feedstuffs, Denmark soon emerged as an important producer of butter, bacon, and eggs. Denmark never sold less than 93 percent of its butter exports to Britain before 1914, of which about 33 percent was sold to the Co-operative Wholesale Society to supply retail societies in the Midlands, the north of England, and Scotland, and 20 percent was purchased by the Maypole Dairy Company to stock its hundreds of stores. About 40 percent of Britain's imports of butter came from Denmark between 1896 and 1913, with Russia, Australia, and, to a lesser extent, France, Sweden, and Holland producing most of the butter consumed in Britain.[102] Imported eggs came primarily from Russia, France, Germany, Denmark, and Belgium, and, following the expansion of sugar beet production in Continental Europe, great quantities of the sweet

Table 1.3
British Empire share of British imports in food commodities, 1854 and 1913

Food commodities	1854 (£m)	share (%)	1913 (£m)	share (%)
Grains	22.9	5.8	105.5	35.3
Sugar	9.6	64.7	10.7	8.7
Tea	5.5	0.7	13.8	87.3
Oilseeds	2.9	26.5	15.9	53.3
Butter	2.2	1.5	24.1	19.0
Meat	1.7	0.9	56.4	24.7
Fruit, nuts	0.8	3.2	11.6	14.3
Cheese	0.9	0	7.0	81.7

Source: Schlote, British Overseas Trade, 164–5.

stuff was imported from Germany, Austria-Hungary, France, Belgium, and Holland, with an important contribution from other countries such as Argentina, Brazil, and Russia. Bacon, cheese, ham, fresh beef, and apples from the United States; margarine, cheese, and onions from Holland; fresh mutton from Argentina; oranges, grapes, and onions from Spain; lemons from Italy; and apples, cherries, plums, pears, potatoes, and onions from France are yet further examples of the vast and expansive geography of food production underpinning the British diet.

The third noticeable trend is the remarkable rise in the Empire's contribution to food imports (table 1.3). Cecil Rhodes was on firm ground when he declared, in 1895, that the British Empire "is a bread and butter question. If you want to avoid civil war, you must become imperialists."[103] While Australia shipped growing quantities of fresh beef, fresh mutton, butter, and wheat, Canada became a key producer of apples, cheese, and wheat, contributing further to Britain's food security by exporting important quantities of bacon, butter, and fresh beef. Meanwhile, increased production of tea and wheat in India and oilseeds in West Africa was instrumental to the growth of the role of the Empire on key items of food consumption. The shift from cane to beet sugar in Continental Europe largely explains why sugar goes against the general trend towards increased reliance on imperial food imports. Despite its growing role, however, the British Empire's share of food imports was never as important as was the share in food commodities taken by foreign countries, except for tea, wheat, and cheese.[104]

The central role of cheap food in the betterment of the British working class was evidenced in the growing proportion of the population that experienced the satisfaction of a full belly and surplus money, a trend reinforced by the mushrooming of slate clubs and co-operative stores. The transition from national to world agriculture and the growing distance it created between farm and fork amounted to an unprecedented rescaling of market dependence and, therefore, contributed dramatically to the international repositioning of the value of labour-power through the exploitation of distant populations and lands. Britain was therefore able to mitigate hunger and starvation by exporting the contradiction between capital and labour through free trade policies, thus linking industrial competitivity and the working class's food security to international and colonial food markets. As we shall see in the following chapters, however, food distributors played a key role in delivering cheap food to the masses. While the persistence of poverty, hunger, and starvation up to 1914 suggests that the sphere of distribution could not solve some of the most important problems plaguing Britain, its active role in the production of cheap food proved essential in mediating the contradiction between capital and labour. It is the study of this relationship to which we now turn.

2

Public Markets

The reorganization of the medieval marketplace along capitalist lines represents one of the most important social and architectural transformations of the urban environment in Britain during the nineteenth century. The marketplace was at the centre of the struggle between a landed aristocracy and a rising capitalist class for the control of urban space, and it represented one of the most powerful elements in the institutional toolkit of the newly formed corporations (i.e., cities) in tackling the problems associated with rapid urbanization. For a growing proportion of the population living in urban settings and dependent upon the market for survival, the transformative adaptation of the public market remained one of, if not the single most powerful institutions for providing them with cheap food. Whatever role small- and large-scale retailers would come to play in how people obtained their food, public markets remained fundamental structures of the food distribution system. Yet the tendency to study retail structures pertaining to the so-called "retailing revolution" – that is, capital-intensive ventures associated with the co-operative movement, multiple shops, and the department store – has resulted in the downplay of public markets as "decaying and moribund institutions."[1] For instance, *The Cambridge Urban History of Britain*, a book of about one thousand pages, which, for all its remarkable achievements, almost entirely avoids the subject, except for rare, scattered references.[2] Part of the problem here is the tendency to universalize the general lack of public markets in London, while failing to register the gradual yet uneven shift in the distributive function of public markets from retailing to wholesaling. However, as we shall see, the idea that the public market – especially in its most developed form, the market hall – was a somewhat archaic medieval institution simply does not stand.[3]

The rise of the new bourgeois order was in part established through the control over the sphere of distribution. Providing sufficient market accommodation to reduce the "friction of space" became central to the system's ability to increase the volume and velocity at which food commodities moved in space and, thereby, lower food prices. As Edward P. Thompson has argued, this entailed a conceptual shift over the very meaning of the marketplace from a concrete space of sociability and politics to an abstract and sanitized economic process of exchange dedicated to mass distribution.[4] The transformation of the marketplace into a capitalist space geared towards the production of cheap food was characterized by three distinct yet complementary changes. The first one relates to the nature of the marketplace as a physical site of conflict between the landed gentry and the bourgeoisie. Local authorities were indeed all too aware that control over the town's food supply was key to securing cheap food, lowering the price of labour-power, and undermining the political threat associated with mass poverty and human insecurity, especially after the Poor Law Amendment Act, 1834. The second major transformation must be understood through the spatial integration of public markets within a growing and increasingly comprehensive national railway system. Successful public markets were those capable of commanding distant sites of production by taking advantage of the growing industrial capacity to transport great quantities of food efficiently over long distances.

Together, the political redefinition of the marketplace and its integration within railway systems furnished the basis for the development of a third major transformation – namely, the gradual rescaling of the public market's function from retailing to wholesaling. Especially after 1870, public markets increasingly became tied to a rapidly developing international food regime that was itself premised upon the distributive capacity to handle large consignments. The gradual repositioning of the historical function of the public market was most visible in London and large provincial cities such as Manchester and Glasgow. However, for the vast majority of public markets across Britain, municipal authorities, while often providing more space and longer hours for wholesaling than they used to, nonetheless maintained their traditional role as a retail space. In this respect, trends towards wholesaling did not fundamentally alter wages and working conditions in the market before 1914, although the restructuring of the distributive space tended to professionalize public markets through the growth of a permanent class of market sellers who did not produce what they sold. The chapter follows this tripartite division.

THE RISE OF THE BOURGEOIS DISTRIBUTIVE ORDER

The Royal Commission on Market Rights and Tolls' definition of the public market as "an authorised public concourse of buyers and sellers of commodities meeting at a place, more or less strictly limited or defined, at an appointed time" was the perfect illustration of the market as a physical space.[5] Most important, it specified the three pillars upon which both market and fair rested: authority, space, and time. The difference between a market and a fair was one of degree rather than nature. A fair was understood quite simply as a larger market that was held less frequently, often over a longer period of time, and that was usually a more general type of space. Whereas fairs were held only a few times a year at set dates, markets were held at least once a week and very frequently two to three days per week, including on Saturdays when the market was open until 11:00 p.m. or 12:00 p.m. The fixed periodicity of markets allowed farmer-retailers and "professional" market sellers to lower marketing time, concentrate their sales, and service multiple markets held on different days and in different towns. In large cities, public markets were held every day except on Sundays.[6] One of the marked features of retail markets between 1830 and 1914 was their key role in selling cheap food to urban-based, market-dependent working classes, including meat, fish, milk, cheese, fruit, vegetables, poultry, eggs, and butter.

Throughout medieval times fairs and great marts served an important commercial function. Held in virtually all the towns of the country and in several villages in spring, when stocks of consumer goods were low, and in autumn, when surpluses from the harvest needed to be disposed of, fairs played an important wholesaling function, which of late came to be met by professional factors scouring the countryside.[7] Fairs were the occasion for shopkeepers, the houses of great landlords, and institutions such as colleges and hospitals to stock up for months to come. They offered a greater variety of common goods, which were not always easily procurable, and introduced novelties. In spite of its general character, however, the distribution of foods and manufactured goods remained the most important commercial function of this bi-annual market. There were also a series of more specialized fairs, such as the statute fair, at which servants and farm labourers were hired, and the cattle fair. Both of these fairs predated and informed modern labour and cattle markets in important ways.

Contemporaries understood well how the development of more efficient means of communication and transportation was a major cause for the waning of the fairs. As an inhabitant from Wolverhampton put it in 1850, "there is no necessity now for fairs, with our weekly markets, capital shops, and railway connection."[8] The very existence of the fair as a commercial concourse was itself tributary of a limited and limiting transportation system as it sought to overcome spatio-temporal difficulties in the movement of commodities, including labour-power, by concentrating commercial activities in a fixed place over a specific period of time.[9] Already in the eighteenth century improvements in roadways were starting to undermine the rationale behind the fairs as provisioning institutions. By the early nineteenth century an important network of canals was in place, contributing further to linking localities and regions with one another. For instance, the importance of the Sturbridge fair, one of England's great marts in the first decades of the eighteenth century, had seriously declined by 1800, notably as a result of the increase in the density and reliability of roadways and waterways.[10] The rapid expansion of the railway in the 1830s and 1840s simply destroyed the raison d'être of the fair as a commercial venture. Even the cattle fair, which benefitted enormously from the new possibilities afforded by railways for livestock transportation, was undermined by the rapid expansion of the dead meat trade during the second half of the nineteenth century.

The fair continued to exist in two main forms. At the sub-national level, the receding economic life of the traditional fair opened the way for increasing the importance of a social function historically attached to the fair – amusement. The rise of the "pleasure fair" during the nineteenth century was less a new development than the accentuation of one of the institution's existing central components. One could watch the performance of conjurers, jugglers, and strong ladies as well as enjoy theatrical presentations, wrestling booths, spectacles, puppet shows, swings, roundabouts, and the like. Pleasure fairs were always anticipated with great impatience for weeks in advance and no doubt constituted an important moment in the town's calendar. The fair also survived through its rescaling at the international level.[11] Very much like the traditional fair, the emergence of the world fair with the Great Exhibition held in London in 1851 fixed a time and place for everyone to congregate, while offering the space for countries and merchants alike to expose their commercial and industrial prowess and cultivate what many saw as civilizational achievements. In this respect, the world fair captured the need for international spaces of distribution where new commodities, technologies, and innovations could be exhibited. The pleasure fair and the world fair gained in popularity while the traditional fair declined. The Fairs Act, 1871, which reflected Victorians' tendency to portray traditional fairs as public nuisances and immoral environments encouraging promiscuous behaviours, empowered municipal authorities to abolish them, with consent of the owner. By 1881, no less than seven hundred English fairs had been abolished.

Meanwhile, the industrial regularity with which railways transported commodities completely transformed the traditional marketplace into one of the institutional pillars of capitalist social relations. The resilience of the public market as a physical place for distribution ultimately lies in its ability to adapt to the reproductive needs and rhythms of urban-based and market-dependent working classes. The traditional marketplace situated at the centre of the town was the perfect model of chaotic development and public nuisance in the context of rapid urbanization. Public markets frequently developed by spilling over adjacent streets, and complaints about animals in the streets as well as the lack of access and mobility were common.[12] As agrarian capitalism produced a new crop of town dwellers, quickly outgrowing medieval market structures, the rising bourgeoisie also became more and more critical of the public market's contribution to unruly and disorderly scenes. The modern, sanitized conception of the marketplace as the encounter between buyers and sellers had yet to be socially accepted, politically enforced, and architecturally constructed. In fact, up until 1850, it remained an important space for politics. People gathered in and around the marketplace not only to buy and sell but also to socialize, gossip, drink, celebrate, seek entertainment, and voice their grievances, sometimes violently. The marketplace offered a space of dissent, a fertile public ground where social discontent could be expressed through (food) riots and public outrage.[13]

Market reforms were desperately needed. Informed by classical political economy's understanding of the relationship between the costs of labour and food, both radicals and reformists became increasingly aware that the marketplace could be, and in fact was, an important bottleneck for capital accumulation and profitability. By obstructing the flow of food commodities and limiting the town's food supply, public markets maintained artificially high food prices, contributed to the inflation of the "natural" price of labour, and cultivated social discontent. In this respect, the realization of the need for reforms in the daily operation and overall organization of the public market, as well as the recognition of its role as a prime institution of capitalist governance, represented nothing short of an early rehearsal for the upcoming struggle over the repeal of the Corn Laws. The battle over the control of market rights was not disinterested, and so-called "radicals" such as shopkeepers did not carry the flame of progress for its own sake. Indeed, the lord of the manor was extremely likely to enforce his rights on market day and, therefore, request goods to be sold exclusively on the site of the market or charge a fee to anybody selling goods outside of it. There can be little doubt that shop-owners greatly resented this economic privilege.

The battle for the authority over public markets thus became a battle for the control over the town's food supply. Growing urbanization in the context of an inherited feudal legal structure of manorial market rights put tremendous pressure on existing market accommodations and distributive infrastructures. From medieval times, the traditional market system had evolved through royal grants and charters that gave the monopoly of market rights to the lord of the manor. For example, by the late 1880s, the Duke of Bedford held the market rights for the sale of vegetables, fruit, and flowers at the Covent Garden Market – rights that were originally granted in 1661 to the Earl of Bedford by King Charles II. Such royal grants usually specified when and where the market would be held, and authorized its owner to levy tolls and other dues.[14] Moreover, under fourteenth-century common law, markets were supposed to be held seven miles apart from one another in order to provide the lord of the manor with exclusive rights over commerce. At the dawn of the nineteenth century, most English and Welsh markets belonged to local manorial families. With very few exceptions, they tended to subject the public interest to their own profits by showing little to no interest in costly improvements and comprehensive reforms to increase the town's food supply. In stark contrast with Scottish markets, which were generally better managed because they were kept under municipal control from the start, English and

Welsh markets were generally inconvenient for both town inhabitants and nearby farmers.[15]

Nineteenth-century Britain witnessed the thorough transformation of the public market as a result of the need to move greater quantities of commodities more quickly. "The natural progression of the public market," James Schmiechen and Kenneth Carls argue, "was from the traditional, open-air marketplace to a combination of market place and street market, to an enclosed market site, to a roofed market hall."[16] Between 1800 and 1850, the floor space of the public markets more than doubled, with Liverpool spending £108,200 between 1822 and 1844 to erect six markets.[17] At the beginning of the 1890s, while "just over half of the country's markets were wholly or partially under cover," the vast majority of them were enclosed markets.[18] Despite the multiplicity of market arrangements, however, no other reformed markets embodied the logic of industrial capitalism quite like the market hall. Essentially a provincial phenomenon concentrated in the North and the Midlands, its construction was often architecturally impressive and the subject of great civic pride. For instance, at the dawn of the twentieth century, the Kirkgate Market Hall in Leeds, a covered area of over 196,000 square feet (4.5 acres) with a complex glass-and-iron roof, a Renaissance façade, and prominent corner entrances, housed 83 shops (20 of which were butchers' shops) and 84 stalls.[19] Uncovered markets in open squares were no proof of bad municipal management, however, as many of them provided good facilities in line with people's needs, such as the ones in Leicester, Northampton, Norwich, and Nottingham.[20]

The market hall also responded to the Victorian ideals of cleanliness and technological progress by offering conveniences such as urinals, water troughs, hot water, and lavatories, and, in some cases, the "unusual luxury" of a telegraph office.[21] Its architectural design and spatial positioning within the urban landscape was aimed towards fostering both speed and fluidity in the distribution of commodities, and its exclusive dedication to economic activities displayed an obvious appreciation for efficiency through the functional compartmentalization and spatial division of economic life. In this respect, the market hall epitomised the hallmark of bourgeois sensibilities for order "in the struggle for urban spatial hegemony."[22] Market halls embodied an elaborate internal division of space and function geared towards high turnover, with stalls regrouped into specialist divisions (e.g., fish, butcher, confectioner, provision, fruit, vegetables) and organized in rows so as to facilitate the orderly movement and efficient circulation of people and goods within the market. As Goronwy Rees puts it, "they resembled some huge proletarian department store ... The difference was that in the market hall the different 'departments' were under separate ownership."[23] Already in 1822, St John's market hall in Liverpool, arguably the first market hall to be constructed, boasted some sixty-two shops and 404 stalls, setting the trend for subsequent market halls.[24] Indeed, most market halls "contained inward-facing lock-up shops around the outside wall, and all had benches and tables for country farmers as well as stalls for regular market traders."[25] The market hall embodied a historical compromise between traditional and modern trading practices, providing a fixed space for local, regional, national, and international food producers to congregate.[26]

Public markets in general and market halls in particular provided working classes with both cheap entertainment and cheap food, especially on Saturday nights when they attracted the biggest crowds. For example, the Flat Iron market in Salford featured "roundabouts, shooting galleries, boxing booths, penalty kick competitions for footballers, and a cheap theatre," all of which were greatly appreciated by local populations.[27] Many contemporaries have fond memories of the Saturday night market: "Here life was at its gayest and rowdiest; the open shop fronts lit by paraffin flares, competing traders bawling their wares, and narrow streets crowded with buyers or gaping sightseers."[28] Living in the village of Mirfield, Joseph H. Hird also looked forward to what were rare outings: "Heckmondwike had a small market place, where we indulged in tripe at a stall. Dewsbury had a large open-air market, where, at a stall illuminated by hissing suspended lamps, we could have a small pork pie, with peas, served on a plate, and consumed under the eye of the stallholder."[29] As Hird suggests, cheap entertainment and cheap food were often one and the same.

One of the main vectors of market reforms between 1800 and 1880 were private and local market improvement acts passed by Parliament (table 2.1). It is significant that the number of market improvement acts reached its peak in the decades preceding the mass import of cheap food in the 1870s and that it dramatically declined as large-scale retailers gained traction in the 1880s. Local market improvement acts served different purposes: the construction of a new market, the purchasing or leasing of market rights from the lord of the manor, the rebuilding or enlarging of an old market, or the changing of market regulations.[30] The shift in the control of markets came with the

Table 2.1
Market improvement acts passed in England and Wales, 1800–90

1800–10	1811–20	1821–30	1831–40	1841–50	1851–60	1861–70	1871–80	1881–90
42	27	34	44	56	78	60	30	3

Source: Shaw and Wild, "Retail Patterns in the Victorian City," 284.

Municipal Reform Act, 1835, which granted borough or corporation status to 179 English and Welsh towns. Later legislations – the Markets and Fairs Clauses Act, 1847; the Local Government Act, 1858; and the Public Health Act, 1875 – upheld the prescriptive right of private market owners while gradually empowering local authorities to establish and regulate public markets, particularly through sanitary inspections.[31] By 1886, out of 769 town markets in England and Wales, excluding the metropolis, 313 were under the control of local authorities, 274 were still in private hands, 64 belonged to private trading companies, 57 did not have owners, 39 were managed by commissioners, and 22 had questionable or unclear market rights.[32]

The transfer of market rights from private to public hands was often costly. With Parliament upholding their prescriptive rights, the lords of the manor were in an excellent bargaining position against desperate local authorities seeking to acquire neglected or otherwise inadequate markets. While Darlington paid the Bishop of Durham £7,854 for the town's markets and Sir John Ramsden received £39,802 for the market rights in Huddersfield, Manchester bought them from the lord of the manor for £200,000 in 1846.[33] For those unable to reach an agreement with the lord of the manor, leasing the market rights was often the only way to gain control over the town's food supply. For instance, in 1866 the Corporation of Bradford leased Miss Rawson's manorial rights for 999 years at £5,000 per year, the corporation being "compelled to obtain the markets at any cost, because the nuisance occasioned by want of accommodation was so great and the wants of the town were not properly supplied."[34] Wakefield was in the same situation, the bad management of the market giving its owners leverage to negotiate by "forcing the hands of the authorities to get rid of the nuisance."[35] Since local authorities almost always made improvements during the leasing period, however, once the lease expired, the lord of the manor was often in possession of a far more valuable property than he was at the beginning, such that manorial rights could then be rented again or sold at higher prices.[36]

Once market rights were acquired, the provision of better market accommodations required substantial capital investments for both general and specialized markets. For instance, by the early 1890s Blackburn had disbursed £54,407 for its markets, including £28,000 for a general market hall, about £8,500 each for a retail fish market and a cattle market, and £9,400 for public slaughterhouses.[37] In Glasgow, £180,353 were spent on the cattle market, the dead meat market, and the fish market, and £54,600 upon the slaughterhouses.[38] By comparison, the new Metropolitan Cattle Market built at Copenhagen Fields in Islington in the mid-1850s was estimated at over £300,000.[39] Despite the lack of retail market accommodations in the metropolis, it was estimated in the early 1890s that the markets in the hands of the Corporation of London had cost £3,091,342, a remarkable sum given that the total capital expanded by forty selected provincial markets was estimated at £2,621,295, including regional powerhouses such as Manchester (£567,989), Liverpool (£246,700), and Birmingham (£235,730).[40] Once broken down, virtually all capital expenditures were piecemeal reorganizations and incremental additions to existing markets.[41]

Whether realized under private or public ownership, market improvements were often very profitable, although for different reasons. For example, the Duke of Norfolk, owner of the market rights in Sheffield, spent £121,000 between 1877 and 1888 to improve his markets and, as a result of increased business, pocketed a net income of £9,700 in 1888.[42] Since most public market authorities tended to adopt a competitive structure of tolls and dues to attract local and regional producers and merchants, low yearly net income was no indication of unpopular markets – rather, it was often the result of good municipal management through the careful balancing of public needs with market expenses.[43] While many provincial markets met their needs through relatively cheap retail infrastructures, virtually all municipal governments recognized that proper market accommodations were key to securing and controlling the flow of food commodities coming into town.[44] Proactive market authorities could also secure a better food supply by encouraging distant producers and retail and wholesale traders to come into town through bylaws, regulatory policies, and other market incentives. For instance, the price of fish in Newcastle dropped significantly after the town invested £7,000 in a fish market and quay for the boats supplying it from the fish mar-ket in Shields. Moreover, the town allowed them the use of the market for free and even paid five to ten pounds a week for "tug boats to tow the smacks up here."[45] Similarly, Preston developed as an impor-tant distributing centre for cheese through lower charges, and local authorities argued that cheaper and better-quality cheeses largely compensated for the decline in revenues.[46]

Everywhere the lesson was clear: "towns with the best market facil-ities had the largest, most varied, and cheapest food supplies."[47] Together high volumes, quick turnovers, and lower rents and over-heads produced a distributive environment conducive to cheap food. The public market was a powerful vector of local and regional inte-gration as well as a strong municipal lever over the control of the quantity, quality, and variety of food supplied. Although they might not have put it in those terms, contemporaries understood very well the vital role of public markets in producing cheap food.[48] Of course, there were still "pannier market" or "pitching sales" in the early 1900s, and farmers were still coming into town on market days to sell poul-try, eggs, butter, fruit, vegetables, and the like. But the trend was un-mistakable as professional stallholders and salespeople increasingly came to mediate the space between consumers and producers. In this respect, the reconfiguration of the marketplace along capitalist lines was the first step in the rise of the bourgeois distributive order. It marked a crucial moment in the battle for the control of the urban environment, while consolidating the vital role of the marketplace in the reproduction of the British working class.

RAILWAYS AND THE SPATIAL EXPANSION
OF THE MARKETPLACE

By 1850, large towns in Britain were still heavily dependent on their immediate surroundings for perishable commodities such as fruit, vegetables, milk, fish, and meat. Articles with a longer marketing life, such as cereals, cheese, or livestock moved on the hoof, usually came from farther afield. Important demographic changes towards urban centres increased the number of people dependent upon the market to purchase their means of subsistence, which put enormous pressure on a town's food supply. This was further complicated by the time-scale of different food commodities, especially perishable articles, and the tensions arising from existing geographies of production.[49] With speedier and more efficient means of transportation becoming essential to delivering mass quantities of cheap food and preserving the quality and overall integrity of the products conveyed, the fate of public markets became increasingly tied to the development of the railway.[50] The capitalization of space-time relations was indeed fundamental to the repositioning of food relations on a scale sufficient to overcome existing spatial limits. Perishable food commodities such as milk, dead meat, fruits, and vegetables from distant places were suddenly made available to mushrooming urban centres.

Few technological developments captured the Victorian mind and imagination as did the railway.[51] Through its ability to move immense quantities of food goods over longer distances and within shorter periods of time, the railway dramatically reduced the circulation time of food commodities, increased the distance that they could travel without deteriorating, and consequently fractured previous geographies of food production and consumption. This revolution on rail carried more than the powerful forces of fixed capital in its movement; it also conveyed profound changes in the ways in which people related to their surrounding environment. While the rapid expansion of the railway from the 1840s onwards tore apart previous notions of space and time and contributed to the harmonization of diets across regions, it also introduced important changes in the cost structure of transport.[52] Even when cheaper alternatives existed, the reliability, efficiency, and rapidity of the railway were convincing arguments to a great number of shopkeepers and salespersons doing business in the food trade.[53]

Despite their importance throughout the period under review, the fate of canals and coastal shipping had been settled early on. In harmonizing closed railway systems through the gradual elimination of goods transferred from one system to another, the establishment of the Railway Clearing House in 1842 undermined the view that canals could still compete against railways.[54] Until then, transhipments at the junction between two lines frequently produced chaotic scenes and wastes of time. The Clearing House played a leading role in the acceleration of commodity flows, which was crucial for time-sensitive food commodities. The proportion of route mileage of railway companies, parties to Clearing House, rose from 50.8 percent to 94.5 percent between 1850 and 1870, before stabilizing at about 91 percent between 1880 and 1910. Tellingly, the proportion of goods cleared per annum remained stable at about 36 percent between 1864 and 1913,[55] thus suggesting an important intra-district trade within the same railway system, including ports. The 1840s thus marked the beginning of an increasingly integrated system of transport aimed towards the reduction of bottlenecks and delays. As the Select Committee on Railway Acts Enactments was forced to conclude in 1846, canals had been "beaten" by railways and the introduction of lower rates.[56]

The expansion of reformed public markets in the middle decades of the nineteenth century was closely linked to these developments. The great mania of the 1840s saw colossal fortunes poured into the construction of railways: total capital raised by railways rose from £54.6 million in 1841 to £228.6 million in 1850 to £1,272.5 million in 1912.[57] One effect of this vast capitalization was the growing comprehensiveness of the whole system as distinct local and regional railway systems were expanded and linked to one another. As the financial pressure to increase the traffic of goods through a reduction in freight charges rose in the post-mania depression, carrying in bulk soon became one of the operative principles of railway companies.[58] By the late 1860s, all the main railway trunks had been built and most companies were now competing over the matter of facilities such as sheds, sidings, and loading banks and cranks to attract new traffic.[59] Reflecting on the dramatic expansion in the traffic of goods carried by railways, the 1867 Royal Commission on railways concluded that it would be "very difficult to institute any comparison with the past."[60] For public authorities seeking to expand the town's food supply, connecting public markets to railway systems was crucial.

In 1905, there were 3,639 miles of canals and navigations in England and Wales and 183 miles in Scotland, compared to 16,223 miles of railways in England and Wales and 3,815 miles in Scotland in 1912.[61] The tonnage conveyed through canals in Britain amounted to 38.7 million tons in 1905, compared to 440 million tons of goods that were conveyed by rail in Britain in 1912.[62] Although canals remained an alternative to railways, they were almost marginal where food was concerned. Markets and factories depending on the canal for their supply, such as the Cadbury's factory in Bournville or the Gloucester's corn market, were exceptions.[63] Of the total tonnage of goods carried on the Grand Junction Canal in 1905, only 5,812 tons (or 0.003 percent) of it were agricultural products.[64] By far the great majority of goods carried on waterways consisted of minerals (e.g., coal, iron ore, pig-iron), building materials (e.g., stone, bricks, tiles, slates, timber, cement), town manure, and refuse. Waterways were simply too slow for the transport of livestock, milk, and butter, and the growing importance of the grain, fish, and meat trade in the ports of Britain made railways more attractive.

The most powerful alternative to railways came from the coastal trade. Sea competition, as the general managers of the different railway companies repeatedly pointed out, was the main reason for the maintenance of low railway rates.[65] Whereas coasters' expenses were generally limited, railways had to sink millions into the buying of land, railway construction, goods vans, locomotives, stations, tunnels, signal boxes, wages, and the like before even carrying the first load.[66] Yet coastal shipping was systematically slower than railways, which was impracticable for perishable commodities such as fruit and vegetables, milk and meat. This is why Francis Craze, market gardener from Penzance, and John Taylor, an important grocer from Swansea, either shipped or received their produce by rail.[67] For them as for many others, the regularity and rapidity afforded by the railways were ultimately much more important than a few more shillings on the ton. As Dodd put it in 1856: "Time is money."[68]

The live cattle trade offered an interesting window on the superiority of the railways in food transportation. Before steam transport opened up new markets, live animals reached distant markets on the hoof. On their journey to the southern markets, Scottish herds from the districts of Aberdeen and Forfar were joined west of the Pennines by Irish cattle landing in Liverpool, and were driven to the grazing districts of Norfolk, Suffolk, and Lincoln to be fattened for the Midlands and London markets.[69] In his study of the cattle trade in Aberdeenshire, J.H. Smith argues that, after its introduction in 1828, the transport of cattle by boat increased rapidly before peaking in the 1840s, at which point between 9,543 and 15,858 heads were shipped per year. With the expansion of the railway after 1840, the waterborne cattle trade fell to one-third of its previous size and never recovered. From 1850 to 1870, between 27,000 and 44,000 cattle per year were sent by rail from Aberdeen to Edinburgh, Glasgow, and London, the latter capturing up to 90 percent of the trade. As one commentator wrote in 1854: "Aberdeen is in fact becoming little else than a London abattoir."[70] Meanwhile, important provincial cattle markets in Bradford, Preston, and Salford emerged as public authorities were able to take advantage of the new geography of food afforded by railways. Table 2.2 shows the early dominance of railways in the livestock trade. Railways also promoted a new spatial division of labour by facilitat-

Table 2.2
Total number of livestock brought to London, 1853

	Oxen	Sheep	Calves	Pigs	Total
By railways					
Eastern Counties	81,744	277,735	3,492	23,427	386,398
London and North Western	70,435	248,445	5,113	24,287	348,280
Great Northern	15,439	120,333	563	8,973	145,308
Great Western	6,813	104,607	2,320	2,909	116,649
London and South Western	4,885	100,960	1,781	516	108,142
South Eastern	875	58,320	114	142	59,451
London and Brighton and South Coast	863	13,690	117	54	14,724
Total by railways	181,054	924,090	13,500	60,308	1,178,952
By sea					
From North of England and Scotland	14,662	11,141	421	3,672	29,896
From Ireland	2,311	3,472	21	5,476	11,280
From the Continent	55,065	229,918	25,720	10,131	320,834
Total by sea	72,038	244,531	26,162	19,279	362,010
Driven in by road	69,096	462,172	62,114	48,265	641,647
Total	322,188	1,630,793	101,776	127,852	2,182,609

Source: Anon., "The London Commissariat," 284.

ing the development of the dead meat trade. The quantity of beef sent by rail from Aberdeen to London rose from 8,000 tons (28,000 carcasses) in 1855 to 10,000 tons (35,000 carcasses) in 1865.[71] By comparison, the amount of dead meat sent by sea peaked at 496 tons in 1857, before dropping to 61 tons in 1865.[72]

The failure to provide public markets with proper railway accommodations could be an importance source of frustration and a strong impediment to their growth. Between 1877 and 1887, the number of beasts exhibited at the cattle market in Birmingham declined from 35,378 to 28,041, calves from 15,616 to 8,185, and sheep from 113,964 to 75,345. The inconvenience of the market, which was situated "in the very heart of the town" where "roads are not good and cattle have to be driven or carted to it from the railway stations," was the main cause of the decline of the market. As Henry Fulford, chairman of the Markets and Fairs Committee, argued: "in several other towns in the midland counties not so important as Birmingham, for instance Wolverhampton, there are live cattle markets larger and more prosperous than our own, and we have been very anxious to remove our cattle market to a larger site to which we should be able to bring in the railways."[73] Even successful markets could have their future development hindered because of their location. Situated outside of the town, yet close to the railway station and private slaughterhouses, the cattle market in Hull flourished rapidly, encouraging growing quantities of cattle from Lincolnshire and Yorkshire to come into it. Its success soon reached its spatial limits, with farmers complaining that they had to send their beasts elsewhere.[74] The relationship between public markets and railway accommodations thus tended to oscillate between untapped possibilities and saturated capacities, which was reinforced by a complex web of power relations as towns competed against each other over the distribution of food goods. In bringing distant producers together in the marketplace, railways encouraged price competition not only between producers but also between market authorities.[75]

The organic relationship that existed between the railway as a technology of mass circulation and the reformed market as a site of mass distribution is perhaps nowhere better illustrated than in the case of the Great Eastern Railway and the lack of sufficient retail facilities in the region through which it travelled. With very few exceptions, the Great Eastern passed almost wholly through agricultural districts, which sent their products to Manchester, Birmingham, Leeds, Bradford, and other districts beyond Peterborough, with London capturing the lion's share. Although the quantity of potatoes carried into London had risen from 16,000 tons in 1869 to 24,000 tons in 1879, the Company's business was increasingly limited by the lack of proper market accommodations.[76] In order to encourage traffic, the Company invested about £17,500 to open its own market in 1879 in the parish of Stratford, West Ham, adjoining an existing railway station.[77] The market was so successful that the Company decided to convert the old passenger station at Bishopsgate into a depot for the sale of vegetables, roots, and fish. It opened in July 1882.

Stratford Market and Bishopsgate Market were of importance both for the booming working-class community of the East End and the producers in Norfolk, Suffolk, and Bedfordshire. The total weight of potatoes, roots, vegetables, and fruits received by rail at the Stratford Market increased from 5,000 tons in 1880 to 33,000 tons in 1887, and by 1886 an extra 12,000 tons of foodstuffs was coming by road through 6,184 carts. In 1880, the total weight of vegetables brought to London by the Great Eastern, irrespective of the markets, amounted to 32,000 tons. In 1882, when the Bishopsgate Market opened, the total weight brought jumped up to 52,000 tons and reached 66,000 tons the following year. Despite its success, however, Bishopsgate Market was forced to close in January 1884 because it was too close – and therefore infringed on the market rights – of Spitalfields Market, which held by ancient charter the exclusive right to sell vegetables, fruit, and market-garden produce.[78] That year the amount of fruit and vegetables brought into London by the Great Eastern only slightly increased to 69,000 tons and reached 87,000 tons in 1887. For William Birt, general manager of the Great Eastern, there was no doubt that, if Bishopsgate Market had been kept open, the total weight of rail-borne food commodities to London would have been much larger.[79] As far as railways were essential to supply public markets with great quantities of cheap food, their respective development was often limited by a legal geography tending to reinforce – rather than to inhibit – the uneven development of retailing.

Railway depots like these were not uncommon. Both the Great Northern Railway Potato Market at King's Cross and the Midland Railway Vegetable Market were important railway depots in London. In places such as Liverpool and Carlisle, railway goods depots often developed into important markets. Some were formal, like the Lancashire and Yorkshire Railway Company which paid the

Corporation of Manchester £1,500 per year to hold an extensive potato and carrot market on its premises in Oldham Road.[80] Broadly speaking, however, it seems fair to say that most railway depots tended to be informal but tolerated – and in some cases secretly celebrated – by municipal authorities for providing a temporary solution to the lack of market accommodations without encroaching on public finance or increasing the "burden" of ratepayers. Hull is a case in point. As a result of insufficient public market infrastructures, the Corporation did not intervene in the development of an important informal market in perishable goods at the Paragon Station. In fact, so valuable was the traffic in game, poultry, fish, and fruit that the railway company spent several thousands to improve the station and cover three thousand yards of space.[81] Railway depots almost always came as a result of insufficient retail infrastructures. Conversely, the provision of proper market accommodations tended to undermine their raison d'être, as in Birmingham, where the London and North Western Railway Company used to carry extensive business at the stations before the borough markets were reformed and made adequate.[82]

As suggested by the case of the Great Eastern, however, the dialectical tension that existed between food retailing and the railway as a technology of mass transportation was the mutually reinforcing relationship that brought them both to life, along with their ability to generate new production opportunities. At the beginning of the 1850s, most of the vegetables and fruit brought to London were grown in the vicinity of the metropolis, even though the effects of urbanization were deeply felt as the lands of Fulham, Battersea, Chelsea, Putney, Brentford, Hammersmith, Mortlake, Mitcham, and Deptford were increasingly yielding a new kind of crop: buildings. The rapid expansion of railways was key to the rescaling of food production from the local and regional levels to the national and international ones. The growing distance separating farm and fork in turn tended to favour certain counties and regions over others, such as the market gardening industry of Bedfordshire. The average annual tonnage of vegetables sent from the Potton railway station to London rose from 4,146 tons between 1857 and 1860 to 13,325 tons between 1896 and 1905. The county also became known for its production of onions and Brussels sprouts in the mid-1900s, forwarding large quantities of carrots to the Glasgow wholesale market and other northern cities.[83] With the expansion of public markets and railway lines in the 1850s, new potatoes from Yorkshire, which had until then supplied the markets of Leeds, Bradford, and other large towns from the county, as well as London, were now daily forwarded in large quantities during the season to Birmingham, Cheltenham, Derby, Leicester, and Sheffield.[84]

The same was true of market gardeners from Penzance sending great quantities of vegetables such as early potatoes, broccoli, peas, and cucumber to Covent Garden from Hayle to Bristol by steamer, and then from Bristol to London by railway. Within twenty years of the opening of the Great Western Railway for through traffic in 1859, market gardening in Cornwall increased fourfold, and most of the vegetables sent for London and the large towns of the industrial districts of Lancashire and Yorkshire were carried by railway. By the early 1880s, West Cornwall forwarded about 18,000 tons of broccoli and 12,000 tons of new potatoes every year to these large towns, with Manchester frequently receiving 20 tons of broccoli per day.[85] The impact of the railway on the geographies of production, distribution, and consumption was vividly captured by John Page in 1880 when he remarked that, as a result of "the revolution in the sources of supply" brought by the "abolition of duties, improved steam navigation, and the more complete development of the railway system," perhaps no more than one-eighth of the supply of Manchester fruit and vegetable markets came from nearby growers coming into town with their carts.[86] In the growing distance separating producers and consumers, public markets came to play a key role in facilitating the flow of food goods.

RESCALING THE PUBLIC MARKET

Nowhere was the distinction between retail and wholesale activities clearer than in the metropolis. As Daniel Tallerman, dealer in meat and fish in the metropolis for twenty-two years, put it, the Central Meat Market "is not a market at all. A market is a place where producers and consumers may meet and exchange their produce, but into this market producers cannot enter at all."[87] Tallerman's anxiety over what constitutes a market is interesting because it reveals how London's wholesale markets represented a clear spatial and scalar break from traditional understandings of the marketplace. Despite their importance, however, these "critical agents in the capitalist system of metropolitan provisioning" were only the most extreme version of what was already happening across the realm, especially in large towns.[88] Public markets in Edinburgh and Glasgow evolved from their old retail function to become chiefly wholesale, supplying a mushrooming class of small-scale retailers as well as regionally distant markets.[89] Moreover, in capturing the bulk of food distribution activities, important wholesale markets tended to reinforce geographically uneven patterns of development. About two-thirds of the market produce in Manchester was sent to a variety of towns all over Lancashire, Cheshire, and Yorkshire, and evidence shows that Bolton, Oldham, and Salford were largely dependent on Manchester for their food supply, as were shopkeepers from Bury, Radcliffe, Ramsbottom, Tottington, and Darwen.[90] Farmer-retailers, still prominent figures of the marketplace in the middle decades of the nineteenth century, had lost their importance in large towns by the late 1880s. Instead, the development of wholesale markets across Britain tended to support a growing army of greengrocers, fishmongers, butchers, fruiterers, and other dealers and tradespersons who did not produce what they sold.

Characteristic of geographically uneven market structures was the existence of a differentiated food price matrix favouring large towns with wholesale markets. This new reality and the geographical paradoxes it raised left many contemporaries perplexed. "Tourists and pleasure-seekers at Brighton, Hastings, and other coast towns, are often puzzled to understand the fact that fish, although caught and landed near at hand, is not cheaper there than in London ... It is, in a similar way, a subject of vexation in the salmon districts that the best salmon are so uniformly sent to London as to leave only the secondary specimens for local consumption."[91] Moreover, wholesalers turning to retail were quite common. In Leeds, for example, the combination of modern infrastructures, competitive market policies, and the practice of letting wholesale dealers sell by retail meant "that the prices of poultry, vegetables, and game would be 25 percent cheaper in the market than in the shops."[92] Even the London Central Meat and Poultry and Provision Markets, a wholesale market supplied from "nearly all parts of the world" and supplying the whole of Great Britain, turned to retail on Saturday afternoon and evening when a considerable trade was said to be carried on.[93] While local economic interests could be an important block against the development of public markets, as we shall see in chapter 4, evidence supports the view that reformist policies, capital investments in proper market accommodations, the development of wholesale markets, and the ability to take advantage of the new opportunities afforded by railways all played a key role in the production of cheap food at the municipal level.

The dead meat trade offers one example of the growing scalar disparities existing in the food distribution sector in mid-century. Already by the early 1850s great quantities of country-killed meat were forwarded to London.[94] The total quantity of dead meat brought by different English railways and "pitched" at Newgate and Leadenhall markets ca. 1853 was about thirty-six thousand tons.[95] Between January and November 1867, no less than 64,924 tons of fresh meat were carried by some of the most important railway lines into the metropolis from the provinces.[96] As the rising importance of the dead meat trade suggests, the metropolis was increasingly divided between a growing class of retail butchers with insufficient capital and inadequate retail and slaughtering facilities to purchase from the live cattle market, on the one hand, and a class of wholesale carcass butchers dealing primarily from Leadenhall, Newgate, and Whitechapel markets, on the other.[97]

Wholesale and large-carcass butchers established in the large industrial towns of the north also purchased their livestock before slaughtering, dressing, and forwarding them to London markets where small retail butchers congregated. The differentiated access to capital among butchers, combined with the new business opportunities generated by the railways, created an extensive spatial division of labour between wholesale carcass butchers and retail butchers.[98] In addition, farmers lacking market accommodations were unable to dispose of hide, rough fat, or skins, and usually preferred to send their animals alive by rail rather than loosing valuable parts of them, thus further concentrating slaughtering activities into the hands of wholesale carcasses butchers.[99] Following the Public Health Act, 1848, many towns introduced controls over slaughterhouses by relocating them – often with the cattle market – outside of the town.[100] In this respect, the old Smithfield cattle market in London captures well the difficulties associated with rapid urbanization. By the late 1840s, "220,000 head of cattle and 1,500,000 sheep [were] violently forced into an area of five acres, in the very heart of London, through its narrowest and most crowded thoroughfares."[101] The market and slaughterhouses were finally relocated at Copenhagen Fields in Islington, where the Metropolitan Cattle Market opened in 1855. A few years later, the City of

London obtained under the Metropolitan Meat and Poultry Market Act the right to construct new buildings on the Smithfield site, which were built above railway lines connecting the market to the whole country and enabling meat to be delivered directly to the market.[102] These new markets represented public authorities' willingness to enforce a new spatial division of labour and thereby clean the Aegean Stables that often were the Victorian cities.[103]

This new spatial division between retailing and wholesaling was also supported by sanitary reforms and policies, which made it more difficult for small urban slaughterhouses to pursue their activities. For instance, the number of private slaughterhouses in London declined from over 1,500 in 1873 to 651 in 1891, and, following a 1892 by-law, 117 licences were not renewed, the premises judged unsuited for the task. The following year, only 526 licences were granted.[104] In addition, a series of Orders in Council (1866, 1879, and 1892) for the compulsory slaughter of all foreign cattle at the port of debarkation to prevent the spread of the cattle plague to British herds had the effect not only of preventing Scottish farmers and the Eastern Counties from importing store cattle or sheep for fattening but also of promoting the dead meat trade, either through the import of chilled and frozen meat or the slaughtering of live animals at their port of discharge. Even the important cattle market in Salford exhibited signs of decline by the end of the century, its profitability undermined by the growth of dead meat imports.[105] Already well advanced by the 1880s, deskilling reached new heights with the growth of the frozen meat trade in the 1890s and 1900s. Presiding over the dramatic decrease in the number of skilled butchers, the frozen meat trade increased the number of unqualified butchers finding employment in shops where no particular skills were required.

As the history of the live cattle trade and the dead meat trade suggests, one of the most significant aspects in the evolution of public markets in the second half of the nineteenth century was the constitution and gradual expansion of wholesale markets of regional, national, and even international importance. The first step in this direction was the market owners' or municipal authorities' ability to physically link public markets to railways. For example, Bradford's fruit and fish wholesale markets, as well as its cattle and dead meat markets, were connected to two different railway systems, thus making them "accessible from every part of the kingdom."[106] As town clerk William Thomas McGowen put it in 1888, the fish trade "used to be a slack trade at Bradford at one time, but facilities being provided for the sale of fish, people have taken premises, and on Saturday the sale of fish is something extraordinary." Fresh consignments coming as late as 8:00 or 9:00 o'clock from Grimsby in lots of fifty to sixty tons were considered to be "an inestimable boon" of the "finest fish," further transforming the market into a regional distributive centre.[107] Similarly, the price of fish in Durham was said to be "at least half what it was before. A large quantity of fish comes from Whitley and Cullercoats, and it is a great boon to the town; the poor get well supplied at a very small sum."[108] The same was true in Blackburn, Birmingham, and other large industrial towns.[109]

The growth of wholesale markets was not only influenced by the ability of market and municipal authorities to link public markets to railways but also by Parliament's willingness to integrate the national railway system into an increasingly international food regime. Thousands upon thousands of pages of parliamentary debates and inquiries attest to the vertiginous anxiety arising from the new possibilities and problems emerging from the acceleration of movement in space. Parliament's indefectible support for a legal framework aligning railway development with the nation's commitment to free trade policies reflected the extent to which railways were key to the development of an international geography of production opposing home to foreign producers. It is certainly a measure of the social benefits associated with cheap food imports that, by the turn of the century, very few British farmers would speak against the idea of free trade. "As a grower," said George Sinclair, a fruit grower from the Preston Kirk neighbourhood, "it [protection] would be a great benefit to me, but I am not convinced that it would be a benefit to the country."[110] What they could not accept, however, was the existence of two different rates for home and foreign producers. For instance, foreign dead meat from Liverpool to London was conveyed at twenty-five shillings per ton, compared to fifty shillings per ton for home meat. Until the emergence of ton-mile statistics in the late-1890s, rates were no more than well-informed guesses made by agents having a general sense of "what the market would bear."[111]

Despite their inability to prove that they were justified in quoting two different rates, railway companies found in the state an unswerving supporter. While upholding the view that undue preferences were justifiable as long as they benefitted the public, which was axiomatic in the case of cheap imported food, Parliament's efforts to promote the "public interest" were tested on 1 January 1893, when many railway companies raised their rates all at once. In an important piece of legislation, the Railway and Canal Traffic Act, 1894, stated that, following any complaint regarding the increase of a rate after 31 December 1892, it was the company's responsibility to prove that the increase was reasonable. The effect of the act, which came to be known as the "Trader's Charter," was to roll back many of the rates to their pre-1893 level, while severely restricting railways' capacity to raise their rates thereafter.[112] By limiting what companies could charge, the act not only proved an important gain when international food prices increased after 1896 but also introduced a strong incentive towards a more efficient and critical approach with regard to defining the costs of operation.

The emergence of ton-mile statistics in the late-1890s and early 1900s settled the whole issue. Examined before the Departmental Committee on Railway Rates in 1905, Sir George Gibb, general manager of the North Eastern Railway, reported that, out of a total of 561,728 tons of grain forwarded by the company in 1904 over its whole system, 295,835 tons (53 percent) were carried from ports – 91 percent of which came from Hull (182,419 tons) and Newcastle (86,803 tons). The difference (265,893 tons) was carried from 467 different stations other than ports, an average of 569 tons per station per year. The average load per train departing from various country stations and serving the inland farmers was about thirty-two tons, compared to 308 tons per train leaving the port of Hull and sent directly. Gibb further noted that, out of seventy ports in England, 94.3 percent of the total value of imports transited through only thirteen of them. "These conditions produce a situation in which railway carriage to and from the ports is necessarily on a more advantageous basis, so far as cost is concerned, than can be the case in inland parts of the country."[113] The British railway system thus promoted the constitution of an international food regime through low rates for large and bulky foreign consignments sent directly from docks. The result was the division of the railway system into distinct, consolidated geographical monopolies competing for goods traffic beyond the limits of their own system, especially from the ports.[114] Perhaps the most significant aspect here was not so much how long it took railway companies to develop the economic argument to support "undue preference" against home producers as it was Parliament's continuous support for it despite any such proof. The growing separation between retail and wholesale market functions must therefore be understood through the need for effective food distribution systems capable of handling mass food transportation.

Despite significant shifts towards wholesaling, however, the vast majority of public markets developed wholesaling capabilities while retaining their original retail function. With a few important exceptions, virtually all public markets allowed both small- and large-scale retailers to trade in the same space. As a result, the public market often continued to be the single major employer in the town's food retail industry as late as 1914. As Michael Winstanley's foray into retail property ownership in Edwardian England suggests, municipal authorities were the largest single owner of retail property "through the construction and ownership of covered market halls, which were erected in almost every northern industrial town in the mid-to-late Victorian period."[115] As a historical compromise between traditional and modern retail practices, public markets in general and market halls in particular tended to house five main groups of retail and wholesale workers. The first group was represented by country farmers. While their presence had diminished in large cities, they retained an important role throughout the period, especially in agricultural districts. Born in Ipswich in 1898, Cyril Angell remembers how "people came in from miles around" on market day, including small-holders and bigger farmers, to sell their produce.[116] As we saw, this was in part the result of their inclusion within reformed market structures, where rows of trestle tables and benches could be had for the day at a low price. Farmers' wives and daughters were still key figures of "pannier markets" and "pitching sales" in the early 1900s, coming to town on market day to sell poultry, eggs, cheese, butter, fruit, milk, meat, vegetables, and the like.

While farmer-retailers continued to play an important role in the towns' food supply, the growing distance between farm and fork contributed to the development of a permanent structure of "professional" traders and market retailers such as butchers, greengrocers, provision dealers, grocers, and confectioners.[117] As such, the establishment of a permanent class of specialized food retailers was most visible in large towns with covered market halls, but it was also noticeable in smaller conurbations where the market was not held every day. For example, many salespeople attending the enclosed market place in St Albans also traded in Luton, Dunstable, Leighton, Hemel Hempstead, and Tring on different market days, thus participating in a rich local retail economy often supported by regional wholesale markets.[118] Albeit diminishing, retail markets continued to play an important role in how people obtained their food. Indeed, about 10 percent of retail outlets in Accrington, Barrow, and Lancaster were permanent market stallholders in the 1900s.[119] Whether trading from an open air site or owning a stall or a shop in a covered market hall, this second group of market traders was probably the most important one as it benefited directly from market reforms. Closely connected to reformed markets was a third group composed of shopkeepers who also owned a stall or a shop in the public market. Although evidence from retail markets in northern and midland England suggest that a substantial majority of market stall- and shop-owners did not have other outlets, it was nonetheless common for shopkeepers such as butchers, poultry dealers, and greengrocers to have market premises as an additional outlet to sell their cheaper cuts of meat and offload perishable surpluses.[120]

A fourth group of retail and wholesale workers was made up of multiple shops, which were numerically less important than farmers-retailers, professional traders, or small shopkeepers. Their strategic development almost always took place outside of the market hall, but some, like Marks and Spencer, did grow out of it. Michael Marks was a licensed hawker trading in the mining and agricultural villages around Leeds before letting a stall in the open market in 1884, which was opened on Tuesdays and Saturdays. Marks added new outlets in Castleford and Wakefield where the markets fell on different days, and after moving his stall to the covered market hall in Leeds, he hired assistants to take care of his different stalls. New locations in covered market halls were added in Warrington (1890), Wigan (1891), Bolton (1892), and Birkenhead (1893), and with Thomas Spencer buying a half share of the business in 1894, the newly formed Marks and Spencer expanded even further. By 1903, the company had 36 branches – 24 were in market halls and 12 were shops. Compared to open markets, covered market halls provided important advantages such as protection from weather, a permanent counter that could be closed off, storage space to keep overstock, and business hours throughout the week.[121] From then on the number of branches in market halls and arcades decreased in both relative and absolute terms, constituting less than 10 percent of the 140 branches by 1914. With shop development becoming the main strategy of expansion after 1903, Marks and Spencer's business model showed the limits of the market hall as a fixed retail space. While multiples like Liptons and Home and Colonial often had a branch in the town's market hall, it was the private shop that gave them the spatial flexibility they needed to expand in the context of rapid urbanization.

A fifth and final group, this time connected with large retail and wholesale markets, comprised market and warehouse porters. Large markets in London, Manchester, Glasgow, and Aberdeen had their own licensed porters to be hired by shoppers and salespeople alike.[122] Very few porters had regular employment and the majority lived precarious lives.[123] Wages were irregular and rarely amounted to more than one pound per week. Alternating between bust and boom, casual porters could earn as little as on shilling per week during the winter and up to two and even three pounds per week for a few weeks during the summer.[124] By the early 1890s, between seven hundred and eight hundred porters were employed at Covent Garden Market, and it was said that they were "of several nationalities, and include[d] not a few Jews. They [were], as a rule, a hard-working lot, but [led] a very hand-to-mouth life."[125] The gendered division of labour within the distributive space meant that women porters were confined to the Flower Market, where they earned no more than six to twelve shillings per week. Many women would get employment in the market during the fruit season as "pea pickers, asparagus tiers, walnut shellers, &c., but these people during the rest of the year ha[d] to get on as best they [could]."[126] In their report to the Royal Commission on the Poor Laws in 1909, factory inspectors described how market porters in Manchester and Salford almost always lived in poverty, forming "a noticeable proportion of the common lodging-house population."[127] There is little evidence that the grim reality of pauperism among market porters changed significantly between 1830 and 1914, and, although their number was comparatively low in relation to street sellers, shopkeepers, shop assistants, and child labourers, their poverty was no less representative of a food distributive sector producing cheap food through cheap labour.

Although little is known about pay and working conditions in public markets, this rapid survey offers us some key insights. To begin with, market retailing was largely a family industry. While this is obvious in the case of farmer-retailers, the domestic nature of market activities was also noticeable among small-scale retailers. Examined before the RCMRT in 1888, Michael Butler, who had been connected for more than thirty years with Covent Garden, reported that shops in the market were generally a family industry passed down from father to son or from uncle to nephew, with some shops staying in the same family for up to fifty years.[128] Ada Carlile was eight years old in 1907 when she began to help her dad, who owned a retail and wholesale fruit and vegetable stall in Nottingham market. Unpaid for many years, her mum, who also helped in the market, gave her two shillings and five pence per week when she got older. After leaving school at fourteen, she started working full-time in the market for about one year before serving in her father's fruit and fish shop. Even after taking on a different job, she still had to help in the shop on Saturdays.[129] Unpaid family labour was rife among country people, permanent stall- or shop-owners, and small shopkeepers owning an additional stall or shop in the market, and no doubt constituted one of the, if not the, main forms of "employment" in public markets across Great Britain.

Another insight comes from the growing role played by women and girls as a source of cheap labour. While the sexual division of labour in agricultural households explained the presence of farm women and girls in public markets, permanent and professional sellers were also increasingly relying on women's work. "In Liverpool's St. John's Market from 1900 to 1930, for example, approximately 40 percent of the nearly three hundred permanent market shop and stallholders or 'occupiers' (not clerks) were women, and most casual country market sellers were women as well. Women dominated the fruit stalls and, as well, made up a sizeable portion of owners of stalls and shops selling poultry, fish, and meat."[130] Similarly, key to Marks and Spencer's business strategy was the systematic hiring of cheap female workers. Yet even with a minimum working week of 63 hours and wages ranging from 5 shillings a week for a girl of 14 to 18 shillings for an adult (girls hired on Saturdays were paid 2 shillings and 6 pence a day), working conditions were comparatively good, as we shall see in chapter 4.[131] More generally, wages and working conditions in public markets must not have differed substantially from those offered by competitors in outside shops. Most market halls were open seventy-five hours per week. After deducting meal times and adding unpaid overtime for the setting up and closing down of the stall or shop, it seems reasonable to say that an average working week of about seventy-five to eighty hours must have been the norm. In addition, market sellers who enjoyed lower overheads by operating from a stall were much more likely to "invest" in their competitiveness in the form of cheap foodstuffs for customers rather than in the form of higher wages in a sector already plagued by an oversupply of labour.

The battle over the political and economic control of the marketplace, its spatial integration within the industrial efficiency of a national railway system, and the rescaling of its activities in line with an emerging international food regime were the key changes underpinning the rise of the bourgeois distributive order. As a physically delimited space, the marketplace showed extraordinary dynamism during a period of intense and profound changes in Britain. Its transformation over the years did not always go smoothly, however, and the marketplace soon proved to be an important site of conflict between landed interests and a rising capitalist class eager to control one of the main levers of municipal power. Public markets continued to be appreciated as an institution of prime importance in smaller towns, whereas in the larger cities, important demographic changes in the context of rapid urbanization meant that more and more inhabitants came to live relatively far from public markets, especially in the booming suburbs of the Victorian era. This is not to say that these populations stopped shopping at the public market, but on a daily basis they became increasingly dependent on other forms of retailing to obtain their food.

To the extent that reformed public markets represented a remarkable transformation in the very structures of food distribution, the expansion of this innovation in space through small-scale retailers constituted another key development in the British retail system between 1830 and 1914. It was indeed the reorganization of the traditional marketplace into capitalist structures geared towards mass distribution that opened up the space for the subsequent expansion of street sellers and small shopkeepers in the urban environment, which, in turn, reinforced the development of the wholesale function in public markets. This symbiotic relationship, though not without its contradictions, actively contributed to the constitution of a more resilient and comprehensive system of food distribution capable of bridging the growing distance between the marketplace and working-class neighbourhoods. It was initially through these small-scale retailers that people stopped experiencing the market as a physical place, with the former becoming a spatially mobile metaphor substituting for the spatial fixity of the latter. In carrying the logic of the marketplace outside its walls, street sellers and small shopkeepers, who depended on the public market for their supplies, contributed to an important shift from the market*place* to the market*space*. It is to one of the main actors of this newly minted spatial mobility that we now turn.

3

Street Sellers

In her lecture at the Economic Club on 10 January 1893, English social reformer Helen Dendy argued that "the industrial residuum" – a class characterized by the inferiority of its labour, the factitiousness of its employment, and the permanent failure to maintain itself – was "economically dead" and had "no real use" in a modern economy. Living at the periphery of an otherwise expanding capitalist universe, Dendy concluded that "the best that can really be hoped for it is that it should gradually wear itself away, or in the coming generation be reabsorbed into the industrial life on which it is at present a mere parasite."[1] Beside her contempt for the poorest segments of the population, which exposed the resilience of poverty amidst unprecedented economic development and showed the ruling class's unwillingness to take responsibility for its own creation, her characterization of "the industrial residuum" as some sort of economic deadwood could not be further from the truth. In fact, many members of "the industrial residuum," such as streets sellers, were of prime economic importance, their existence playing a key role in keeping wages and working conditions in check. Far from being anachronistic figures, these castaways of industrial capitalism were indeed essential to its functioning. As we shall see, their competitive edge in the retail environment came at a heavy price for it was precisely the wretchedness of their lives that constituted the basis of their economic function as cheap food distributors.[2]

As we saw in the last chapter, the retail revolution was in part based on the architectural transformation and spatial reconfiguration of the marketplace in the context of increasingly dense and complex urban environments. Accompanying this reorganization of food distribution was the rise of an important class of street sellers, commonly referred to as costermongers, hawkers, hucksters, or pedlars. While the overwhelming majority carried trays or baskets of goods, some rose "to the dignity of a wheelbarrow," often alternating between dealing from a fixed stand and doing rounds in the streets.[3] As Reverend W. Rogers put it in 1857, only "the most aristocratic" could afford to keep a pony or donkey with a cart.[4] The vast majority of street sellers lived in chronic poverty and inhabited overcrowded, filthy, and dilapidated dwellings. They were also fierce competitors who sold food cheaper than anybody else and therefore performed a vital function in providing working-class people with the necessities of life. While the growing number of people taking to the streets in the second half of the nineteenth century tended to reinforce the competitive nature of the sector, it also reinforced their vital economic function as cheap food distributors and contributed to their spatial dispersion in rapidly changing urban landscapes. The result was not simply the growing presence of street sellers in Victorian and Edwardian Britain but also the rising proportion of customers, municipal governments, and market authorities recognizing the central economic role that they played in delivering cheap food.

Combined with the absence of a social safety net, the inability of the economic system to provide stable and full-time jobs to all of those looking for work reinforced the formation of a reserve army of labour, which, in turn, changed the social composition of the costermongering class. Although street selling remained in part a hereditary occupation up until 1914, especially in London, the mass import of cheap food confirmed its role as an economic refuge by further facilitating one's ability to take to the streets.[5] From the 1870s onwards, street selling increasingly became "the ploy of immigrants, the unskilled, the unemployed, the old, the sick, the victimised and the injured," as well as of criminals who, having lost their name, could not get work in the labour market again, except as hawkers.[6] The growing presence of costermongers in the streets of Britain and the general appreciation of their role as purveyors of cheap food was itself a strong counterpoint to the bourgeois idea of social progress. The painful irony of an underfed population selling cheap food to the masses clashed with the bourgeoisie's seemingly sanitized, modern, and rationalized approach to economic growth and urban development. Moreover, the growing legal apparatus designed to deal with this "dangerous class" reinforced the vulnerability of the hawker's economic position and secured its role as an essential component of the food supply system.

A MOST USEFUL CLASS

The etymology of the word "costermonger" comes from a deformation of the word "custard," a kind of apple that was said to be "round and bulky like the head." A "coster-monger" or "custard-monger" was someone who sold apples.[7] The presence of the coster in the streets of London can be traced back to at least the sixteenth century, with Christopher Marlowe's *Doctor Faustus* and William Shakespeare's *Henry IV* referring to the famous itinerant trader.[8] The geographical origin of the term partly explains why "costermonger" was mainly used in London, while the term "hawker" was generally employed outside of the metropolis. Although there were social, cultural, and regional differences in the ways in which the terms "costermongers," "hawkers," and "pedlars" were used, competing and contradictory definitions often coexisted. For instance, some made a spatial distinction by associating costermongers with intra-urban trade and hawkers with inter-urban trade, even though many contemporaries referred to street sellers dealing exclusively in Manchester or Glasgow as hawkers.[9] In order to avoid confusion, I use the terms "costermongers," "hawkers," and "pedlars" in their larger sense of street sellers or itinerant traders and, therefore, follow Alexander's inclusive definition of itinerant distribution "as all retail trading outside fixed shops," excluding formal markets.[10]

We can identify three major transformations in the nature of itinerant distribution, all of which must be situated in the context of capitalist development. The first one is associated with the rise of an important intra-urban trading class and the decline in the number of country itinerants – commonly called Cheap Johns – who specialized in inter-urban trade, although pedlars continued to play an important role in some villages such as Tysoe and Moss Ferry.[11] Already noticeable in the metropolis in the 1830s, an urban-based costermongering class quickly developed outside of London in the second half of the century. A second transformation, this time linked to the constitution of a landless, market-dependent working class, was the growing proportion of those dealing in foodstuffs. While street sellers engaged in an impressive variety of trades, including stationery, ink and literature, flowers, matches, clothes, and newspapers, most of

Table 3.1
Number of street sellers in Britain, 1851–1911

	England and Wales		Scotland	
	Number	Per person	Number	Per person
1851	25,747	696	4,744	609
1861	37,671	533	5,526	554
1871	49,775	456	–	–
1881	47,111	551	6,202	602
1891	58,919	492	6,446	625
1901	61,339	530	6,200	721
1911	69,437	520	6,845	696

Source: BPP 1852–53a, "Census of Great Britain 1851," ccxxii, ccxxvi; BPP 1852–53b, "Census of Great Britain 1851," 908, 912; BPP 1863a, "Census of England and Wales 1861," xxxiii–iv; BPP 1864, "Census of Scotland 1861," 96, 107; BPP 1873a, "Census of England and Wales 1871," xxxviii, xliv; BPP 1873b, "Census of Scotland 1871," 468; BPP 1904c, "Census of England and Wales 1901," 280; BPP 1917–18, "Census of England and Wales 1911," 144–5; BPP1913b, "Census of Scotland 1911," lxxxvi. Data on total population to calculate the number of street hawkers per inhabitant are taken from: BPP 1917–18, "Census of England and Wales 1911," 21; BPP 1913b, "Census of Scotland 1911," xxii.

them sold eatables and drinkables such as fruit and vegetables, fish, nuts, meat, tea, bread, hot potatoes, pies, cheese, milk, and coffee. The third major transformation is linked to the remarkable increase in the number of street sellers. At a time during which there was no social safety net, except for the workhouse, which offered little more than semi-starvation, taking to the street was often one's last resort before complete destitution.

Table 3.1 shows official estimates of the number of street sellers in Britain between 1851 and 1911. Given the difficulties associated with the porous and informal nature of the trade, however, official figures were never more than a pale reflection of the actual size of the coster-mongering class as the vast majority escaped the administrative net. In his well-known survey of London, social commentator Henry Mayhew described the 1851 census return of 3,723 street sellers as "absurdly small," estimating that about thirty-five thousand men, women, and children subsisted in the streets of London alone on the sale of fish, fruit, and vegetables.[12] Extremely low numbers in Manchester, Salford, Liverpool, Glasgow, Leeds, Newcastle, and South Wales also suggest important problems with government figures.[13] Hollingshead estimated the population of street hawkers and street minstrels in the metropolis, including their dependent, at 100,000 in 1861.[14] Arguably, the 1891 census returns estimating the number of costers and street sellers in London at 11,992 do not make much sense.[15] Building on Charles Booth's work, Arthur Sherwell estimated at 24,094 the number of costers or street-seller heads of families in the mid-1890s in London. As Sherwell carefully noted, however, this number excluded the majority of those depending on street selling as it referred exclusively to families in which the heads were engaged in such trade and, therefore, excluded both women and children and those costers who were not heads of families.[16]

There are three main reasons that explain the discrepancies between government returns and the actual size of the costermongering class. To begin with, most hawkers were illiterate and could not (or simply would not) complete the census returns. Many did not know their age, and "not one in twenty of the costermongers troubled themselves to fill up the census returns."[17] While literacy rates increased from the 1870s onwards as a result of the Elementary Education Act, 1870, in England and Wales and the Education (Scotland) Act, 1872, costers' distrust of any forms of authority, especially the much hated police, made them question the purpose of census returns. Street sellers disregarded such inquiries as a useless and inappropriately intrusive formality that would not change anything about their economic condition. Moreover, the social and cultural stigma associated with street selling must have been an important hindrance to properly filling in the census returns. For instance, bankrupt shopkeepers or skilled workers forced to take to the street because of illness, unemployment, or underemployment would not have accepted their new social status so easily.

Second, throughout the period under review there was always an important proportion of country people coming into town to hawk their products in the streets. Their presence was generally greatly appreciated by town inhabitants both for the cheapness of their articles and the convenience of having the goods delivered at their door. The rescaling of the marketplace from retailing to wholesaling tended to favour large-scale producers while marginalizing small farmers. Although farmers continued to attend to the market, hawking their produce often gave them the ability to avoid paying market tolls. While their presence was probably more important in small towns, farmers taking to the street was not uncommon in large urban centres either, especially those situated within agricultural districts such as

Hull, Birmingham, and Exeter, where a great deal of fruits, vegetables, milk, cheese, and butter were sold.[18] Greengrocer William Pepler complained about "hundreds of horses and carts coming into Bristol from the country daily with greengrocery, and they hawk the streets of Bristol and go from door to door and sell their goods."[19] Farmers coming into town to make ends meet were very unlikely to describe themselves as street sellers at the time of the census as most of them would have despised being associated with street hawking, a sure reference to the lowest order of society.

Finally, and perhaps more importantly, many workers temporarily took to the street in times of economic hardship. As we saw, coster-mongering and hawking were "residual occupations for casual workers" offering a last occupational refuge before complete destitution, homelessness, or the much-feared workhouse.[20] Unemployment and underemployment, economic fluctuations, trade cycles, and seasonal employment forced many dockers, builders, bricklayers, brickmakers, and casual workers into hawking in order to stave off hunger. Of course, the necessity of taking to the streets depended on one's capacity to earn enough in "normal" times to save for periods of unemployment or illness. While workers in virtually every trade experienced periods of adversity, the stratification of the labour market between skilled, semi-skilled, and unskilled workers greatly influenced the extent to which one could weather market fluctuations, especially during winter months and the seasonal interruption in the supply of raw materials. As historian Gareth Stedman Jones puts it, "undertakers took on extra workers at the beginning of November to cope with the extra supply of corpses."[21] Official returns must therefore be regarded with great precaution. At best, they represent a very low estimate of the "permanent core" of full-time street sellers.[22]

Notwithstanding the problem of counting an elusive and mobile workforce, the number of costers in London was proportionally much higher than in provincial towns as there was "no parallel in any other city."[23] To a great extent, this was linked to the lack of retail markets in the metropolis. Between 1800 and 1840, population per market increased from 39,900 to 114,600, while the number of retail markets declined from 24 to 17 during the same period. This meant that "by 1840 only 0.34 million out of 2 million Londoners were able to obtain their provisions from formal retail markets."[24] It was in the growing space left by inadequate retail markets that costers came to be "accepted by the mass of Londoners as a metropolitan institution of primary importance. The 'coster' has his place, in song and story, in verse and picture, as one of London's best-known characters. He is of the people; for the people."[25] The lack of retail markets underpinned the tendency for street traders "to settle into fixed sites, creating new markets, albeit that these were informal gatherings with no buildings or infrastructure." Informal markets made up of costers and hawkers such as the Newport Market, Oxford Market, Paddington Market, New Cut, Whitecross Street, Whitechapel, and Mile End Road mushroomed, rising from 37 in the early 1850s to 112 in 1893 to 130 in the early 1900s. The majority of the stalls sold perishable foodstuffs, and, although the 1888–91 Royal Commission of Market Rights and Tolls had all but ignored unauthorized markets in its thirteen volumes, a special report to the London County Council (LCC) in 1893 concluded that at least thirteen of these informal markets were important enough to be considered retail markets in the ordinary sense of the term.[26]

In Manchester, Leeds, Newcastle, and Glasgow, rising urban and suburban density also triggered the transformation of public markets into regional wholesale distributive centres, which, in turn, created the space for a costermongering class to grow.[27] Hawkers in Bolton and Ashton-under-Lyne generally bought wholesale in Manchester before selling from door to door, a practice appreciated by town dwellers but despised by market stallholders and shopkeepers.[28] Alice Foley and Albert Williams, who grew up in Bolton in the 1890s and 1900s, remember vividly the importance of street trading and the remarkably varied nature of the commodities that they sold on the streets.[29] In Chorley, the "problem" of street hawkers was considered particularly acute for, while the market days were on Tuesdays and Saturdays, hawkers roamed in the streets every day, seriously depriving market stallholders from their custom.[30] In some places, like Rochdale, where hawkers played an important role in the distribution of food, they formed associations.[31] In order to control this growing class of itinerant traders, many corporations, such as Halifax and Huddersfield, adopted licensing systems.[32] Yet statistics from licensing systems rarely (if ever) captured the reality on the ground. There was also a clear concentration in the counties along the south and east coasts.[33] While stallholders in the Eastgate Market in Gloucester complained about the unfair competition of hawkers coming from Cheltenham,[34] the market in Torquay was not very popular because hawkers supplied the town with an impressive range of food goods, such as fish, meat, poultry, fruit, butter, vegetables, and eggs, brought from Dartmouth, Newton, Exeter, and Totnes. Their importance was such that hawking tolls were the main source of income of the private company holding the market rights.[35]

This quick summary of the composition and geography of the costermongering class gives us a better appreciation of the economic importance of this ubiquitous figure of Victorian and Edwardian Britain. For the bulk of the working class earning less than thirty shillings a week, the coster was key to rising living standards. Contrary to shopkeepers who often charged up to 150 percent on the articles bought, the coster was "satisfied" with very tiny profits.[36] As John Denton, costermonger at Spitalfields, put it: "We have to buy cheap, because if we did not buy cheap we could not sell cheap, and if we could not sell cheap we could not sell a quantity, and if we did not sell a quantity it would not pay us."[37] Attending the informal Whitecross Street Market on a Saturday night of November 1868, Greenwood counted no less than thirteen hundred people coming out of the street between eight and nine o'clock, most of which were "of the decent working order."[38] As James William Sullivan put it in 1913: "Working-class London in general, and much of middle-class London as well, buy the bulk of their perishable necessaries from ambulant pushcart vendors or at the open-air markets. The system is at once the most ancient and the most modern. It is the cheapest of all systems – efficient, natural, democratic, rightfully communistic. It often gives the masses double rations."[39] For the poorest segments of the working class, costers' low prices were the surest way to stave off hunger. Whether in the metropolis or outside of it, careful housewives hunting for bargains could count on the coster as an important ally in their quest to make their money go further.

As Sullivan suggested, the costermonger's custom was not limited to the working class, as important as it was. Already in the 1850s, John Page – writing under the pseudonym of Felix Folio – noted how middle-class housewives buying cheap food from hawkers in the industrial towns of the north was not so uncommon a scene as one might have believed.[40] By 1880, the practice was ordinary and many municipal authorities encouraged it, often by abolishing tolls on hawking activities. In Bedford, for instance, public authorities argued that the loss in municipal revenues was largely compensated by the greater availability of cheaper food for its inhabitants, ratepayers themselves taking advantage of these bargains.[41] As George Robert

Shorto, managing clerk in Exeter, put it: "If ... it should be attempted to do away with selling from door to door, it would occasion the greatest possible inconvenience to a very large class of householders, because the city spreads a great way, about 2.5 miles in one direction, so that a great deal of hawking must be done. I should say that a certain class of householders, the lower middle class, are entirely supplied by people who come to the door."[42] Although, comparatively, working classes benefitted the most from these cheap bargains, there were no fixed rules over which classes frequented the costers, and countless variations existed. While many working-class families were tied to the corner shop through debt, costers were, as a rule, simply too poor to allow credit.[43] Yet their ability to sell cheaper than their competitors ensured their presence in the working class's household economy.[44] Skilled workers, anxious to retain social status and respectability, could choose to bring their custom to the shop instead, and in places where a strong culture of mutuality existed, the politics of consumption was likely to tie an important part of the household budget to the co-op. Yet since most co-operative societies did not sell perishables at the time, there was always a potentially important custom for those costermongers who "specialized" in such articles.

Local governments and market authorities were all too aware of street sellers' vital economic function in clearing markets of unsold domestic and imported food items and redistributing surplus produce to the poorer classes. Tables 3.2 and 3.3 give an idea of their importance in the sale of fish, fruit, and vegetables in London around 1850. By the late 1880s, George Packer, secretary to the London Fish Trade Association, and Robert Horner, owner of the Spitalfields Market, praised costermongers, respectively, as "the best customers to Billingsgate Market" and as "very useful people in clearing the market."[45] All recognized costers' key importance in the distribution of cheap food, further noting that if, from bad weather, fish or any other commodities were scarce in the market, they would buy something else to supply their customers with whatever was available that day. Street sellers not only delivered cheap food, they also mediated the worst effects of rapid urbanization and urban sprawl through their ability to overcome the spatial fixity of other retail actors, such as public markets. Hollingshead's reference to them as those "who follow the markets" and Hardy's appreciation of their role as "taking the market" to their customers capture well the spatial capacity of street sellers to displace the marketplace from its geographical fixity.[46]

Table 3.2
Proportion of fish from Billingsgate sold by costermongers, ca.1850

Fish	Number	Weight (lbs.)	Proportion sold by costermongers
Salmon and salmon trout	406,000	3,480,000	One-twentieth
Live cod	400,000	4,000,000	One-fourth
Soles	97,520,000	26,880,000	One-fifteenth
Whiting	17,920,000	6,720,000	One-fourth
Plaice	33,600,000	33,600,000	Seven-eighths
Mackerel	23,520,000	23,520,000	Two-thirds
Fresh herrings (per bar)	175,000,000	42,000,000	One-half
Fresh herrings (in bulk)	1,050,000,000	252,000,000	Three-fourths
Dried salt cod	1,600,000	8,000,000	One-tenth
Bloaters	147,000,000	10,600,000	One-fourth
Oysters	495,896,000		One-fourth

Source: Mayhew, London Labour, 63.

In places such as London, where wholesale markets were extremely developed, the scalar interface existing between costermongers and wholesalers could prove difficult to reconcile. Since large sellers handling great quantities of foodstuffs were chiefly uninterested in dealing with small-scale retailers, a new class of "semi-wholesalers" or "wholesale-retail men" – known as "higglers" (fruit and vegetable) or "bummarees" (fish) – emerged to bridge the gap between the two.[47] The conditions of existence of these "speculative dealers" thus largely depended upon their ability to control the market supply by enacting planned scarcity.[48] This helps to explain why they were present in Billingsgate Market, Covent Garden, and Farringdon Fruit and Vegetable Market, where powerful salespeople operated, and absent from Shadwell Fish Market and Spitalfields Market, where wholesale traders did not control the supply of goods.[49] While costermongers often depicted higglers and bummarees as a parasitic class of dealers standing between them and the market, their mediating role and function remained central as they reconciled two seemingly contradictory yet deeply complementary aspects: (1) the formation of large-scale distribution facilities through the creation of colossal wholesale markets, the constitution of a national railway system, and the consolidation of an international food regime; and (2) the resilience and daily importance of labour-intensive methods of street selling amidst booming urbanization and suburbanization.

Table 3.3
Proportion of home-grown fruit and vegetables from the metropolitan wholesale markets sold by costermongers, ca.1850

Fruit and vegetables	Covent Garden	Borough	Spitalfields	Total	Proportion sold by costermongers
Apples (bushels)	360,000	25,000	250,000	686,000	One-half
Pears (bushels)	230,000	10,000	83,000	353,000	One-half
Gooseberries (bushels)	140,000	26,200	91,500	276,700	Three-fourths
Strawberries (pottles)	638,000	330,000	396,000	1,527,500	One-half
Potatoes (lbs.)	161,280,000	48,384,000	64,512,000	310,096,000	One-fifteenth
Cabbages (plants)	33,600,000	19,200,000	12,000,000	89,672,000	One-third
Turnips (roots)	18,300,000	4,800,000	4,800,000	32,648,000	One-tenth
Peas (bushels)	270,000	50,000	100,000	438,000	One-half
Onions (bushels)	500,000	398,000	400,000	1,489,600	One-third

Source: Mayhew, *London Labour*, 80.

POLICING THE "DARK CONTINENT"

In arguing that "the British public know more of the social misery of savage nations, than they do of their own poor," social reformer William Dodd captured both the ruling class's mounting feeling of insecurity over "the dangerous classes" at home and the extent to which the colonial empire reached at the very core of Britain's geographical imagination.[50] It is indeed remarkable, as English historian Asa Briggs points out, "how often the exploration of the unknown city was compared with the exploration of Africa and Asia."[51] For the "respectable society," slums and poverty-stricken neighbourhoods were dangerous places threatening the social order – that is, internal colonies that had yet to be blessed by the bourgeois civilizing mission.[52] From religious missions to journalists and social commentators exploring the maze of poverty in British slums, the metaphor of a dark underworld captured both the anxiety and contempt of a ruling class presiding over the accumulation of wealth and destitution.

Street sellers belonged to the "dark continent" as surely as Prometheus was chained to a rock. Even the progressive Charles Booth referred to the costers' children as "dirty, filthy, rough, and savage."[53] As a class they were considered unruly and prone to gratify bodily pleasures over intellectual achievements. The racialization and lower economic status of the costermongering class went hand in hand, reinforcing the need to police the borders of the bourgeois sanitized urban space against the threat of corruption and degeneration from below. Frequently harassed by the police to keep them on the move and legally surveilled by a growing juridical apparatus, costermongers lived under the perennial risk of being taken into custody or having their goods confiscated. At a meeting held in London in December 1860, street vendors complained that they "were subjected to fine and imprisonment, and were told when they were following their occupation that they were violating the law. The great objection made against them was that they obstructed the thoroughfares."[54] The clarification of their legal status came in 1867 with the Metropolitan Streets Act, which at first seemed to confirm their illicit status. Later that year, section 6 of the act, which prohibited the deposit of goods in the streets, was amended so that it "shall not apply to costermongers, street hawkers, or itinerant traders, so long as they carry on their business in accordance with the regulations from time to time made by the Commissioner of Police, with the approval of the Secretary of

State."[55] The amendment reflected the core tension between an idealized bourgeois urban order and the economic necessity of the costermongering class for the city's food.

By the end of 1869, regulations were in place and stipulated that no barrow, cart, or stall could exceed nine feet in length by three feet in width. Most important, regulations specified that street sellers were "liable to be removed from any street or public way in which they create an obstruction to the traffic, or where they are an annoyance to the inhabitants."[56] While the spirit of the law was that none of them would be interfered with as long as they followed the regulations, its effect was to give the police full power over them, and evidence suggests that what constituted "obstruction" or "annoyance" could be interpreted quite liberally. Even the LCC, which acknowledged the importance of informal markets, saw them as a source of serious nuisance. As Hardy perceptively noted, however, "the nuisance is theoretic rather than practical, an offence against a rather visionary idea of civic order."[57] Costers belonged to what Victorians called the dangerous classes, "whose very manner of living seemed a challenge to ordered society and the tissue of laws, moralities and taboos holding it together."[58] The presence of the coster in the streets was itself an important reminder that the "civic order" to which Victorians aspired as well as their ideals of "progress" and "improvement" were ultimately founded upon the explicit social, economic, and political marginalization of an important segment of the working poor. And it was precisely costers' indigence and lack of bourgeois "respectability" that made them at once economically valuable and socially threatening.[59]

With the slow transfer of legal responsibilities and political control to local authorities, municipal governments outside the metropolis also became very active in regulating food distribution activities. For instance, the Public Health Act, 1848, gave public authorities the power to legislate over street selling, a legal capacity that local boards – often composed of many influential grocers and tradespeople – were not slow to implement. "By 1886, two-thirds of Britain's principal municipal boroughs had, in theory at least, prohibited marketing on the street, except for the occasional designated locations."[60] Notwithstanding the growing legal apparatus of municipal restrictions on street selling, most public authorities turned a blind eye. Large provincial towns with important public markets generally recognized the complementary role played by hawkers in the distribu-

tion of food. In Birmingham, Edinburgh, Glasgow, Hull, Leeds, Liverpool, Manchester, and Newcastle, hawkers, licensed or not, did not
pay any charges. Even in smaller towns such as Preston, Sheffield, and
Stockton, where public markets were very popular, no charges were
demanded as long as they stayed outside the precinct of the market.[61]
Where hawkers worked under a system of licences like in Bradford,
Halifax and Huddersfield, complaints against hawkers, especially by
stallholders in the market, were almost non-existent.[62]

This extensive legal apparatus offered a flexible political tool that
could be used either assiduously or with laxity, according to the bal-
ance of power at the municipal level between shopkeepers, ratepayers,
and working classes. Yet even where costers were popular, police
harassment was frequent, and Roberts recalls how, in the slum of Salford, "the police made drives against 'illegal street traders'" at regular
intervals in the early twentieth century.[63] The situation was not better
in Rochdale, where hawker John A. Tolon reported that many of those
who "were prosecuted were without arms, and some of them without
legs, and some of them very old, they were people quite unfit to get
their living at ordinary work."[64] Such distasteful police actions, however, even in places where costers were very much appreciated, must
be understood in the context of local interests. As we shall see in the
next chapter, shopkeepers' influence over municipal politics often
coalesced into stringent local regulations or arbitrary police actions.
The criminalization of street sellers was the surest way for the "shop-
ocracy" to influence the politics of consumption through the spatial
control of the competitive environment.

Police interference with the costers' business explains their extreme
hatred of the police. Many of the costers "could not understand why
Chartist leaders exhorted them to peace and quietness, when they
might as well fight it out with the police at once." As one costermonger told Mayhew: "Can you wonder at it, sir, that I hate the police?
They drive us about, we must move on, we can't stand here, and we
can't pitch there." The collective hostility arising from their shared
experience of repression often gave way to a strong political sense,
which was visible in countless daily acts of mutual aid. "One very
common procedure, if the policeman has seized a barrow, is to whip
off a wheel, while the officers have gone for assistance; for a large and
loaded barrow requires two men to convey it to the green-yard. This
is done with great dexterity; and the next step is to dispose of the stock
to any passing costers, or to any 'standing' in the neighbourhood, and

it is honestly accounted for. The policemen, on their return, find an empty, and unwheelable barrow, which they must carry off by main strength, amid the jeers of the populace."[65] Any attempts at controlling their lives tended to reinforce bonds of solidarity and mutual assistance as well as to cultivate radical political ideas.

Costermongers' political consciousness did not escape contemporaries. Reverend W. Rogers referred to the costermongers as "the people who, in times of disturbance, would be the first to band themselves against the authorities."[66] Mayhew was more blunt: "I'm assured that in case of a political riot every 'coster' would seize his policeman." To injure a policeman was indeed considered an important feat of arms that would be celebrated "by a whip-round from his fellows' meagre earnings."[67] Costers made their appearance under the Police rubric of the *Times* on a regular basis. For instance, not appreciating that his mother was "pushed up the court towards her home" by two constables trying to disperse a crowd, hawker John Belham hurled a brick at a policeman, hitting him on the upper lip. When assistance arrived, "a desperate crowd of some 200 roughs tried to rescue him. The police were stoned and kicked in all directions" by a mob principally composed of women. Similarly, costermonger John Andrews was convicted for aggravated assault, the policeman being "so seriously assaulted ... that he had never since been able to be on duty."[68] For this precarious retailing class earning its pittance on the streets of the wealthiest nation on earth, being "moved on" or having one's goods confiscated could make all the difference between bare subsistence and semi-starvation. Hence costermongers' bitter attitude towards the police and moments of solidarity from the populations they served, especially poor people who understood that, through the control they exerted over street sellers, authorities were indirectly attacking their own ability to survive.

By the late 1890s, the issue of control started shifting towards the policing of a rapidly increasing labour force in the urban landscape – child labour. According to the Report of the Board of Education for 1906–07, there were 82,328 children in Great Britain under the "half time system," most of whom were concentrated in Lancashire, the West Riding of Yorkshire, and the county boroughs of Bradford, Burnley, Oldham, and Sheffield. "These half timers are children over twelve years of age who have obtained a labor certificate, and who are then allowed by the law to be sent to work half a day in mills or factories, provided that they are sent to school the other half of the day."[69] There were a certain number of regulations attached to this system, such as a mandatory limit of 27.5 hours of work per week. These children, who fell under the jurisdiction of the Factory and Workshops Act, 1901, represented only a fraction of those working for a wage, and children working in domestic work, street trading, agriculture, and shops constituted a veritable little army of cheap hands.

In June 1898, the Education Department sent a circular to all the 20,022 public elementary schools in England and Wales to inquire about the number of children working for wages. About 9,949 circulars were returned blank, indicating that, according to the managers of these schools, wage-earning children did not exist at their address. Despite the "defective nature of many of the returns," it was found that, out of 9,433 schedules filled in, no fewer than 144,026 full-time school children worked for wages, exclusive of the 409 schedules (3,323 children) that were returned late. Of them, 2,435 were considered hawkers and 76,173 worked in shops or ran errands for shopkeepers, delivering goods such as milk, groceries, and the like. The department also found that 99,623 (69.1 percent) of these apprentice wage labourers worked twenty hours or less, and that 39,752 (27.6 percent) were employed for twenty-one hours or more. Over 85 percent of them earned three shillings or less per week, and 72 percent two shillings or less per week, a level of exploitation that would have put any working adults in a sure state of starvation.[70] The political economy underpinning child labour only made sense as a livelihood strategy whereby households used the limited assets they possessed to make ends meet.

The findings of the Education Department were unreasonably low, if only taking into account the number of street sellers. The Inter-Departmental Committee on Employment of School Children conducted a more exhaustive survey a few years later, which led to a substantial reassessment of previous estimates. Reporting in 1902, the committee estimated the number of children working for wages in 1898 at about 300,000, over twice as much as previously thought. Furthermore, it revised upwards the number of street sellers to 25,000 and the number of children working in shops to about 100,000. As the report concluded: "if all children employed at any time of the year, however irregularly or for however short a period, could be included, it is probable that the figure should be considerably increased."[71] The previous year the Public Control Department of the LCC had estimated "that between 12,000 and 20,000 children [were] employed in connection with street markets," thus suggesting that the number of children employed in street trading in Britain was much more important than was suggested by these new figures.[72] More generally, in defining street trading as any activities carried on in streets or public places for profit, public authorities tended to underestimate the number of child street vendors.[73] While costermongers buying their wares at the public market and disposing of them in the streets operated on their own small capital and profits, children employed as street sellers usually worked for a wage.[74] Tens of thousands of them were errand boys employed by a shop to deliver milk and groceries to customers in the morning, often turning to street selling for the same shop once deliveries were completed.

Alarmed by the growing number of schoolchildren working for a wage, Parliament passed the Employment of Children Act in 1903. The act prohibited children under the age of eleven from engaging in street trading and gave local authorities the power to make bylaws for persons less than sixteen years of age in relation to street trading. It also contained a statutory provision prohibiting children less than fourteen years of age to work before 6:00 a.m. and after 9:00 p.m., although local governments could change these hours. Appointed to inquire into the functioning of the 1903 act, the report of the 1910 Departmental Committee concluded that it had largely been a failure. Although 50 out of 74 county boroughs in England and Wales had made street trading bylaws under section 2 of the act, only 41 out of 191 small boroughs and urban districts had done so. London, which made bylaws only in 1906, did not even start enforcing them until 1908. While the commissioners were "satisfied that a considerable amount of street trading is still done by children under eleven," they also concluded that the act was "almost a dead letter" in Scotland. None of the 33 county councils, 3 out of the 56 burghs (Glasgow, Partick, and Perth), and only 27 out of 979 school boards had adopted bylaws regulating street trading, and evidence received from Scotland showed "that the statutory provisions of the Act are violated in a very flagrant manner."[75] The problem of street selling by children, already challenging south of the border, was also rampant in Scotland, especially in the slums of Edinburgh, Glasgow, and Dundee.

Control over this young generation of street sellers was typically carried through municipal licensing systems. Total number of licences issued from 1904 to 1908 in England and Wales increased from 5,043 to 22,194, excluding London. In London, 13,873 badges where issued in 1909 to boys between 11 and 16 years of age. Badges were not issued to girls since London, as in the majority of cases in England and Wales, had bylaws prohibiting street trading for girls younger than sixteen years old on the basis that the trade was morally compromising. In Scotland, where authorities had almost systematically failed to adopt bylaws and where the statutory provisions of the act were not carried out, only three hundred boys and three girls were registered or licensed as street sellers for Edinburgh, Glasgow, Perth, and Partick.[76] Despite London and Liverpool arguing that they were in control of the situation, the commissioners received strong evidence that thousands of children escaped the licensing net. John Mulvany, superintendent of the Metropolitan Police in the Whitechapel and Spitalfields divisions, not only stated that there was "very much more" street trading by children in London than there used to be but also that many children lent their badges when not using them.[77]

Licensing systems upheld a form of bourgeois paternalism whereby, in an attempt to produce orderly subjects, the state and local authorities could blame "irresponsible" parents. In Liverpool, where bylaws prohibiting street trading for boys under fourteen and girls under sixteen were adopted as early as 1898, unless licensed by the corporation, children seeking to obtain a licence were required to appear "neat and clean" before the Children Trading in Streets Sub-Committee. Failure to do so would result in the adjournment of the process until the child was "able to attend clean and fairly well clothed." As it happened, children simply borrowed clothes for the occasion.[78] Somehow, the forced individualization and accountability of children was supposed to compensate for the fact that a large number of them lived in dire poverty in "unsuitable homes." In certain localities, such as Birmingham and London, badges of different colours to denote that a child was or was not free from school were used. Though often limited, resistance to these different forms of control was nonetheless ever present. Apart from unlicensed children playing hide-and-seek with the police or borrowing badges, boys in London, ashamed of having to wear a badge, turned it inside out, left the strap outside, or simply put it in their pockets.[79]

The police did not make the lives of these children easy. In Liverpool, 265 children were arrested for trading without licences in 1901, and 647 offences and breaches of the regulations were reported for those with a licence. In 460 cases the child was cautioned, but 187 of them either saw their licence revoked or temporarily suspended. By 1910, 12 percent of juvenile-adult prisoners and ex-prisoners at Wormwood Scrubbs Prison were streets sellers. Reverend S.P.H. Statham reported that 13.2 percent of the lads between sixteen and twenty-one years of age committed to the Wakefield prison between 1 April 1908 and 31 July 1909 were street sellers, most of whom had been jailed for minor offences such as sleeping out, trespassing on the railway stations, or obstructing the footpath. In 1905, about one thousand prosecutions were issued in the metropolis, and, in 1908, 70,263 tickets for violations of the street trading bylaws were given. Over a six-month period from 1909 to 1910, London authorities reported 3,582 infringements by children between 11 and 16 years of age, 2,512 of which (70 percent) were committed by children less than 14 years of age.[80]

For children earning as little as two shillings per week and working very long hours, these fines were a serious hindrance to their contribution to the household. Legislation that sought to redress what it identified as a social problem often ended up reinforcing it by punishing the poor for attempting to escape poverty. This was apparently well understood by the members of the Minority Report on the working of the Employment of Children Act, 1903, as they opposed the Majority Report's recommendation for the immediate prohibition of street trading by children. Choosing this path, they argued, "will tend to aggravate rather than improve the present state of things ... Street trading cannot, in our view, be treated as an isolated problem without regard to the social conditions in which it exists."[81] Poverty, they recognized, was key to understanding why so many children roamed in the streets of Britain. It was indeed no great insight that children from poor neighbourhoods were disproportionally working outside school hours. As long as wages remained insufficient to provide for a minimum of material comfort for the family, child labour would continue to be a key livelihood strategy to improve households' economic position, especially among the working poor.

KEEPING THE WOLF FROM THE DOOR

It remained a bitter irony that those providing the population with cheap food were themselves chronically poor and hungry. Going foodless for more than twenty-four hours was not uncommon, and the vast majority of them lived in abject conditions in overcrowded and filthy houses. They often lacked the comfort of heat, decent furniture, and proper utensils and cookery. Speaking about the northern English manufacturing districts in the late 1850s, Folio argued that forcing hawkers to pay a licence "would be tantamount to taking the bread out of the mouths of many hundreds of our fellow-creatures, and driving them to seek relief from the poor law guardians." This class of people, Folio maintained, was already heavily taxed, compelled as it was "to travel with a heavy load many miles a day under a burning sun, or to sit at a stall all day, enduring the bitter, biting blast of winter, to get saturated with the driving storm, and then to retire at night to a cold and badly furnished habitation, where no steaming kettle, warm slippers, or change of raiment await them, or seek the scanty comforts of an overcrowded lodging-house, with only a very few pence as the reward of the day's misery, patience, and toil."[82] The same issue was raised in the late 1880s when hawker James Foster handed out a petition condemning licencing fees in Bolton: "Your Memorialists, can prove by evidence numerous cases where the profits of hawking are barely sufficient to keep their families and in many an instance has reduced an already poor family to starvation."[83] Costermongers embodied an entirely different story from that contained in the sanitized tale of bourgeois civilization, trading their health, well-being, and physical and psychological integrity on a daily basis.

Their poverty was visible in that a great many of them did not own their baskets, barrows, trucks, and carts. Some were so poor that they had to borrow the money with which to purchase their stock.[84] A barrow could be hired for three pence per day or one shilling per week, with interest rate on money-lending at about two pence on the shilling.[85] For the average coster earning about ten shillings per week in the 1850s, the purchase of a barrow costing somewhere between twenty-five and forty shillings remained an unattainable dream. By the early 1870s, not one coster in twenty possessed his own barrow.[86] Moreover, usurious rates on rented baskets and barrows often put them in debt. The continuous arrival of newcomers taking to the streets tended to further divide meagre gains into a growing number of hungry bellies. The transformation of street selling from a hereditary occupation – although this was never fully the case – into an economic refuge during the second half of the century reinforced competition among costers and within the food distribution sector more broadly, as more and more people from the population took to the streets in times of need.[87]

The costers' dwellings were reminders of their own destitution. In the maze of courts and alleys where they lived, in these rickety and rotting "palaces" where no kings or queens would venture, poverty and squalor were the norm. By the late 1840s, most of them lived in filthy slums populated by dilapidated, badly drained and overcrowded houses, where ten to twelve persons could occupy a single room.[88] Given the very nature of their trade, costermongers could not live far from the markets from which they obtained their stock, and they could only afford a place at the price of severe overcrowding.[89] Small pools of inky water and vegetable refuse covered the ground of the slum courts where most of them lived.[90] In the "pestilent colony" of Brandon Road in Belle Isle, an industrial slum situated just north of King's Cross station, costers were said to live in overcrowded "fever-dens."[91] There is little evidence to suggest that housing conditions improved during the period under review – rather, reforms aimed at solving the problem often worsened it.

Under Prime Minister Benjamin Disraeli's second Conservative government, the Artizans' and Labourers' Dwellings Improvement Act, 1875, was passed. One of Disraeli's chief social reforms, the act gave local authorities the power to demolish slum houses and replace them with modern dwellings. In London, the act proved catastrophic for the poor in general and costermongers in particular, amounting, as it did, to a legalized mass eviction.[92] No less than 42 acres from 14 different sites of slum property were demolished, displacing 22,868 persons from 5,555 separate tenements and clearing the ground for the upcoming housing crisis of the 1880s. Moreover, the Metropolitan Board lost over £1.1 million through the excessive compensation of slum owners' dilapidated houses and the drop in the value of land. Virtually all of the targeted areas concentrated on the inner industrial perimeter of central London where a high proportion of costermongers lived. Projects seeking to improve the dwellings of the working class were often contradictory schemes in that they permanently evicted those they sought to help. For instance, the Peabody Dwellings in London accepted applications only from those who could attach an employer's reference, required rents to be paid in advance, restricted homework to narrow activities, and did not allow arrears. Only prosperous artisans, skilled workers, and clerks were able to afford these new model dwellings, forcing the poorest segments to live in even more dilapidated, overcrowded houses.[93] Indeed, almost half of the land cleared was still vacant in the mid-1880s.[94] By the end of the decade, costermongers spent one-third of their miserable wages of about fifteen shillings on rent, and more than half of them lived three or more to a room.[95]

Greenwood was certainly right when he wrote that slum dwellings were "one of the safest investments in the world for a heartless speculator." In Turnmill Street, Clerkenwell, where numerous costermongers lived in "abodes of dirt and squalor," rain meant that "every available scrap of crockery, with tubs, and pots, and kettles, ha[d] to be spread about the floor to catch the descending downpour."[96] The "owners of these piggeries" knew all too well that their lodgers were "of a class that wouldn't be accepted anywhere else but in a slum" and, therefore, that they were highly unlikely to complain about housing conditions and overcrowding.[97] In 1884, Reverend Archibald Brown reported that, in one small district in Shadwell, 260 families (or 1,244 individuals) occupied 340 rooms and that in another district in Bromley, 64 families lived in 79 rooms.[98] Had the Public Health (London) Act, 1891, been enforced, which made it illegal for people to live in less than four hundred cubic feet of space, no less than 900,000 people would have been forced to evacuate their houses and wait for the construction of 500,000 new rooms. It was this lack of affordable accommodations that gave rise to the "three-relay system," whereby the same bed was let to three different tenants who occupied it for eight hours each, and very often the space under the bed was let to further tenants. And for those with time to waste and more "luxurious" tastes, there was always the "two-relay system."[99]

Working conditions were hardly better. Costers worked up to eighteen hours a day and still starved at the end of it. "Of all the population of London," wrote Charles Dickens Jr, "there are none who work longer hours for a living than do these itinerant vendors; their labour commencing at daybreak, and extending until eleven or twelve at night."[100] For the "humblest of the humbler class," an unviable title that costers shared with immigrant bakers, agricultural workers, dockers, market porters, and general labourers, life was anything but easy. "Our homes are squalid and unhealthy," one coster told Greenwood, "and hundreds of us find the length of even a summer's day entirely too short for our main purpose, which is to keep the wolf from the door, that we work Sundays as well as week days."[101] Alfred Ailion, president of the Bethnal Green Traders' and Costermongers' Union, examined before the Select Committee on Sunday Trading in 1906, said that if Sunday trading were to be abolished, "it would be taking away their right of living" by forcing them into starvation.[102] The spirit is willing but the flesh is weak, one might say, for none ever chose to rest on the Lord's Day.

The growing number of costermongers fuelled competition among them, resulting in the maintenance of long hours of work to realize meagre profits on very low prices and high volumes. In the early 1900s, Olive Christian Malvery, a middle-class reformer, tried to better understand their reality by taking to the street. Unable to endure the demanding life of the coster, she quit after a month. "It was a hard life enough," she wrote, "up at four each morning, to bed never before eleven, the long walks to the market, and the standing by that blessed barrow in rain and shine ... This was the hardest work I think I have ever done. My arms ached, and my legs almost refused to move."[103] The vagaries of weather were also an important factor in determining the fortune (or lack thereof) of costers, as a series of rainy days was likely to bring them "to the brink of starvation."[104] Dr John Thomas Arlidge, consulting physician to the North Staffordshire Royal Infirmary, reported in 1892 that hawkers constituted the largest "proportion of hospital and dispensary patients" and that they often died from tuberculosis. "Exposure to weather," he added, "prolonged standing and sitting in the open air, insufficient food and clothing, and in their homes the absence of most or all sanitary requirements, are doubtless the principal causes of the sickness, suffering, and mortality of the class in question."[105] Given the low incomes of both women and children and the precariousness of the whole family, the premature death or illness of the father would irremediably bring the household into extreme forms of privation.[106]

Children selling in the streets were particularly affected by hard work, chronic poverty, and hunger. Physical sufferings were "constant, and at times extremely severe," and their distress was easily visible to anyone who dared to look at it. "Her little face," Mayhew wrote about an eight-year-old girl, "pale and thin with privation, was wrinkled where the dimples ought to have been." She had to be at the Farringdon market between four and five o'clock in the morning and never made more than four pence per day. She got two slices of bread with butter and a cup of tea for breakfast and the same for dinner, with bits of meat on Sunday.[107] The situation did not change much in the following decades.[108] By the early 1890s, Mary C. Tabor did not find much to commend about the state of the costers' children, describing the girls as "stunted in growth, anxious-eyed, with faces beyond their years," and the boys as looking "dazed, and beaten, their faces worried and vacant." Working long hours and having no regular meal times, their chronic state of hunger made them unfit to attend the duty of school.[109] In poor neighbourhoods of the east and central south of London where costermongers lived in large numbers, such as Bermondsey, Blackfriars, Southwark, and Lambeth, destitution was rampant, with at least two-thirds of them living in dire poverty in the 1880s.[110]

Dr Alfred Eichholz, one of His Majesty's inspectors of schools, reported in 1904 that, at the Johanna Street Board School, Lambeth, 90 percent of the children could not attend the duties of school in a proper way because of the insufficiency, irregularity, and low quality of food.[111] He also deplored the poor physical constitution and "dullness of mind" of these children, and the same was said in Newington and Walworth about the children attending the Costers' School.[112] This chronic state of semi-starvation produced very low endurance, with boys lacking the staying power to get through a match of football. Eichholz also noted the lack of memory and concentration as well as the low stature of these children, and estimated that about 90 percent of the boys were anaemic: "A good many children suffer from blight in the eyes and sore eyelids. The hair is badly nourished and wispy, and the skin is tough, dry, pale, and shrivelled, giving a very old look very early in life."[113] James Niven, medical officer for Manchester, gave similar evidence on the inadequate diet of the families living in the central district, one of the poorest places of the city, where a disproportionate number of costermongers lived.[114]

A particularly distressing case of child labour concerned Italian children employed in the ice cream trade. While street musicianship remained an important occupation for many Italian immigrants, their dramatic expansion as costers from 1861 to 1901 was largely the result of the growth in ice cream manufacturing.[115] Mostly a treat for well-off people in the 1850s and 1860s, growing consumer spending power from the 1870s onwards, combined with the rising availability of ice depots and liquid milk, contributed to the skyrocketing popularity of the trade. By the early 1900s, the association between the trade and the Italians was well entrenched, Sims even referring to Little Italy in Holborn, London, as "Halfpenny Iceland."[116] A decisive shift in labour relations arrived in the 1880s with the establishment of the Padrone system, which W.H. Wilkins described as "a veritable slavery."[117] Recruitment was organized around the *padroni*, who "frequently recruit[ed] directly from Italy [especially from Calabria in the south of Italy], often from their own villages, thereby using their regional and kingship ties."[118] As Lucio Sponza explained, the system "entailed the obligation for the youngsters to serve their masters as apprentices for 18, 24 or 30 months, for a yearly pay ranging from £12 to £16, and for working days lasting 14 to 16 hours. The lads were to be fed, lodged, clothed ('one suit a year'), and the expenses of one return journey from Italy were to be met by the *padroni*."[119] In reality, they often worked longer hours, slept four or five in a bed (when they had one), were not infrequently paid less than originally agreed, and lived in filthy, dilapidated, and overcrowded dwellings.[120]

With children bringing home up to ten shillings or more a day, and with up to fifty children under his rule, the *padrone* was often running a very lucrative business. Thousands of these young Italian immigrants plied the streets of large towns and seaside resorts selling ice cream. By 1914, the medical officer of health in Manchester counted no less than 729 places where ice cream was manufactured.[121] Successful *padroni* often opened ice cream shops as well, thus adding fixed premises to the spatial mobility of their cheap workforce. For instance, it was estimated that there were one thousand shops selling ice cream in Scotland in 1911, especially in the Clyde and Forth districts, and that 350 of them were situated in Glasgow.[122] This was not surprising given that the city was the main area of settlement for the community in Scotland. Employees in ice cream shops did not fare better, however, working from 15 to 17 hours per day and up to 20 hours on Saturdays, 7 days a week.[123]

The growth in the number of immigrants taking to the street during the second half of the nineteenth century was sufficient enough to worry the so-called "English" costers. Although the literature showcases many negative racial references to Italian immigrants,[124] they were not the only group to dwell in the streets with the same purpose and thus suffer the same scorn. This was particularly the case of Irish immigrants, widely represented in London, Manchester, and other large urban centres.[125] Even the most progressive social writers did not fail to uphold anti-Irish sentiments, often describing them essentially as uncivilized beasts of work prone to drunkenness.[126] The poorest districts of London almost invariably housed "separate colonies" of Irish costermongers, most of whom lived in filthy, overcrowded and

Table 3.4
Death rates of males in England in selected occupations

Occupation	Mean annual death-rates per 1000 living				Comparative mortality figure, 1880–82
	1860/61–1871		1880–82		
	Years of age		Years of age		Years of age
	25–45	45–65	25–45	45–65	25–65
All males	11.27	23.98	10.16	25.27	1000
General shopkeeper	–	–	9.12	21.23	865
Cheesemonger, milk, butterman	–	–	9.48	26.90	1009
Greengrocer, fruiterer	11.41	24.51	10.04	26.57	1025
Fishmonger, poulterer	15.62	29.21	10.53	23.45	974
Butcher	13.19	28.37	12.16	29.08	1170
Baker, confectioner	10.72	26.39	8.70	26.12	958
Costermonger, hawker, street seller	20.09	37.82	20.26	45.33	1879
General labourer (London)	18.35	40.64	20.62	50.85	2020

Source: Ogle, "Supplement to the forty-fifth annual report of the Registrar-General of Births," xxv–vi.

ill-furnished apartments, some of them infested with vermin. Poor immigrant Jews were also affected by economic hardship. As Sims noted in 1905, many of them arrived as early as four o'clock in the morning to reserve a space for a barrow. "These men will stand patiently guarding the spot which is theirs by right of 'the first comer.' They have nothing as yet to sell themselves, so they sell the space" to prospective "English" hawkers offended by the fact that they had to buy the right to a "pitch."[127] As a rule, anti-immigrant attitudes tended to reinforce the social exclusion and economic marginalization of these communities, entrenching them further into poverty.

All in all, street selling was extremely detrimental to health and well-being. In his study of the male population from one hundred different occupations of the early 1880s, Dr William Ogle found the rate of mortality among street sellers to be almost twice as high as the average rate from all occupations, second only to London's casual workers (table 3.4). Ogle also found out that, in relation to industries with the highest mortalities, street sellers ranked tenth for liver disease, eighth for gout, fourth for urinary infections, second for diseases of the nervous system, first for diseases of the circulatory system, and first for suicide, leading the latter category hands down with more than three times the average ratio.[128] By 1909, out of the twelve occupations with the highest mortality in England and Wales, costermongers ranked third. Their life expectancy at age 25 was 29.0 years, preceded only by general labourers (27.8 years) and tin miners (28.5 years).[129] Costermongering was no sinecure as these "wrecks of civilised society" embodied capital's deep contradictions of hunger amidst plenty, poverty despite hard work, and social marginalization despite their vital economic function.[130]

Far from being archaic and inefficient figures of the food distributive system, street sellers were instrumental to the rise of the working class's living standards and purchasing power. While providing comparatively cheap food to growing segments of the population between 1830 and 1870, their ability to offer low prices on domestic food items and pass on the full benefits of cheap food imports from the 1870s onwards made them a deeply appreciated class of retailers. However, their ability to transform the benefits of cheap food imports into low food prices for their customers came at a heavy price.

Indeed, it would not have been possible without the growing competitive nature of the occupation and the growing matrix of legal control and political repression surrounding their lives, which locked them into chronic poverty and hunger, and forced them to survive by selling food goods more cheaply than any other retailers. As the growth of the costermongering class reinforced its role in the distributive environment, notably in contributing further to a highly competitive retail sector, street sellers increasingly came to affect – either positively or negatively – shopkeepers' economic interests and social status. As we shall see in the next chapter, shopkeepers struggled to survive in a distributive environment increasingly detrimental to the aspirations of their trade.

4

A Nation of Shopkeepers

"The small shop is rapidly losing its place in the economy of distribution," declared a Fabian tract in 1897, "and the 'respectable shopkeeper' is disappearing as the Store and the Limited Liability Company step in to do his work."[1] A few years later the *Times* published an article on "the passing of the grocer" as the main victim of the competition from co-operative stores and multiple shops, further noting that 1901 had broken new records of bankruptcy in the grocery trade. This "process of attrition" was so advanced, the correspondent predicted, that the single-shop grocer "will soon have almost disappeared" from many districts. Changes in the trade since the 1850s were indeed so profound that they had transformed "the old-fashioned grocer, who required to know many things about the 'art and mystery' of his trade, into a vendor of packet goods, so that a large proportion of the grocer's work of the present-day could be accomplished almost equally well by an automatic machine delivering a packet of goods in exchange for a coin."[2] While contemporaries were wrong to predict the imminent death of the small shopkeeper, they were right to recognize the impacts of the capitalization of the British retail environment and its rapid evolution towards mass food distribution.[3]

As it happened, small shopkeepers died a thousand deaths. In declaring the patient economically dead, most contemporaries underestimated shopkeepers' resourcefulness and wrongly identified the source of their economic precarity in the emergence of large-scale retailers in the 1880s. While co-operative stores and multiple shops effectively transformed the competitive environment within which shopkeepers evolved, the gap between shopkeepers' middle-class aspirations and the reality of economic hardship was nothing new.

Already in the 1830s, shopkeepers in London and other large towns had to deal with the pressure of increased competition in the food distribution sector. Very few had the financial capacity, managerial skills, and personal willingness to fight back through capital investments and the introduction of labour-saving technologies. Moreover, long-term solidarities among tradespeople were constantly broken by individualist tendencies as well as by the reality of a wide range of operations. In this context, the vast majority of shopkeepers tended to weather the competitive storm through a combination of municipal and associational politics to control the food distribution environment, fraudulent practices to increase profit margins, and labour-intensive methods to secure a custom amidst cutthroat competition.

Although it is dangerous to over-simplify, it is possible to distinguish broadly between two groups of independent shopkeepers. Primarily serving more affluent consumers, the first group of tradespeople was generally able to maintain some degree of skills and retain its wider status and political influence, especially in smaller urban centres. Their existence was arguably not of itself precarious, but their economic status relied increasingly on the precariousness of paid employees. The experience of this group may be contrasted with that of the increasing number of small shopkeepers chiefly serving the urban working class. Such individuals had few pretentions to commercial skills or status. Any social or political role that they might have had was almost certainly confined to their immediate neighbourhood, and few participated in traders' associations. Small-scale shop dealing in many food trades was easy to enter as the bar was set low in terms of skills, knowledge, and initial capital requirements. But this, in turn, meant that precariousness also extended to frequent failures of small retail businesses, so that there was a constantly churning population moving in and out of retailing. Small-scale retail businesses were much less likely to employ paid labour, and efforts to reduce labour costs therefore primarily involved self-exploitation and unpaid family labour. It is also significant that some of the smallest shops were not intended to provide a family income but, rather, were kept by wives and (female) children to supplement the wages earned elsewhere by fathers and other adult (male) household members, thus effectively normalizing self-exploitation.

The mass import of cheap food and the rise of large-scale retailers during the last quarter of the nineteenth century triggered a fundamental change in shopkeepers' strategies of reproduction, which were linked to their social and economic positioning within the distributive environment. As we shall see, food prices between the 1830s to the 1870s were kept artificially low and profits fraudulently high through the widespread adulteration of food and drinks as well as the generalized use of false weights and measures. These practices were reinforced by municipal politics aimed at protecting shopkeepers from retail competition and state intervention. However, the flooding of the food markets with cheap imported goods in the 1870s, combined with stricter state regulations and greater regulatory powers at the municipal level, shifted the reproductive dynamics of the shopkeeping class towards the extensive use of cheap labour. From the 1880s onwards, most shopkeepers responded to the imperatives of market competition through heightened labour exploitation. This exploitation was achieved through measures such as wage reduction through long hours of work, unpaid overtime, the introduction of cheap juvenile and female labour, and the extended use of family labour.[4] On the collective side, the rescaling of shopkeepers' activism from municipal politics to regionally and nationally based associational powers was largely a failed attempt at protecting big shopkeepers from the new horizon of large-scale competition carried by co-operative stores and multiple shops. Already showing signs of economic fragility in the 1830s and 1840s, shopkeepers' social status was largely an empty shell by 1914, which further reinforced the relationship between cheap food and cheap labour.

THE POLITICS OF PRECARIOUSNESS

Historically, the grocer or shopkeeper referred to a wealthy trader who dealt in foreign produce such as dried fruits, condiments, spices, tea, coffee, and sugar from fixed premises for the "better class." Traders in butter, cheese, bacon, and the like were provision dealers, and both grocers and provision dealers could specialize in a particular trade.[5] By 1850, the term "grocer" was generally preferred, with "shopkeeper" increasingly reserved for small, non-specialized retailers lacking capital and social standing.[6] Small shopkeepers encompassed a range of operations showing important differences in types, scales, incomes, social status, and economic vulnerability. It is also during this period that we see the emergence of a more encompassing definition of grocery, such as the Bolton-based grocers Mr Kitchen, who "did a thriving business in packaged goods, dairy products and vegetables," and Edward Heyes, whose shop "was crowded with merchandise – sacks of potatoes, onions, carrots and long, shallow, wooded boxes full of Irish eggs."[7] Integration was also common in villages, such as Neville Bros' corner shop in north Warnborough selling grocery and provisions, and proudly advertising that its owners were also bacon curers, bakers, and corn merchants.[8]

The growth of small shopkeepers after 1850 was nothing short of phenomenal, rising from 330,000 in 1881 to 625,000 in 1911.[9] According to Gareth Shaw, the average rate of population per shop fell from about 136 in 1801 to 56 in 1881, with food shops in Beverley, Halifax, Huddersfield, Hull, Lancaster, Leeds, Oldham, Rochdale, Wakefield, and York constituting about 57 percent of retail shops at that time.[10] The growing army of greengrocers, fruiterers, confectioners, bakers, grocers, butchers, fishmongers, and cheesemongers was a strong reminder that the backbone of the retailing revolution relied both on the regionally uneven expansion of a market-dependent working class and the consolidation of an international food regime that was increasingly visible in wholesale public markets supplying shopkeepers with their produce.[11] During these years, retail commerce experienced a shift from general to specialized shops. Rising real wages not only allowed the purchase of a greater quantity and variety of food but also permitted the consumption of a growing range of commodities and services, including hairdressers, furniture retailers, and baby linen dealers. Another key aspect was the growth in the number of shops that sold convenience foods after 1880, as illustrated by the rise in the number of fried fish shops in the United Kingdom from about 11,000 in 1888 to 25,000 in 1910.[12] Similarly, the number of confectioners selling pies and cakes rose from 1 for 853 people to 1 for 472 during the same period.[13] The growth in food shops was tied to employment structures and the availability of cooking facilities at home, and large swaths of the working class took advantage of the basin meal during the Edwardian era, especially where women constituted an appreciable proportion of the working force.[14]

Studies of shops' spatial development highlight the deepening relation between shop location and population distribution through a process of linear extension in retail facilities as shops were moving away from city centres and towards suburban locations.[15] As Alexander Harris, deputy town clerk of Edinburgh, put it: "The whole habits of the people have completely changed; the city has spread out into the fields so much, and the citizens have retail shops of every kind in their immediate vicinity, and they prefer to go to those to coming into the centre of the old town as they used to do."[16] Food shops dominated the distributive network in these newly formed and fast expanding suburbs, and by 1880 the bulk of food shops in smaller towns were located in suburban areas, a trend already apparent in larger settlements thirty years earlier.[17] The reorganization of public market activities towards wholesaling and the decentralization of retailing through the migration of shops to suburban areas were therefore complementary processes. Despite their respective distributive functions, a myriad of retail arrangements existed between them, especially in smaller towns where it was not uncommon for shopkeepers – especially butchers – to own a shop in the main shopping street and to take a stall in the market.[18] The relationship between the two was not always courteous, however, as many shopkeepers complained about wholesale market hours. Since greengrocers, butchers, fishmongers, and other shopkeepers went to the market early in the morning to get their goods, wholesalers who turned into retailers during the day were often seen as unfair competitors.[19] Despite the existence of bylaws prohibiting them from doing so, market authorities in Blackburn ignored them entirely, and evidence suggests that they were far from the only ones to do so.[20] Since wholesalers provided towns with great quantities of cheap food, market authorities were likely to turn a blind eye when some of them turned into retailers during the day.

Small shopkeepers' ability to survive depended on their ability to position themselves at the centre of their community's economic life.[21] Diligently and judiciously using their power to grant credit (or "tick" as it was called), the economic success of these "bankers of the poor" was regulated by the economic pulse of their constituency.[22] Their ability to offer a temporal fix through credit was an integral part of the working-class household economy as well as an important pillar to the shopkeeper's power over the reproductive life of the community. At the same time, small shopkeepers "feared that by refusing credit they would lose long-time customers once hardship was over."[23] As such, most shopkeepers nurtured a culture of gossip by offering a welcoming space for women to meet during the day and acted as an important network of information to assess the credit worthiness of each family in the neighbourhood.[24] The rise of large-scale retailers, the heightened financial autonomy of the working class, and the growth in manufactured items such as proprietary or pre-packaged goods tended to erode the symbiotic relationship existing between shopkeepers and their communities, while contributing further to the competitive nature of the food distribution sector.[25] The retail grocer who blended tea, cut sugar, mixed spices, pickled chutneys, made sauces, bottled fruit, potted meat, and roasted coffee beans became an endangered species. As we saw in the case of the dead meat trade, the relocation of cattle markets and slaughterhouses outside of the cities largely contributed to the deskilling of the butcher trade through a new spatial division of labour between wholesale carcass butchers and retail butchers.[26] Combined with the new prosperity of the late Victorian period, deskilling lowered barriers to entry, which in turn encouraged working-class families to start their own domestic shop, thus reinforcing further market competition in the lower rungs of food retailing.[27]

Shopkeepers also sought to control their distributive environment through municipal politics. Public markets were a contentious issue in many boroughs where the need to provide the town with cheap food often foundered on the rocky shores of local economic interests.[28] While leading capitalists such as manufacturers and merchants never represented less than 50 percent of the membership of municipal corporations in mid- and late Victorian Lancashire, the period also witnessed the rising political influence of dealers and shopkeepers within municipal governments.[29] William Augustus Casson, clerk in the Local Government Office, pointed out that "one finds cases where the local board is composed to a large extent of shopkeepers, and those shopkeepers find it to their interest to fix such scales of tolls and to take such stallages and rents as will make it unprofitable to outsiders to come into the town to trade, so that the goods cannot be sold at a less price than the shopkeepers themselves can sell at."[30] For the Glasgow United Fleshers' Society, however, the issue was that dues paid for the use of the public slaughterhouses should serve exclusively to cover the fees associated with them. The substantial profits made by the slaughterhouses, they argued, was an unfair and disguised tax on their earnings as surpluses were used for other expenses like the reimbursement of the debt upon all markets in Glasgow, which was estimated at £160,000 in 1889.[31] The politicization of market governance in the second half of the nineteenth century was one key strategy to weather the competitive storm.

Street sellers also represented a menace to shopkeepers' economic interests.[32] While evidence suggests that shopkeepers wielding political power to legislate or implement strict regulations over street selling were not uncommon, the relationship between them was largely determined by the level of support each had at the municipal level. For instance, the removal of the costermongers from the Leather Lane Market following local shopkeepers' appeal to the police is a particularly instructive case of the tense yet symbiotic relationship that could exist between the two. Housewives in the neighbourhood liked "to make one errand do," buying from both costermongers and shopkeepers according to what they needed. Moreover, most of them could not "be persuaded that they [could] buy as cheap at the shops; and besides they [were] apt to think shopkeepers [were] rich and street-sellers poor, and that they may as well encourage the poor." Following the abolition of the informal market, they simply transferred their business to another "unauthorized" market and to other shopkeepers located in a different part of London. Within two weeks, after further appeals to the police by the shopkeepers, the Leather Lane market was allowed to resume its activities.[33] Despite ongoing tension, shopkeepers, especially in large towns, generally welcomed costers in their streets as they recognized the strong correlation between their presence and increased trade. By the early 1890s, the LCC reported that 790 out of the 5,292 stalls in the 112 "unauthorized" markets established by costermongers belonged to shopkeepers. Furthermore, the report stated that out of 70 local shopkeepers interviewed, 60 were favourable to these informal markets, while 6 were indifferent and 4 were hostile.[34] In towns like Bolton and Portsmouth, small shopkeepers competed directly against street sellers by going round with their carts and vans, while their wives looked after the shop.[35]

Another advantage that costermongers held over shopkeepers was the favour of the public. For instance, in Rochdale, town clerk Zachary Mellor recognized "that great advantage accrues to the poor people of the town by their having the facility of buying marketable commodities from hawkers."[36] Working under a licensing system between 1875 and 1887, hawkers became illegal after the system was barred due to a legal technicality. Despite the prohibition, street selling continued unabated, and shopkeepers were not slow to seize the occasion to summon hawkers. The matter was "brought up so frequently before the magistrates, they came to the conclusion that in place of fining the hawkers 5s. or 10s. with costs, they would fine them only 1s. without costs."[37] In other words, the magistrates created an informal licensing system that recognized the vital role played by costermongers as cheap food distributors. The decision to stave off competition by applying stringent licence fees or by prohibiting hawking activities entirely was often met by unimpressed local residents whose interests as consumers lay first and foremost in the availability of cheap food.[38] Shopkeepers seeking to protect their economic interests had to navigate these contentious waters.

Although public markets and costermongers were constant economic threats to the shopkeepers' well-being, co-operative societies (from the 1860s) and multiple shops (from the 1880s) became more worrisome.[39] Their structural and organizational ability to lower food prices by taking advantage of the economies of scale offered by an expanding international food regime was contrary to shopkeepers' ideals of independence, security, and comfort. The shopkeepers' initial response to heightened competition was to reinforce individual actions and methods such as advertising, window dressing, and bookkeeping, all of which were in line with their ideals of independence and self-help.[40] While there is no doubt that many shopkeepers were successful in applying modern retail techniques, especially those catering to the middle and upper classes, such individualized methods did very little to change the competitive nature of the retail environment. As the need for a more united front emerged, trade associations came to play a growing social and economic role in the protection of shopkeepers' interests.[41] Associations introduced bulk-buying schemes, reduced price competition, provided education in traditional and developing trade skills, and offered a space for companionship between members.[42] However, shopkeepers were far from being a homogenous group, and calls to solidarity by the better-off sections very often clashed with the economic pragmatism of a trade divided by social status and incomes. In this respect, "their efforts were usually entirely reactive, fitful and short-lived; they served only to illustrate the lack of a collective trade consciousness within the retailing community."[43] Shopkeepers' operations could be worlds apart, and, although their economic interests were similar in theory, they rarely (if ever) coalesced into a coherent and organized counter-movement.

The limits of associational life were also visible in the difficulty experienced by trades associations trying to take advantage of the new possibilities afforded by large-scale infrastructures of distribution and transportation. For instance, the Birmingham and Midland Counties Grocers' Protection and Benevolent Association complained that the "scale charge" on goods delivered by railway was both "excessive" and "unjust." While the petitioners did not ask for the "entire abolition of an extra charge being made on small items," they nonetheless requested "that such items be confined to weight of 100 lbs."[44] Similarly, John Taylor, owner of four shops in Swansea, South Wales, and a fifth one in Ilfracombe, England, on the other side of the Bristol Channel, complained that goods delivered by railway, though coming faster, suffered from high rates on small quantities. Sugar and fruit he generally obtained from Bristol, but most of his goods such as tea, coffee, seeds, arrowroot, oranges, jams, macaroni, and sago came from London. Since the bulk of these goods came in quantities ranging from one to five hundredweight, Taylor was rarely in a position to take advantage of lower freight rates for consignments exceeding five hundred pounds.[45] Both examples are interesting not only because they highlight the limitations placed on even the most successful shopkeepers, such as those with economic means and associational power, but also because they reveal the growing tension that existed between small-scale distribution and large-scale transportation. Contrary to co-ops and multiples, shopkeepers' associations ultimately lacked the internal cohesion that made their competitors so effective. Rising prices after 1896 only sharpened the economic advantage of large-scale retailers.[46]

"I AM AS HONEST AS I CAN AFFORD TO BE"[47]

Strategies to mitigate retail competition in the middle decades of the nineteenth century took many forms, and shopkeepers drew on a wide range of fraudulent practices to protect their economic interests, including food adulteration and the use of false weights and measures. Essentially an individual response to the difficulties associated with cutthroat competition in the food distributive sector, the general use of such methods betrayed the economic and moral frailty of the so-called "respectable shopkeeper." Food adulteration generally involved altering food by adding weight and bulk, enhancing colour, and improving smell, flavour, and pungency.[48] While food adulteration in the 1820s and 1830s can be understood as a strategy to achieve higher profit margins in the context of very low working-class purchasing power, the widespread adoption of these fraudulent methods by 1850 had exhausted most of their economic benefits. The result was twofold: the production of artificially low food prices through chronic food degradation and the dependency of the shopkeeping class on dishonest practices to survive. In 1850, finding pure or unadulterated food had become virtually impossible. Things started to change when Dr Arthur Hill Hassall, chief analyst of the Analytical Sanitary Commission of the *Lancet* from 1851 to 1854, published the result of his analyses and listed the names and addresses of shopkeepers practising culinary sophistry. While a handful of social reformers were well aware of the social plague of adulteration, including the co-operative movement promising pure food to its customers, its sheer ubiquity in the 1850s was in and of itself a strong testimony to the blind faith in laissez-faire precepts. The widespread frauds practised by a "respectable" class of tradespeople made many question the economic morality of the retail class itself.

Following the devastating revelations of the *Lancet*, the government appointed in 1856 the Select Committee on Adulteration of Food, which revealed the widespread – and in some cases poisonous – adulteration of food and drink.[49] Bread was often made by adding barley, ground beans, peas, and potatoes to the mix, and other impurities such as chalk, plaster, sand, sawdust, and ground stone found their way in as well. Decayed and spoiled grades of flour could be "recovered" by the addition of alum to produce a whiter bread to be sold at a higher price. The addition of arrowroot, farina, potato starch, and soda to butter all sought to incorporate as much water as it would hold. Coffee almost always contained large proportions of chicory, and cocoa was commonly adulterated with starches and sugar. Large quantities of tea were manufactured by mixing genuine tea with hedgerows, shrubs, and plants as well as ash, sloe, and elder leaves. The watering down of milk and beer was another common practice, the original taste of beer recovered through the addition of ginger root, alum, coriander seed, and orange peels. Other forms of adulteration included adding chalk, plaster, pipeclay, and sawdust to sugar; making sugar confectionery from poisonous colouring matters such as chrome yellow and white lead; using copper to add colour to, and incidentally poison, pickles; colouring the rind of

Gloucester cheese with vermilion and red lead; and adulterating pepper with dust and sweepings from the warehouse floors. In 1863, the scale of the trade in cheap offal and old and diseased meat was also the subject of an extensive survey by John Gamgee, which revealed that one-fifth of the meat sold in the United Kingdom (beef, veal, mutton, lamb, and pork) came from diseased cattle.[50] Overall, the quality of food was probably at its lowest in the 1850s and 1860s.[51]

Widespread adulteration was not the brain-child of greedy shop-keepers – rather, it was the structural outcome of an expanding class of retailers desperately trying to survive amidst intense competition and the working class's low purchasing power. Despite the appalling quality of food in the middle decades of the nineteenth century, the state was slow to act and largely uninterested in doing so. Indeed, free market principles very much informed the 1856 Select Committee's report: "If, as regards the adulteration of articles with substances of a cheaper and innocuous character, the public derive the full benefit of this cheapness in a lower price, it would be difficult, if not unwise, for the Legislature to interfere."[52] In so doing, the committee explicitly recognized the key role that food adulteration played in producing cheap food before the start of mass food imports in the 1870s. Unsurprisingly, the first Food Act of 1860 was a complete failure, as the legislators imparted the optional responsibility for the quality of food to local authorities without funding to help them cover the costs associated with the implementation and daily management of the act. Hassall, who predicted that the 1860 act would be a dead letter, found it difficult to believe "that these vestries, composed as in great part they are of tradespeople, will be desirous of carrying out the Bill efficiently."[53] Corporations and town councils, whose members were often shopkeepers, were indeed unlikely to voluntarily finance and carry out a system to monitor themselves.

At least until the late 1860s, the great majority of local inspectors were simply unqualified to perform their duty, their jobs not uncommonly "regarded as sinecures for worn-out men."[54] Inspectors were often put in the difficult position of having to scrutinize those who hired (and could dismiss) them, and not infrequently came from the same class of tradespeople subjected to inspections. Despite the fact that the 1860 act was a toothless piece of legislation, it nonetheless represented the first attempt by the state to act upon the problem, the scale and scope of which had reached dangerous proportions. While the act contributed to increased public consciousness, food adulteration continued unabated throughout the decade. Meanwhile, many condemned shopkeepers' kleptomaniac tendencies. Greenwood, for example, saw the adulteration of food and drink as a "much safer system of robbery" than robbery itself.[55] In was in this context of heightened outrage that the Adulteration of Food, Drink and Drugs Act, 1872, was enacted. Although it went further than the 1860 act in imposing a stricter regulatory apparatus, its overall performance was called into question when a Select Committee appointed to evaluate it concluded that it might be of "some consolation to the public to know that in the matter of adulteration they are *cheated* rather than *poisoned*".[56] The elimination of the worst forms of food adulteration was undoubtedly an important achievement, but many continued to see the ongoing degradation of their food as it became more and more unpalatable.

The landmark piece of legislation in the regulation of food came with the Sale of Food and Drugs Act, 1875, which constituted the first comprehensive framework fully dedicated to the establishment of pure food, notably through the more systematic appointment of analysts, easier proceedings against offenders, and harsher penalties[57] Already in 1878 the overall proportion of adulterated samples in the retail trade was down to 19.2 percent, despite the growing number of samples examined by local authorities. While the adulteration of milk remained high at 24.1 percent, bread and beer demonstrated a noticeable improvement at 7.4 percent and 9.3 percent, respectively.[58] Adulterated samples declined to 15.07 percent in 1882, before reaching 10.8 percent in 1888.[59] Out of 49,555 samples examined in 1898, 8.7 percent were found adulterated, the lowest percentage ever recorded until then.[60] Given the resilience of adulteration in milk, butter, coffee, and spirits, this figure tends to mask the extent to which articles of heavy consumption like bread, flour, beer, sugar, jam, and tea exhibited comparatively low levels of adulteration. And while it was still possible to find low-quality meats at the beginning of the twentieth century,[61] the general quality of meat had dramatically improved. Mass food imports from the 1870s onwards also contributed to the rising food quality as lower food prices undermined the economic basis for adulteration by rendering pure food as cheap as its previous substitutes.[62] The shift away from deadly adulteration and the decrease in the widespread use of cheaper substances of lower nutritional value represented nothing short of a daily revolution in consumption and a drastic improvement in people's health and living standards. It also meant the decline of a nationwide fraud on working people's finances.

Another important weapon in the shopkeeper's arsenal was the use of false weights and measures. The commissioners appointed to inquiry into the Exchequer Standards revealed that virtually all offenders under the Weights and Measures Act, 1835, were shopkeepers dealing in food, including beershop keepers, licensed victuallers, greengrocers, fishmongers, confectioners, corn dealers, cheesemongers, butchers, and bakers. In 1866, local inspectors reported that 222,602 false and defective weights, measures, and balances required adjustment in Great Britain, and that an additional 18,060 were seized by inspectors during that same year, resulting in 6,094 convictions. Despite the fact that five counties and sixty cities and burghs made no returns, the report also revealed that the inspection of weights and measures largely remained under the control of corporations, town councils, municipal boroughs, and similar bodies.[63] Given the low conviction rates and penalties and costs averaging about fifteen and five shillings, respectively, cheating the working class no doubt remained a very profitable business. As the commissioners noted, "it appears to us to be wrong in principle and injurious in practice, that such authority should be exercised in towns and boroughs by Corporations and Town Councils, members of which frequently are tradesmen using weights and measures subject by law to inspection." Indeed, the magistrates whose role it was to summon the offenders were "frequently taken from the same class of tradesmen."[64]

Arguably, the 1866 figures are not representative of the scale of the fraud on the working class's meagre incomes. Greenwood did not mince his words: "more insatiable than the leech, you [the shopkeeper] are not content with cheating him [the customer] to the extent of twenty-five percent. by means of abominable mixtures and adulteration, you must pass him through the mill, and cut him yet a little finer when he comes to scale!"[65] It was indeed not uncommon for traders to have weights of either fifteen ounces or seventeen ounces in the pound, according to the occasion. Greenwood was appalled by the thirteen hundred convictions for false weights and measures in 1868 in London for he knew all too well that convictions represented only a fraction of the actual number of false and defective weights seized, which, in turn, represented only a fraction of those in use. And while the districts of Southwark, Newington, St George's, Hanover Square, Paddington, and the Strand did not even bother sending returns to the municipal authorities, it was discovered that 70 percent of the persons convicted over a period of six months in the district of Westminster were provision dealers, including dairymen, greengrocers, licensed victuallers, and cheesemongers. "When the last batch of shopkeeper-swindlers of St. Pancras were tried and convicted," Greenwood wrote, "the ugly fact transpired that not a few of them were gentlemen holding official positions in the parish."[66]

The commissioners made clear "that much of the unwillingness and negligence shown by the local authorities of many districts in carrying out the provisions of the existing laws has been caused by their reluctance to entail any material increase in the burden of their local rates."[67] Class politics was essential in upholding the shopkeeper's social status. In fact, the best political course for a class of shopkeepers largely uninterested in having its private business overseen by public powers and zealous inspectors was to foster inaction or limited capacities from underfunded local authorities. Tellingly, complaints made by shopkeepers about the use of false weights and measures by hawkers in London in the 1890s triggered the following reaction on the part of one of the inspectors: "the shopkeepers whose names are attached are, in my opinion, only one degree removed in class from the hawker. The neighbourhood is a very poor one. All of the grocers in the original complaint had already received cautions ... Their instruments for weighing were approximate to those of the costers of whom they complained." The LCC's trust must not have been high for, in 1894–95, its inspectors visited thirty-five thousand premises during which 800,000 glasses were measured to ensure that they did contain the required volume of drink.[68] Street sellers also succumbed to the temptation of using fraudulent practices to increase their profit, and those who appeared to keep true weights and measures often were the keenest in their ability to give less than what customers perceived.[69] That being said, more comprehensive legislative controls and better funding of the inspectorate at the municipal level did result in some progress. Between 1893–94 and 1900–01, the proportion of incorrect measuring devices tested in London dropped from 4.5 percent to 0.2 percent among shopkeepers, and from 9.1 percent to 4 percent among hawkers.[70]

Although the existence of fraudulent practices persisted until 1914, their economic importance after 1880 declined rapidly and became marginal. What did rise, however, was shopkeepers' dependency on cheap labour. Legislative controls over food adulteration and weights and measures, the professionalization of municipal administrations, the erosion of the economic role played by shopkeepers in their communities, the inefficiency of associational politics, and the rise of large-scale retailers all placed severe limits on the strategic possibilities available for shopkeepers to survive. While it is true that labour conditions in the food distribution sector were never satisfactory, changes in the structure of food retailing during the last quarter of the nineteenth century only served to intensify the use of labour-intensive methods.

"A DOG'S LIFE":
SHOP ASSISTANTS AND CHILD LABOUR[71]

The level of exploitation and economic hardship experienced by shop workers was excruciating, and there were no shortage of social commentators and medical doctors to testify to the unhealthy nature of the shop life.[72] In their attempt to deliver cheap food in a highly competitive environment, big shopkeepers relied on four main strategies of labour exploitation: the feminization of the workforce, the use of child labour, the enforcement of long hours of work, and the recourse to the living-in system. This section describes these different strategies to cut labour costs in detail, and it concludes with a discussion of shop workers' efforts to resist exploitation through unionization.

The first strategy to cut labour costs was the gradual feminization of the workforce from the 1860s onwards, beyond the wives and daughters who were "the original 'shopgirls.'"[73] Absent from all except for small, family-run shops in the 1850s, by the 1890s, there were about 250,000 shopgirls in Britain.[74] They played a key role in lowering wage expenditure by costing, on average, between 50 and 66 percent of men's wages.[75] Heavily concentrated in the drapery, millenary, and dressmaking trades, women also tended to be employed in cities and bigger stores where their presence behind the counter was less likely to be frowned upon.[76] Despite their growing presence in retailing, however, inroads into the food distributive sector proved more difficult, with grocery, provisions, and butchery remaining firmly male-dominated even in 1914, with some presence in greengrocery. The major exception in the food sector was the confectionary trade, where shopgirls represented the vast majority of the workforce. In London, 90 percent of the twenty thousand female workers employed in confectionary shops worked on average ninety hours a week. In seaside resorts such as Blackpool, for example, working hours of over one hundred hours a week during the summer months was common.[77] By the late 1900s, a girl working in a café in Manchester would have earned between seven and twelve shillings for up to ninety-four hours of work. "She is an underpaid slave, working under bad conditions, and often under unscrupulous, tyrannical managers and manageresses."[78] Although the employment of women constituted an important strategy to cut costs and stay economically afloat, their presence in food distribution remained limited before 1914, a situation that dramatically changed as a result of the First World War and the ensuing need to replace drafted men.

A second and much more important strategy to cut costs was the rapid expansion of child labour.[79] Most shopkeepers avoided employees with social conditions such as married men who required higher wages, and evidence suggests that the practice of replacing adult male assistants with younger ones was quite common.[80] The Royal Commission on Labour did not have trouble finding cases of juvenile shop workers toiling from 90 to 110 hours per week on starvation wages, thus making a mockery of the 1886 act.[81] No less than 100,000 children were employed in shops by the late 1890s, albeit their actual number was probably much more important than the official figures. Indeed, close to a third of all the shops in London employed juveniles by that time, and by 1906 it was estimated that 55,000 out of 750,000 schoolchildren in the metropolis worked for a wage.[82] Alfred George Chamings, one of the principal assistants to the education officer of the LCC, thought that up to 18 percent of the boys between eleven and fourteen years of age were employed in 1910.[83] In places such as Blackburn and Preston, the proportion could reach over one-third, whereas in Liverpool, over half of the child labour force in the early 1900s were employed by grocers, milk dealers, butchers, greengrocers, fish and chip shops, cafés, and restaurants.[84] These figures demonstrate that food distribution relied heavily on the exploitation of children. Unsurprisingly, memoirs and biographies from that time talk of how often people had started their lives as shop boys and girls.[85]

Taking the measure of the scourge, the report of the 1909 Royal Commission on the Poor Laws and Relief of Distress concluded that the "great prominence of boy labour ... is, perhaps, the most serious of the phenomena which we have encountered in our study of employment."[86] The commissioners were particularly attentive to the relationship between a rapidly expanding sphere of distribution and the new openings it created for errand boys, milk boys, street sellers, shop boys, and the like. Particularly distressing was the striking number of schoolchildren working while attending full-time school.[87] By 1909, it was estimated that up to 80 percent of boys leaving elementary school entered unskilled occupations with little prospect of learning a trade, most of them working for shopkeepers.[88] This army of cheap hands fuelled what contemporaries referred to as "blind-alley" labour, which "is boy and girl labour employed in an industry from which it will be ejected towards the end of adolescence ... The essence of the blind-alley job is that it is a juvenile job, offering little opportunity for absorption into the higher grades of the industry."[89] As children grew older, shopkeepers simply dismissed them and hired younger (and cheaper) ones. As Paine put it, "their only chance of being employed again is to put back their age a year or two until their faces belie them, and even that pathetic ruse avails no more."[90] Census returns for England and Wales revealed that, with the exception of greengrocers in 1901, the number of males between the ages of fifteen and twenty employed by milksellers, butchers, grocers, greengrocers and bakers (makers and dealers) was greater than those between the ages of twenty and twenty-five in both 1901 and 1911, and this does not count the large numbers of errand boys employed as messengers and clerks.[91]

The work itself was hard and long hours were frequent, especially on Saturdays when up to sixteen hours of work could be accomplished. For instance, the young John Birch Thomas worked seventy-four hours from Monday morning to Saturday night in a shop in London for eight shillings a week, being most grateful to the shopkeeper's wife, who gave him a cup of coffee and some bread and cheese on Saturday night for his supper. He lived in a common lodging-house, a cheap accommodation where lodgers lived together. Surviving on his meagre income was a constant battle and demanded that every halfpenny be accounted for. Despite his efforts, however, Thomas could not afford better than his "worn and shabby" clothes and "often went hungry at the end of the week." He was thus forced to take on other small jobs to survive. Before going to the shop, he went to two other shops "to take down the shutters in the morning, sweep out the shop and now and then give the windows a rub-over, and then come at night and put the shutters up." For this work, which took him about two hours per day, he received seven shillings per week, almost doubling his earnings. Working 74 hours for 8 shillings or close to 90 hours for 15 shillings was a no-brainer as it not only "meant a good dinner every day" but the financial capacity "to get another pair of trousers" and a means of "saving some money."[92] The frugality of Thomas's existence was no accident in a distributive sector largely dependent upon cheap labour and overwork.

One of the principal occupations of children was to deliver orders to customers, something that had become very popular as shopkeepers tried to stand out by offering new conveniences and services to secure the latter.[93] Compared to adult shop assistants, children were a cheap bargain, young boys earning on average 5 or 6 shillings and girls from 2 shillings and 6 pence to five shillings a week.[94] Unsurprisingly, most of these young wage labourers came from poverty-stricken neighbourhoods, their incomes, however small, making a much appreciated contribution to the household budget. According to Dr Thomas, assistant medical officer of the LCC who investigated the physical condition of 2,000 schoolchildren from 14 different schools, 233 out of 384 wage earners showed signs of fatigue, 140 were anaemic, 131 had severe nerve signs, 64 were suffering from deformities from carrying heavy weights, and 51 had severe heart signs.[95] Similarly, Mr Christie, headmaster of North Corporation Street Board School, located in one of the poorest districts of Liverpool, reported that 12.5 percent of the boys were employed outside school hours and that they were all "poor, stunted, little, ill-developed children."[96] The grinding mill of poverty awaiting this class of unskilled boys and girls made few exceptions, and occupations such as errand boys, shop boys, messengers, and van boys were disproportionally represented in the army and distress committees.[97] In London, for instance, 42.6 percent of army recruits aged fourteen were shop and errand boys driven in by economic necessity.[98] Roland Williams, the superintendent of the Divisional Office in charge of the London Exchange in the northwest of England, reported that, out of 1,302 casual labourers applying for relief in Liverpool, 369 (28.34 percent) had been errand messengers and shop boys after leaving school.[99]

The third main strategy pertained to long hours of work. While working hours in most trades had fallen to fifty-six to sixty hours per week during the Victorian era, shop assistants' work-week actually increased during this period. In the context of growing urbanization and retail competition, the dissemination of gas lightings played a major role in extending business hours beyond daylight. Long hours were very much the norm by the early 1840s,[100] and many commentators did not hesitate to talk about shop slavery and condemn the "evils" of late hours as being injurious to shopworkers[101] Most assistants worked from 80 to 90 hours a week, and from 90 to 100 hours a week in shops trading on Sunday.[102] Although most shops were open between seventy-five to eighty-five hours per week, working hours were generally longer as "the shop had to be cleared, stock put back on the shelves, counters scrubbed, and in the case of some of the 'multiples', stocktaking had to be done."[103] The gap between paid and unpaid work was even sharper at Christmas time when unpaid overtime could easily reach over eighty hours during the month of December.[104]

Founded in 1842 to dismantle the system of late hours and abolish Sunday trading through voluntary closing, the Early Closing Association, despite good intentions and small, short-lived victories, failed to reform shop hours. Indeed, the Select Committee on Shop Hours Regulation Bill admitted in 1886 that a great many shop assistants still worked eighty-five hours a week.[105] Despite evidence that most shopkeepers and shop assistants would welcome compulsory closing hours, the government elected not to introduce compulsory controls over shop hours. Instead, the Shop Hours Regulation Act, 1886, stipulated that persons under eighteen years of age could not work more than seventy-four hours per week, including meal times. As Fabian socialist William Johnson remarked, the act "contained no provisions to ensure its enforcement – which was left optional with the local authorities – or penalties for non-compliance with its regulations. The promoters of the measure relied solely upon its moral effect, and, in consequence, it remained practically a dead letter."[106] The 1892 and 1893 acts did little to address this major loophole, making the appointment of inspectors by town councils permissive rather than mandatory and stipulating that salaries incurred should be defrayed by the council of a county. As such, by 1896 there were only five inspectors in England and Wales and two inspectors in Scotland to enforce the act.[107]

The animosity between the proponents of voluntary and those of compulsory closing reached its climax with "the battle of the Bills," a meeting organized by the London district council of the Shop Assistants' Union in support of Sir Charles Dilke's bill for a maximum working week of sixty hours, including mealtimes, and against Lord Avebury's (formerly Sir John Lubbock) vision of voluntary closing.[108] In its attempt to reconcile the irreconcilable, the Shop Hours Act, 1904, introduced a system based on the compulsory enforcement of voluntary early closing. The act sought to capitalize on the tendency in better class shops to institute an early closing day once a week and thus empowered local authorities to fix shop closing hours by local government order, provided that two-thirds of the shop-owners agreed. By 1907, only 112 local authorities had made orders under the 1904 act, affecting "a mere 9,000 shops, [and] covering perhaps 15,000 persons 'out of a possible total of some 800,000 assistants besides shopkeepers.'"[109] It was not until the Shops Act, 1911, that a statutory half-day weekly holiday for all staff members was finally introduced. The 1912 and 1913 Shops Acts consolidated the 1886, 1904, and 1911 acts regulating employment in shops and mandated a maximum workweek of sixty-six hours. However, they continued to suffer from permissive rather than mandatory inspections and enforcement regulations.[110] In 1916, the home secretary introduced compulsory shop closing at 8:00 p.m. as a wartime measure to save fuel. The order remained in effect after the war and finally became permanent with the Shops Act, 1928.[111]

The truck or living-in system constituted a fourth key strategy to reduce labour costs. Growing out of the old custom of boarding and lodging apprentices, especially in the drapery and grocery trades, the system was brutish and morally degrading, designed more to produce cheap labour than to train the next generation of practitioners. Considered apprentices rather than permanent wage-earners, shop assistants were initially excluded from the Truck Act, 1831, which had generally outlawed the truck system – or "company store" system – whereby wages were paid in part or wholly in goods whose prices were set by the employers. While union agitation succeeded in extending the protection of the Truck Act to shop assistants through sections 1, 5, and 6 of the Amending Truck Act, 1896, and some of the best firms started abandoning the living-in system in the 1900s, it still remained prevalent in England and Wales.[112] Moreover, under the Reform Act, 1884, all living-in male shop assistants continued to be excluded from political life as the right to vote only extended to adult men who were either householders or renting lodgings to the value of ten pounds a year.[113] By the late 1900s, it was estimated that from 400,000 to 450,000 out of some 750,000 assistants were still operating under the living-in system.[114]

This regime of labour control gave unscrupulous employers the ability to lower the costs of labour in many ways, notably through a series of house rules.[115] For instance, the 1886 staff rulebook of the "Universal Provider" William Whiteley "contained no less than 176 separate rules and potential offences … For good measure, rule 176 covered 'any mistake not before mentioned.'"[116] House rules covered almost every imaginable aspect of life, prohibiting everything from hanging pictures on the wall and sleeping out without permission to leaning out of windows or putting flowers in water glasses or bottles.[117] Rules were enforced through a rigid system of fines by shopkeepers who assiduously robbed their employees from one pence to two shillings sixpence at a time. Some fined assistants for going into the kitchen, standing in groups, gossiping, making unnecessary noise in the bedroom or arriving after the closing of the house door at night. Given that most shop workers would not finish their day until 9:00 p.m., the almost universal curfew at 11:00 p.m. was nothing if not a reminder of their complete lack of autonomy and liberty. Shop workers were also subjected to a series of shop rules and fines, including unbusinesslike conduct, soiled shirts, and dirty boots and collars. One could easily loose five shillings per month on mistakes in bills, the loss of duplicate bills, incorrect entry in the books, lateness, or sending a parcel to the wrong address. Fines also took more subtle forms. For instance, it was common to enforce the employee's subscription to a medical fund – the physician conveniently chosen by the employer – and employees often made compulsory contributions to shop funds for the use of the library, the sitting room, the piano, a bath, and clean sheets.[118]Although the best firms tended towards the abolition of fines, before 1914 they remained central to the disciplining environment of most shops.[119]

The low quality, quantity, and variety of food was yet another way to lower overheads. Tea, bread, and butter were usually all that was provided for breakfast, coming cheap to employers and bringing low nutritional value to employees. Bread, butter, cheese, and perhaps ale or milk were all that was provided for supper. Dinner broke slightly from the monotony of this anaemic diet, offering cold or hot meat, generally beef or mutton, with one vegetable, usually potatoes. In shops where a second course was offered, pastry or pudding was served every other day. Fruit and green vegetables were, as a rule, copiously absent. In places where food was insufficient in quantity, workers were forced to depart from precious shillings to buy foodstuffs to supplement their ration.[120] Much resentment arose from badly cooked and undercooked food as well as from food of inferior quality such as rancid butter, stale bread, rotten meat, and weak tea from exhausted leaves. Shop workers were also reminded of their inferior position as many had to have their breakfast alongside shop managers who were "tucking in to eggs and bacon and toast."[121] Very little time was allowed for meals – generally half an hour for dinner and twenty minutes for tea – and shop assistants were liable to interruption during meals.[122] After a tea break around 4:00 p.m., shop assistants very rarely stopped for supper until the closing of the shop, which happened as late as midnight on Saturday. Chronic health problems were therefore frequent, and most women suffered from ill health, including indigestion, anaemia, headache, backaches, and swollen legs because of standing for long periods of time.[123]

There were also more indirect forms of savings for shopkeepers. Shopkeepers often insisted that employees be well dressed in order to uphold their own social status and respectability, thus forcing employees to spend a disproportionate amount of money on clothes and washing, which was particularly devastating for women who earned less than their male shop companions.[124] Employers also saved money by offering poor living conditions such as cold bedrooms during the winter. Similarly, it was common for employees to sleep two in the same bed, and many suffered from headaches as a result of the foul air characteristic of small, overcrowded rooms. Some employers only provided one small jug of hot water per week per employee, and houses providing bathrooms were deemed "quite exceptional."[125] In some places bugs, rats, and black beetles were tenants as well, and most employers offered no privacy as all the space allocated, including the furniture, was shared with the other employees.[126] Moreover, the old practice of forcing shop assistants to go out on Sundays was still common in the 1890s. Justified as a moment for shopkeepers to enjoy the Sabbath with their family, the practice was not disinterested either as it allowed them to save on meals while forcing shop workers to depart from precious shillings to cover food and travelling expenses during that day. Even those who were allowed to stay on Sundays often felt that the owner's family preferred to eat together and have the house for themselves, and consequently left the premises.[127]

Although organizing shop assistants proved to be a difficult task, the "New Unionism" of the 1880s provided the necessary catalyst to organize unskilled and semi-skilled workers by making it clear that "no body of workers, however apparently fragmented and demoralised, was outside the scope of successful collective action."[128] This surge in labour militancy oversaw the creation of the United Shop Assistants Union (USAU) of London in 1889 and the founding of the National Union of Shop Assistants (NUSA) in Birmingham in 1891.[129] Both unions merged in 1898 to become the National Amalgamated Union of Shop Assistants, Warehousemen & Clerks (NAUSAWC), also known as the Shop Assistants' Union. Co-operative distributive workers were also active and formed the Amalgamated Union of Co-operative Employees (AUCE) in 1895 (see chapter 5). However, by 1910, after two decades of labour activism, no more than 2 percent of the total workforce was unionized.[130] On the one hand, uneven power relations between employers and employees tended to undermine labour militancy. Shopkeepers did not hesitate to discharge employees when they learned that they were part of a union, and, given the importance of references from past employers, anyone interested in working their way up the retailing ladder had to remain obedient.[131] On the other hand, the paternalism of the shop, with its fiction of gentility, tended to promote a false notion of superiority that was expressed through shop assistants' "half-conscious feeling that each one is an employer in embryo."[132] Harsh working conditions were therefore often seen as temporary and unions rejected as going against the economic interests of these future employers. While some assistants did become successful shopkeepers or secure better working conditions in higher-end shops, most continued to suffer in an economic sector characterized by long hours and low wages.

In 1911, union membership increased dramatically as a result of the National Insurance Act. Workers gained access to the scheme through approved societies such as the NAUSAWC or the AUCE, which were in charge of the daily administration of the act through collecting the contributions and paying out health and unemployment benefits. Even though the membership of the Shop Assistants' Union rose from 21,426 in 1910 to 85,945 in 1913, the combined membership of both the NAUSAWC and the AUCE represented only 13 percent of all distributive workers by 1914.[133] Despite the limited reach of the labour movement in the food distribution sector, the Shop Assistants' Union played a key role in campaigning for progressive conditions in that sector. As for the NAUSAWC, in addition to its ongoing demand for shorter working hours, it started a campaign for the abolition of the living-in system in 1907, and it was able to secure few victories before 1914, mainly among grocers and drapers in South Wales. That being said, the system remained firmly in place, albeit increasingly discredited in public opinion.[134]

The NAUSAWC also agitated for the institution of a minimum rate of wages. Apart from scattered evidence, often from better-off shops,[135] little is known about shop assistants' wages before the 1880s, in part because of the lack of trade unions to collect data and in part because of an important culture of secrecy surrounding wages. Following the AUCE's 1907 drive for a minimum wage, the Shop Assistants' Union created a minimum wage committee to collect data. Based on the wage returns of nearly two thousand members, or about 10 percent of the total membership, the 1909 report of the committee revealed the complete absence of progress during the Victorian era, with an average wage of 3.25 pence an hour for grocers, butchers, and confectioners, compared to eight to ten pence an hour for engineers, printers, joiners, and other trades. Even dockers earned sixpence an hour.[136] Yet these figures "are indicative only of the wages of what might be called the aristocracy of shop assistants – the best paid and best protected."[137] After agreeing to the principle of a minimum wage in 1910, the Shop Assistants' Union started a campaign to establish a national scale of wages in various parts of the country. For instance, an important campaign was started in 1913 to negotiate better wages with the Master Butchers' Association in Edinburgh, where many assistants received as little as eighteen shillings a week. While the association refused to pay the rates established by the union, the union had become much more militant by that time and it resorted to direct action. "Union officers waited on employers at their shops, and if refused an interview, the staff downed knives and cleavers … Some started dismissing members of the staff so as to intimidate the rest. Down went the knives again … Only one actual strike took place, but eventually agreements were signed covering more than 700 butchers' assistants."[138] Other victories took place among large-scale retailers, as we shall see in chapter 5.[139]

DOMESTIC SHOPS AND FAMILY LABOUR

Contemporaries often referred to self-employed and family-run businesses without employees as domestic shops.[140] It is difficult to know exactly how many domestic shops existed in Great Britain, but the 1911 census stated a total of 607,300 shops in England and Wales, of which only 28 percent were not used as dwellings. Given the informal nature of domestic shops, the census most probably underestimated the actual number of shops. Moreover, the number of residential shops rented at £20 or over per annum (or 7s. 8d. per week) assessed by the Inland Revenue Commissioners rose from 177,000 in 1869–72 to 310,000 in 1909–11 in Great Britain, excluding hotels, public-houses, coffee-houses, and "lock-up shops." While there are some difficulties with these figures, we can nonetheless argue that the actual number of residential shops must have been much higher as many small shopkeepers would not have been able to afford spending close to eight shillings a week on rent alone. As a rough estimate, domestic shops probably represented somewhere between 50 and 60 percent of all shops, which is consequent with the key importance of the shopkeeping class as a whole before 1914.[141] At the very least, there is no reason to question the opinion of John Blundell Maple, member of the House of Commons for Camberwell and president of the Voluntary Early Closing Association, who stated that he had "not the slightest doubt that there are throughout Great Britain and Ireland hundreds of thousands of these small shops with not a single shop assistants in the place; and in those cases very often the keeper of the shop and the family work in the back parlour, and when a tinkling bell rings, announcing a customer, they go and serve the customer."[142]

Domestic shops varied considerably, ranging from the ubiquitous corner and parlour shops to small shops or cellars located in back streets.[143] Some lived a very comfortable life, such as Annie Deacock's father, a dairyman established in Leather Lane in 1863, who paid one thousand pounds for a house in Hornsey in 1879.[144] Yet the reality for the majority was quite different. For instance, an investigation of eighty-six shopkeeping families in Birmingham in 1907 revealed "that an average family of three workers (*i.e.*, over fourteen years of age) and two children (under fourteen) has an income of 39s. per week when the father is not on short time," which amounted to an average weekly profit of about eleven shillings.[145] Although there were many shops in which both husband and wife worked together, it was common for the husband to be employed while his wife managed the shop, often with the help of their children during peak hours. Combined with the husband's wage, even a low weekly profit in the shop would give the shopkeeper a higher living standard and the economic ability to extend credit to trusted customers in order to secure a custom. Small shopkeepers were poor, but they were rich compared to most of their neighbours.[146] Moreover, the central importance of family labour meant that the great majority of these small shopkeepers traded from one shop only, with most families living either above or behind the shop premises. There were also some men who owned and managed a few shops with their wives and children, sometimes with the help of young errand boys, but progress beyond that point was difficult without hiring assistants and renting larger premises.[147]

Domestic shops devised countless strategies to make money go further. For instance, country shopkeepers who fattened and killed their own cattle, cured their own bacon, and made their own lard were able to cut intermediaries and increase their profit margins. Although self-sufficiency was more difficult to achieve for urban shopkeepers, there were nonetheless some possibilities for those with some spare space to garden or breed rabbits for Christmas.[148] The shopkeeper could also increase his profits through reciprocal arrangements. For instance, those with a small capital and a high turnover on one or two commodities could benefit from economies of scale in buying in bulk with fellow traders. Similarly, urban shopkeepers located in or close to agricultural areas often took advantage of small farmers willing to exchange produces such as butter, eggs, and vegetables for credit in the shop.[149] In addition to advertising, extending credit to trusted customers, and resorting to dishonest practices such as food adulteration and short measures, small shopkeepers could increase their trade

through the addition of new lines, such as greengrocers selling proprietary items, sweets, tinned food, or coal.[150] Similarly, about nine-
tenths of the 20,301 off-licence holders in England and Wales in 1894
were domestic shops that did not employ assistants and were managed by a man and his wife, perhaps with another adult member of
his family. Although these domestic shop owners could be butchers,
greengrocers, bakers, or even confectioners, it was estimated that 90
percent were grocers and provision dealers. Given the highly competitive nature of both trades, it was arguably an invaluable trait.[151]

The economic viability of the domestic shop would not have
been possible without family labour and long hours of work. The
domestic shop was a "productive unit," which, as a rule, did not
uphold the Victorian separation between the public and private
spheres.[152] While the presence or absence of family work was influenced by class structure and the nature of the trade (e.g., wives of
"respectable" grocers and gentlemen's outfitters rarely helped in
the shop), most of them depended on family labour. A study of
twenty-nine shopkeeping families revealed that at least 41 percent
of them "had wives and mothers taking an equal or greater share in
shopkeeping than their husbands."[153] Even in businesses where the
whole family worked in the shop, women were often implicitly in
charge of running it. "One gentleman described how he and his
father had refined the technique of half-rising from the dining
table upon hearing the shop bell whilst hoping that his mother
would forestall them. They were considerably discomfited on the
rare occasions when she remained firmly seated."[154] Many wives
also provided the shop with some of its stock, converting surpluses
into jams, wines, and ketchups, or preparing home-made ginger
beer, soups, cakes, and pickled cabbage, walnuts, and onions. Others
added to the trade by cooking breakfasts or dinners for workers.[155]
Children also helped by running errands, making deliveries, serving customers, or, in the case of older girls, by running the house
while their mother was working in the shop.[156] Some went even
further, such as Mr Bennet, fruiterer and greengrocer in Chatham,
who "used to take the boys out of the cottage homes, orphans,
before we [his children] were old enough, and keep them until they
were old enough to go into the services."[157] Domestic shops sometimes hired boys to run errands and deliver orders, and Mr Bennet's
daughter remembers how they "used to be able to get help for
almost nothing. If you gave a kid a few sweets he'd come and do

anything. He'd work all week for a shilling after school hours, and they'd go on the round on Saturdays."[158]

Working hours were excruciatingly long. Daniel Noel, who owned and managed three small shops in the parish of Shoreditch with the help of his wife and three daughters, was open eighty-five hours a week.[159] Off-licence holders, generally open fifteen hours a day, very often traded on Sundays too. Considering the fact that opening a certain number of hours meant working even more, average weekly working hours ranging from ninety to one hundred were the norm.[160] Like its competitors, Robert Roberts's corner shop in Salford was open sixteen hours a day, seven days a week and only closed one full day per year.[161] His mom, who put in 112 hours a week for the shop, "went on working, scrubbing bare bedroom floors, kitchen, shop; washing, baking and caring for the children in between looking after the business."[162] Women's double burden was at its worst in small domestic shops where the husband provided little to no help. Working hours were also kept long because of a generalized lack of labour-saving technologies such as grinding mills, fruit cleaners, tea mixers, coffee roasters, and dough-kneading machines. While most small shopkeepers had neither the capital nor the turnover to justify such investments, the introduction of machinery would also have "brought retail premises under the Factory Acts which laid down minimum requirements for health and safety and restricted the employment of women and children. The most widely adopted labour-saving devices were those which simplified bookkeeping or lowered delivery costs."[163] The food distribution sector remained a labour-intensive business before 1914.

A numerically strong voting bloc, domestic shopkeepers were not a group that either Conservative or Liberal governments were willing to alienate, which explains the unwillingness of the state to enact compulsory early closing. As Thomas Sutherst explained in 1886, "one difficulty in the way of compulsory closing is the interference with small shopkeepers. A man and his wife, who keep a small shop, and probably earn a little to supplement wages made at some calling outside the shop, would feel it an injustice to be deprived of the power of earning a small sum of money in that honest way."[164] Although shopkeepers with employees argued that the exclusion of domestic shops from legislative controls gave them an undue advantage, legislators knew that bringing them under the scope of the law would have undermined their main competitive weapons – unpaid family labour and long hours – and put them out of business.[165] While there were many family-run businesses that did not believe in voluntary efforts to shorten hours, and therefore argued that all should be compelled to close earlier,[166] others, such as off-licence holders and some food retailers, did not favour compulsory closing.[167] Meanwhile, both small and big shopkeepers with employees argued that in domestic shops members of the family should be considered as employees, thus making clear how their immediate economic interests trumped free market principles.[168] In upholding the status quo, the state only reinforced the labour-intensive tendency of the sector by forcing everyone to compete over extremely long hours.

Ideals of respectability and independence were often just that, unrealized promises of a better life through hard labour and devotion. Despite the introduction of modern sales techniques such as advertising and window display, the sinful practices through which the majority of small shopkeepers sought economic redemption were a constant reminder of the intrinsic fragility of their social status. Their attempt to reduce labour costs through the use of child and female labour, their use of the living-in system to produce cheap and dependent assistants, and their willingness to enforce long hours of work were as many strategies to survive in a competitive retail environment. Given the establishment and growing efficiency of legislative controls over food frauds, shopkeepers increasingly survived by degrading labour conditions, either through their own exploitation and that of their relatives in the case of domestic shops or by downloading the impacts of competition onto assistants in the case of employers. The result of this ongoing process of attrition was the gradual erosion of shopkeepers' economic wellbeing, to the extent that by the early 1910s their social status was largely an empty shell. As Herbert G. Wells put it: "Essentially their lives are failures, not the sharp and tragic failure of the labourer who gets out of work and starves, but a slow, chronic process of consecutive small losses which may end if the individual is exceptionally fortunate in an impoverished death but before actual bankruptcy or destitution supervenes."[169] While there were many shopkeepers whose successful businesses allowed them to live a comfortable life and retire without economic constraints, most struggled to make ends meet in a competitive environment witnessing the arrival of two new competitors. It is to them that we now turn.

5

Large-Scale Retailers

In the last three chapters we have explored the transformation of the marketplace from a retail institution dedicated to the provision of food for people to a wholesale function devoted to securing the town's food supply. We have also problematized how small-scale retailers such as street sellers and shopkeepers were connected to this change, and how they in turn transformed the absolute fixity of the marketplace into a relative one. By extending the marketplace in space, they served a growing urban population living in neighbourhoods situated farther and farther from town and city centres. Although their respective dynamics were often conflicting, the largely symbiotic nature of the food distribution system gave the flexibility and comprehensiveness that the new bourgeois urban order needed to grow. Despite their importance throughout the period under review, however, the marginalization of small-scale retailers was accomplished through the immiseration and impoverishment of their social and economic position within the distributive system. Contrasting with the slow but constant process of attrition experienced by small-scale retailers, large-scale retailers grew rapidly through economies of scale based on capital-intensive methods. These methods were anchored at once in Britain's more intensive, market-oriented agriculture and the rapid development of manufacturing in the food sector as well as in the new possibilities afforded by an international food regime. Benefitting from free trade policies and thriving on recent developments in transport and refrigeration technologies, co-operative societies and multiple shops expanded through their ability to organize a more reliable and regular international food supply. Many achieved vertical integration through acquisitions in circulation technologies or production works or both.

This chapter explores how far and in what ways co-operative stores and multiple shops were able expand while delivering cheap food. Their growth was nothing short of phenomenal. Playing no important role at the national level in the early 1880s, albeit some co-ops and multiples were already key local and regional retailers in the 1860s and 1870s, large-scale retailers had become central to the dynamics of food distribution in 1914, even though they had not yet achieved sufficient concentration to control the majority of market shares in any of the food trade. Their organizational means and structural capacities gave them the ability to shape the competitive environment through a price structure based on economies of scale and high turnover. While both shared a common concern for economic growth, co-operative societies and multiple shops relied on entirely different precepts, and the politics informing their respective growth strategies revolved upon entirely different normative assumptions regarding the role of consumption in society. As we shall see, however, the key role played by large-scale retailers in the provisioning of cheap food not only sprang from their ability to take advantage of the gradual rescaling of food relations at the international level but also from their capacity to impose cheap labour practices. This chapter is divided in two sections dealing with co-ops and multiples. In each section I offer a brief review of the means by which they expanded their market share before discussing the extent to which cheap labour was key to their business model and ability to deliver cheap food.

THE "STATE WITHIN A STATE"[1]

A counterpoint to the expansion of capitalist social relations in the period under study was the co-operative movement. The fact that it had a long history arching back to the last third of the eighteenth century was no accident. Emerging as a response to the enclosure movement and heightened market dependence, co-operation was from its beginning a self-help movement of workers, families, and communities animated by principles of independence and mutual support. At first, it represented a communal expression of injustice over the fact that impersonal, market-driven mechanisms were being substituted for the more traditional paternalistic norms of obligations and solidarities. In this respect, the concentration of activities around the organization of co-operative milling and flour clubs at the end of the eighteenth century was as much a refusal of the new capitalist order, entrenched as it was in the uprooting and forced displacement of peasants from the land, as it was a reaction against the disintegration of previous social norms and cultural points of reference. The historical specificity of co-operation is to be found in its attempt to restore a sense of "moral economy" in trade from within the structures and dynamics of capital accumulation through workers' self-empowerment. In this bottom-up approach to social and economic inequalities, co-operators proposed a "co-operative commonwealth" driven by ideals of responsible consumption and decent working conditions that remain nonetheless dedicated to capital's competitive logic and bourgeois individualism.[2] Especially in the late eighteenth and early nineteenth centuries, as food and labour markets expanded greatly, co-operation was a response to price fluctuations and the growing difficulties associated with poverty. Despite its social and cultural importance, however, one should not exaggerate the movement's political role. Most associations were small and there were probably no more than fifty thousand members at the national level before 1844.[3]

Rising from the ashes of Owenite Socialism and the Chartist inspired co-operation of the 1820s, 1830s, and early 1840s, the Rochdale Pioneers were astute pragmatists who, in 1844, introduced a series of ideas whose particular combination radically departed from earlier movements.[4] One key principle was the democratization of power as membership was open to everyone who could make the down payment of one shilling and whom the ownership then conferred with a one-pound share. Second, cash-only trading sought to avoid the rocky shores of credit lending upon which many early societies had foundered, though it also tended to exclude the poorest segments of the working class from the benefits of mutuality. Exceptions were sometimes made during times of economic hardship.[5] Third, the Pioneers were committed to providing their members with pure and unadulterated food and true weight and measure, a remarkable stance given the widespread practice of tampering with food in the retail sector.[6] Fourth, the introduction of fixed and limited interest on capital invested allowed retail societies to retain the benefits of capital in order to finance their own development without allowing lenders to appropriate all surpluses.[7] As modest as it was, this measure allowed them to secure the full extent of what ought to be a member-owned business. Finally, and most important for the future success of the movement, dividends (or "divi") on purchases were redistributed quarterly after interests on capital paid and could be used to pay for one's membership. "Working-class women, who frequently had to negotiate a narrow path between scarcity and survival, made up an ardent rank and file. The dividend was often used for major purchases – coal, clothes, furniture, holidays. The usefulness of this form became part of the common sense, which helped working-class families make ends meet."[8] Surpluses were realized through the difference between economies of scale realized by buying in bulk and selling at average market retail prices. Dividends generally ranged from two to four shillings on the pound, or 10 to 20 percent.[9]

A strong tradition of mutuality in Lancashire, Northumberland, Durham, the West Riding, and central Scotland proved essential to the renewal of the movement, especially in industrial towns where regular employment in factories and mines tended to create a more homogeneous working-class experience and where economic prosperity from the 1870s onwards was accompanied by a sense of working-class identity and traditions of collective organization. In 1914, the Northwest, Northeast, and Yorkshire regions accounted for more than two-thirds of co-operators and three-quarters of the total retail trade in England and Wales.[10] Naval dockyard towns such as Plymouth, Sheerness, and Southampton; railway workers in Stratford; and munitions workers at the Royal Arsenal in Woolwich also enjoyed the benefits of co-operation, as did the South Wales valleys. Pockets of co-operation also existed in Banbury, Oxford, and Reading as well as in Cambridge, Ipswich, and Norwich in eastern England. By and large, cosmopolitan cities and ports and holiday resorts such as London, Liverpool, Blackpool, and rural areas were co-operative deserts as casual labour, seasonal work, high rates of immigration, residential mobility, the high cost of rates, rents, and buildings as well as low levels of demand tended to undermine co-operative efforts.[11] As the Commissioners of the Royal Commission on the Poor Laws and Relief of Distress rightly concluded in 1909: "it may be said that the chief success of co-operation has been among the artisan class – not to any considerable extent either among the poorest classes or the better off."[12]

Despite some limitations, the success of co-operation was nothing short of phenomenal. Although very few of the early societies survived the second quarter of the nineteenth century and struggled to survive throughout the 1850s and 1860s in Wales, the west Midlands, and the South East,[13] the movement slowly gathered pace after 1844 and membership passed the 100,000 mark in the early 1860s with a combined turnover of about £2.5 million. By 1914, Britain counted 1,385 societies regrouping over 3 million members with an annual turnover close to £148 million.[14] In his study of the co-operative movement, sociologist Johnston Birchall describes three main avenues by which co-operation expanded.[15] First, the simplest method, through the stocking of new lines of products and the opening of new departments supervised by specialist managers. Although there was no shortage of hand-to-mouth stores, all of them invariably started with groceries and provisions, dealing in flour, tea, sugar, coffee, dried fruit, bacon, hams, butter, and cheese as well as manufactured goods like marmalade, biscuits, and cocoa. Foodstuff represented on average 80 percent of total co-operative retail sales up until 1914.[16] Other products and services such as drapery, furniture, insurance, clothes, boots, convalescent homes, and funeral care came later as the movement gathered speed.[17] Large societies with strong membership and high turnovers often opened bakeries, confectionaries, and meat departments, although integration in the meat trade was almost non-existent given that each retail society bought and slaughtered its own beasts. For instance, the bakery of the Royal Arsenal Co-operative Society, Woolwich, produced close to 4.5 million two-pound loaves per year in the mid-1900s, and the United Baking Society of Glasgow, a federation of co-operative stores, was not doing badly with annual sales of £482,500.[18] Similarly, the newly formed Bristol Society produced over 2.5 million quartern loaves in 1909, and a new, highly modern bakery with greater capacity was opened the following year.[19] Perishable goods such as meat, milk, and greengrocery only made their appearance in co-operative stores in the early 1900s, with the exception of large societies where they were introduced earlier.

The second way by which retail societies grew was through the early adoption of the branch system.[20] "Co-operatives were thus in the vanguard of the suburbanisation of shopping, providing many of the essentials for day-to-day living without having to venture into the centre of town."[21] This was done by setting up branch stores either by taking over smaller societies or owing to the pressure of populations in outlying areas, and evidence suggests that, by the 1900s, co-operative societies had become the largest owner-occupiers of retail property in towns such as Accrington, Barrow, and Lancaster.[22] As geographer Ronald Jones's study of co-operation in Edinburgh has revealed, however, members were policy makers, too. In Edinburgh as elsewhere, the democratic organizational structure of the co-operative society influenced commercial considerations as much as it affected decisions on where to open shops or the availability of van deliveries.[23] Although the stabilization of working-class neighbourhoods through the rise of more stable forms of employment, rising standards of living, the development of intra-urban means of transportation, and the steady growth of new structures in retailing and wholesaling tended to rationalize the spatial dispersion of retail stores through amalgamations, a strong culture of localism also meant that local societies were often loath to amalgamate.[24] Despite such dynamics, however, the average number of members per society rose from 564 to 2,205 between 1881 and 1914, and the number of distributive societies declined after reaching its peak in 1903.[25] For example, through amalgamation, the St Cuthbert's Co-operative Association of Edinburgh went from 1,310 members in 1879 to 20,000 members at the turn of the century, making it the largest retail co-operative society in Scotland and the fourth largest in the United Kingdom.[26] Some greatly benefitted from these rationalizations, with the Keynsham Society, before its amalgamation with the Bristol Society, described as nothing more than "'hand-to-mouth' dealers."[27]

The third and probably most important way by which the co-operative movement grew was through wholesale trading. While the Industrial and Provident Societies Act, 1852, protected co-operative societies' funds against fraud, it also forbade them "to engage in banking, mining, or wholesaling or to hold land," the right to own land being granted under the Amendment Act, 1855.[28] The key piece of legislation underpinning the future development of the union was the Companies Act, 1862, which gave the movement the legal basis to expand through limited liability, which gave way to the creation of the Co-operative Wholesale Society (CWS) in 1863 and its Scottish (SCWS) counterpart in 1868. Marx understood all too well that the co-operative movement was shifting gears when he referred to it as a "greater victory of the political economy of labor over the political economy of property" in his inaugural address to the International Working Men's Association in 1864.[29] These wholesale societies were federations of member societies with the mandate to realize economies of scale for the exclusive benefit of co-operative stores, as free to buy on competitive markets as their member societies were. As this loose federative structure dramatically extended the movement's ability to cut out the intermediaries, it gave co-operators considerably more control over the organization of the sphere of distribution. Quickly outgrowing the capacity of local and regional suppliers, wholesale societies were capable of influencing larger suppliers, specialist wholesalers, as well as food processors and manufacturers. With wholesale societies moving into production, the co-operative movement resolutely entered into a phase of vertical integration.

The expansion of wholesale societies was nothing short of spectacular. Whereas the annual turnover of the cws rose from £51,875 in 1864 to about £35 million in 1914, total sales of the scws increased from £81,094 in 1869 to £9,425,383 in 1914.[30] The percentage of productions to total sales increased from 3.72 in 1881 to 16.37 in 1900 to 25.93 in 1914 for the cws, and from 26.73 in 1900 to 33.30 in 1914 for the scws.[31] As we shall see, however, while the scale of co-operative wholesaling and production was substantial in absolute terms, it remained disappointing relative to the amount of goods sold by retail co-ops. For the remaining 75 percent that was bought on competitive markets, the cws could count on a small battalion of buyers and salespeople stationed in Manchester, London, Cork, and New York and who organized the wholesale purchasing and shipping of food goods. The cws also owned a whole series of home, foreign, and colonial depots, whose location and opening year reveal important trends in the spatial evolution of food sourcing. Ireland characterized the early phase with the opening of depots in Tipperary (1866), Kilmallock (1868), Limerick (1869), Armagh (1873), Waterford (1873), Tralee (1874), and Cork (1877). The establishment of forwarding depots in Garston (1879) and Goole (1879), as well as the opening of depots in Bristol (1884) and Longton (1886), marked an important step towards greater distributive capacities in the handling of growing quantities of imported food in Britain. The establishment of depots in New York (1876), Rouen (1879), Copenhagen (1881), Hamburg (1884), Aarhus (1891), Montreal (1894), Gothenburg (1895), Denia (1896), Sydney (1897), Odense (1898), Esbjerg (1905), Makene (1914), and Accra (1914) reflected the international sourcing of the co-operative movement and the wider trend within British society towards food import dependency. Meanwhile, the cws extended its capacities by investing £20,000 in the construction of the Manchester Ship Canal,[32] which opened on 1 January 1894, and purchasing numerous vessels so as to further cut out the intermediaries.[33] By the end of the 1900s, the scws had 1,595 employees in the distributive departments and 5,514 in productive works. By comparison, the cws, whose productive works were concentrated mainly in Manchester, Newcastle, and London, had on its payroll 6,691 employees in distribution and 10,291 in production.[34] This is all the more impressive when we consider that, by the end of the 1870s, "the C.W.S., with its annual trade of £2,705,000 was managed by a committee of working men who met on Saturday afternoons and received a 5s. fee for their attendance."[35]

Although co-operative stores continued to stock proprietary brands such as Epp's cocoa, Hudson's soap, and Keiller's marmalade, the variety of goods produced by wholesale societies increased remarkably: boots, brush, drapery, tobacco, underclothing, furniture, hosiery, ironworks, shirt, mantle, paint, soap, candle, and printing, among other things. Despite such a range of articles, however, food preparation remained the most significant sector of these new inroads into production. In 1873, the cws bought Crumpsall Biscuit Works and started to produce biscuits, sweets, currant bread, and the like. The manufacture of cocoa and chocolate and pepper grinding commenced in 1887, and bacon factories were purchased in Denmark in 1900 and Ireland in 1901. From the 1890s onwards, the cws moved more seriously towards large-scale flour milling, beginning at Dunston-on-Tyne in 1891 and acquiring mills in Oldham, Bristol, and London in the following years.[36] The cws soon diversified into agricultural production, acquiring land and buildings to grow plums, tomatoes, cucumber, apples, gooseberries, potatoes, peas, onions, grain, strawberries, raspberries, and currants. By 1914, the cws had extended its activities to cattle breeding at home and acquired tea estates in Ceylon.[37] In addition, a whole series of factories, creameries, and estates produced and processed goods such as bacon, preserves, confectionery, sweets, biscuits, butter, margarine, flour, tea, fruit and vegetables, ground spices, candied peels, mincemeat, vinegar, sauce, pickle, cocoa and chocolate, milk, bottled and canned fruit, and jellies.

This "democracy in business," or "republic of consumers," as co-operator Percy Redfern put it, was not without its own contradictions.[38] As Holyoake revealingly argued, the dying body of the early co-operator would not have survived "if the solid-headed and sagacious men of Rochdale had not discovered the method of *feeding it on profits* – the most nutritious diet known to social philosophy."[39] Adam Smith's ideas were not far when Abraham Howarth, president of the Pioneers' Society, declared that the movement joins "together the means, the energies, and the talent of all for the benefit of each" by "a common bond, that of self-interest."[40] Examined before the Royal

Commission on the Poor Laws and Relief of Distress, William Maxwell, president of the scws, made a similar statement in declaring: "With the growing feeling towards temperance and the possession of capital by the working classes, the future, I think, is extremely hopeful."[41] The idea that capital could be a tool for labour rather than its master was fundamental to the growth of the movement after 1844. "However, prioritizing consumption within this strategy conferred mixed blessings. In the cooperative ideology of the majority movement understanding and transforming capitalist relations of production were subordinated to the transformation of exchange relations."[42] In this respect, the principles inherited from the Rochdale Pioneers marked an important transition from revolutionary politics to a more reformist, morally based approach to shopkeeping.[43] And while one cannot reduce the post-1844 movement to mere economic calculations without running the risk of severely amputating its social and cultural dimensions – co-operation was, after all, a way of life for a great many[44] – it is difficult not to conclude that at least for a substantial minority, co-operation was the vehicle to an end rather than the end itself.

Co-operators' loyalty always remained a source of preoccupation.[45] Even after the opening of a cws branch in Newcastle in 1872, which quickly became the largest single supplier to retail societies in northeast England, over one-third of the societies were not shareholders and thereby continued to get all of their supplies from competitive markets. Moreover, despite an appreciable increase in sales from £203,083 in 1872 to £596,201 in 1877, the business conducted by the cws with northeastern co-operators represented no more than a quarter of the total sales of these retail societies.[46] Already in the 1860s, co-operative stores could count on an extensive network of "discerning and friendly dealers" in Newcastle, Glasgow, Greenock, London, Leeds, and Liverpool for their grocery and provisions.[47] Societies did not hesitate to use several competing firms to obtain their grocery and provisions, and it seems that "the majority of co-operators subscribed to a more limited vision of the practical utility of their own store as a collective endeavour rooted in the immediacy of their particular community."[48] Despite the key role of the Women's Co-operative Guild in keeping "an eye on societies' loyalty to co-operative products,"[49] retail stores continued to rely extensively on competitive markets. Between 1881 and 1914, total wholesale to retail sales within the co-operative movement in the United Kingdom rose from about 23 percent to 43 percent, thus leaving about £60 million to capitalist markets.[50] Given that 52 percent of Scottish co-operative retail sales came from the SCWS, we can conclude that the ratio between wholesale and retail sales in England and Wales was below 40 percent. However impressive the scale of co-operative wholesaling and production was, the power of brands and the desire of consumers to exercise choice in their purchasing constantly diminished its relative importance.

There were always important local and regional variations. In 1909, the Bristol Society purchased 77.7 percent of its supply from the CWS.[51] At the Murton Colliery Society in Durham, average purchases per member per year amounted to an impressive £55 in 1905, compared to £33 in Gateshead and Burnley, £20 in Woolwich, and £18 in the periphery of Plymouth.[52] As George D.H. Cole noted, however, we "see real trade per head rising during the period of falling retail prices which ended in 1896, and then, after a few years of minor oscillations, falling off sharply from 1901 to 1919."[53] Indeed, rising food prices after 1896 triggered one of the main contradictions inherent to the movement, although it continued to grow in the following years. Rising prices forced many co-operators either to curb their living standards in order to stay loyal to the movement or to shop around for the best bargains. Since dividends were a temporally differed discount on goods sold at average market prices, this meant that dividends paid quarterly in the context of falling food prices between 1873 and 1896 tended to command a greater quantity of goods once available. The flipside was that, after 1896, dividends lost part of their value, thus creating a situation where, from a purely economic point of view, consumers benefitted from shopping around. And given the importance of the costermongering and shopkeeping classes and their ability to lower food prices amidst heightened competition, prospective housewives looking for cheap bargains did not have difficulties finding them outside co-operative stores.

The growing anxiety over what Ernest Aves called the "disorganized buying" and lack of loyalty of "the comparatively well-to-do working-man's wife" was indicative of the sexual division of labour and responsibilities to which a great many co-operators subscribed.[54] Given that women were in charge of the household budget, they were likely to be blamed for bringing their customs outside co-operative stores – indeed, it never occurred to Aves that he could have equally blamed the men for failing to bring enough money to afford their politics. The association of men with production and women with consumption, as well as the differentiated politics to which it gave rise, was captured by co-operator Margaret Llewelyn Davies: "Trade Unionism and

Co-operation are woven into the very fabric of the workers' lives. Trade Unionists stretch the warp of a decent wage ... Isolated in their own individual homes, it is through their common everyday interests as buyers that married working-women have come together, and found their place in the labour world and national life."[55] Whereas the politics of production confined men to trade unionism and the fight for better wages, the politics of consumption demanded that women tied most of the household budget to the co-operative stores. To the extent that these politics of consumption were only viable in households headed by well-paid skilled workers with stable employment, it was always precarious and limited. As many co-operators discovered in the late-1890s, cheap food trumped political principles.

That being said, there was no doubt that the movement, which arose out of the "hungry forties," had helped millions of working-class people buy themselves out of poverty. Economies of scale, dividends, and vertical integration combined to create one of the most powerful organizations in the British food distribution system. With total retail sales increasing from £27.5 million in 1882 to £147.5 million in 1914, and with the proportion of national salary spent in co-operative stores rising from 4.2 percent in 1880 to 11.4 percent in 1913, many retailers (such as shopkeepers) expressed anxiety – and even deep resentment – over the movement's success.[56] Ironically, many of the values cherished by shopkeepers (e.g., self-help, independence) were core principles of co-operators' socialized approach to shopkeeping. Already in the late 1880s, market authorities in Bolton and Gloucester complained that the success of the co-operative movement had negatively affected public markets.[57] Despite its remarkable achievements, however, it was the inability of the movement to go beyond the politics of consumption that weakened it. With the exception of the bread and flour confectionery trade, co-operative production never accounted for more than a fraction of its sales, with the bulk of the goods supplied by the co-operative wholesale and retail societies purchased from private firms at home and abroad.[58] In this respect, co-operative culture and politics flourished through – rather than in opposition to – capitalist production.

A Model Employer?

Very little is known about working conditions before the 1880s.[59] While the number of bankruptcies in the third quarter of the nineteenth century provides one explanation for the lack of information, in smaller societies committee members often did most of the work voluntarily at the beginning, being responsible for most "behind-the-counter" work and deliveries.[60] The initial extent of voluntary labour in retail co-ops demonstrated that, beyond ideas of self-help and independence, very few co-operative stores would have survived their beginnings without the benign self-exploitation of a determined few. The lack of information also betrays the employment structure and the low status of shopworkers in the co-operative movement. Co-operators were not always model employers, and long hours and poor wages were not uncommon in many societies. Key to labour conditions was the role that consumer dividends played in opposing members' economic interests to co-operative employees' welfare, which, as J. Thompson, secretary of the Ashton-under-Lyne Society, admitted in 1889, reduced workers to "divi-making machines."[61] Management committees often insisted that they had to "follow the level of shop hours and wages prevailing in their localities" to maintain high consumer dividends.[62] The managerial tension within co-operation between elected officials and paid employees was also the result of the rapid growth of the movement, which had forced many societies to appoint "managers who, although experienced in retail trading, had been trained in private trade, had the outlook of private traders and were ignorant of, or out of sympathy with, the purpose of the co-operative societies."[63] There were also distributive societies paying bonuses on wages and therefore using profit-sharing to pay less than a decent wage.[64] Despite the resilience of cheap labour in the co-operative movement, co-operative employees, especially from the 1890s onwards, were generally better treated than those in private shops: they enjoyed shorter hours and little unemployment, living-in and radius agreements were virtually unknown, and annual holidays were generous by contemporary standards.[65]

While there were no shortage of bad spots in the co-operative movement, there were also a great many co-operators who saw it as an attempt "to build a bridge, materially and ideologically, between the competitive present and the cooperative future."[66] According to this vision, co-operators should have been practising what they preached by granting living wages and progressive labour conditions to their employees. In this respect, the Women's Co-operative Guild – founded in 1883 as the Women's League for the Spread of Co-operation – was instrumental in exposing problematic co-operative stores, organizing

Table 5.1
Estimated shares in selected food trades, 1900–15

	Groceries and provisions			Bread and flour			Meat		
	Co-ops	Multiples	Others	Co-ops	Multiples	Others	Co-ops	Multiples	Others
1900	15.0	5.5	79.5	4.0	0.5	95.5	4.0	5.8	90.3
1905	16.0	7.5	76.5	5.3	1.0	93.8	4.8	8.5	86.8
1910	17.0	10.5	72.5	7.0	2.0	91.0	5.0	11.8	83.3
1915	18.0	13.0	69.0	8.0	3.8	88.3	6.5	10.3	83.3

Source: Jefferys, Retail Trading in Britain, 163, 201, 223.

against sweating, and agitating for better wages and conditions for co-operative employees.[67] Employees too became more active, at first by airing their grievances in the pages of the Co-operative News. Although there existed small associations of employees in Bolton and London in 1887, it was the formation of the Manchester and District Co-operative Employees' Association (MDCEA) in 1891 that truly began the construction of a national union. Interestingly, the MDCEA was formed by delegates representing both employees' and societies' committees, thus highlighting how co-operators, even as employers, could also be invaluable allies in the battle for better working conditions.[68] Already in the early 1890s, many of these workers benefited from a weekly half holiday, thus suggesting a quite progressive co-operative culture from management committees in and around Manchester. At the first annual meeting of the association in July 1892, some 738 members from forty-seven different societies were represented (out of an estimated thirty thousand co-operative employees in retail societies).[69]

The march towards a national union for co-operative employees culminated with the formation of the Amalgamated Union of Co-operative Employees (AUCE) in 1895, which brought together benefit and mutual improvement associations such as the MDCEA and the Bolton and District Association.[70] The AUCE always took a holistic approach centred on co-operative employment, whether productive or distributive. Female workers were comparatively few as they were often regarded with suspicion, their low wages considered a threat to the position of men. This tended to reinforce a gendered division of labour whereby women and girls were confined to drapery, millenary, and dressmaking departments, while grocery, provisions, butchery, and, to a lesser extent, greengrocery were overwhelmingly attended to by men before 1914 – the First World War dramatically changed the situation. Whereas the total number of co-operative employees grew from 80,000 in 1900 to 150,000 in 1914, distributive workers in retail societies represented on average slightly more than half of them. The membership of the AUCE on the other hand increased at a much slower pace: from 2,179 members in 1896 to 4,320 in 1898 to 32,741 in 1912. As for female membership, it always represented a fraction of union members, from 127 in 1898 to 3,014 in 1912.[71] Although levels of unionization were not high, they were substantially greater than in private trade, including multiples. Indeed, the co-operative movement did not share the active hostility (sometimes masked by paternalism) of many private retailers to unions.

On the issue of hours, the majority of co-operative employees worked less than sixty-six hours per week, which at the time was typical in high-end shops. Already in 1893 some ninety societies had accepted reducing working hours, with at least ten of them – all located in Northumberland and Durham – lowering the working week to forty-eight hours. Though encouraging, these early successes left the vast majority of retail societies untouched. At the 1893 Co-operative Congress, William Maxwell, leader of the Scottish Co-operators and president of the SCWS, gave evidence of "sweating" in the movement: 1,096 out of the 1,172 societies (93.5 percent) in the United Kingdom worked their employees for more than 60 hours, 509 (43.4 percent) for more than 66 hours, and 163 (13.9 percent) from 70 to 85 hours.[72] The congress adopted a resolution to the effect that long hours of work and low wages were "opposed to the principles and aims of Co-operation," which was ignored by most local societies as resolutions adopted at the congress were not mandatory.[73] Long hours were nonetheless hard to reconcile with "the average hours of skilled artisans, factory operatives, general labourers, and miners, the classes of people that very largely make up the membership of co-operative societies," all of whom worked on average between 48 and 52 hours per week by the late 1900s.[74] Important gains were achieved ca. 1900, and by 1909 76.7 percent had net working hours greater than 52.5 hours but only 9.9 percent had over 58.5 hours, and only 3.2 percent between 62.5 and 73 hours. By then, the vast majority of societies were open for less than sixty hours a week, with shorter hours in Durham, Cumberland, Northumberland, North Yorkshire, and Westmorland, and longer hours in London and the south and southwest.[75]

Wages were generally lower than in private shops. "In 1891, for example, in the Manchester area the wages of branch managers and head countermen in the Co-operative Stores ranged from 18s. to 40s. a week, and those of other countermen from 7s. to 25s. These were adult men's wages, not boys': women were at that date hardly employed at all."[76] Evidence from Oldham Industrial and Bolton societies in the late 1890s ranged from 12 shillings for an 18-year-old to 28 shillings for a butcher of 31 years of age, with branch managers earning from 30 to 38 shillings. At the Ayrshire Co-operative in 1910, men in the grocery department earned from 15 to 30 shillings and women from 10 to 17 shillings.[77] Reporting wages from 23 to 25 shillings per week for male employees in the late 1900s, Hallsworth and Davies argued that these "are descriptive chiefly of the position of the organised and best-paid co-operative shopworkers. We have frequently had brought to our notice cases of men receiving no more and much less than £1 per week."[78] Indeed, the General Co-operative Survey of 1919 revealed that the average annual wage of distributive workers in retail societies rose from £53.99 in 1906 to £59.74 in 1914, thus suggesting that many did not earn more than twenty shillings a week.[79] The Women's Co-operative Guild showed that well over a third of women employed in the north of England and more than half of those working for societies in the south, southwest, and Yorkshire were paid under thirteen shillings a week.[80] The practice of employing large numbers of low-wage juniors and sacking them by the time that they came of age was also common, and some societies dealt with a downturn in trade by forcing their assistants to go on unpaid leave and reaping the benefits of the resulting wage cuts.[81]

Although the AUCE had adopted a resolution for a minimum wage of twenty-four shillings a week for male shopworkers at twenty-one years of age in 1897, the battle for a compulsory minimum wage proved to be long and difficult. The movement gathered pace in 1905 when the AUCE and the Women's Co-operative Guild came together and started a living wage campaign. The issue of a minimum wage for co-operative employees was brought before the Newport Co-operative Congress of 1908, which approved the principle and appointed a committee to propose minimum wage scales for the following year. The Newcastle Co-operative Congress of 1909 accepted the scale worked out by the committee and recommended its adoption by all retail societies. Rates began at 6 shillings for boys at 14 years of age and rose to 24 shillings at 21 years of age, and ranged from 5 shillings for girls at 14 years up to 17 shillings at 20 years.[82] While there was nothing remarkable in these rates, the fact is that "minimum scales were being established and what was equally significant, they were being *negotiated* by organised employees."[83] It took twelve years to transform the 1897 resolution of the AUCE for a trade union wage into a national guideline approved by the Co-operative Congress, but, as the AUCE soon realized, many local societies opposed the wage scale. The Plymouth Co-operative Congress of 1910 revealed that only 195 societies had replied to the Co-operative Union's circular, which recommended the general adoption of the wage scales. Of those, only 79 societies said that they were ready to implement the new scales and 116 declared that they were unable to do so, thus suggesting that some 1,056 societies "were still on the bad old system of arbitrarily determined and frequently beggarly wage rates."[84]

Progress was slow but the AUCE continued to push for the adoption of a minimum wage for co-operative employees. Following a request for information by the Co-operative Union, it was revealed in July 1913 that out of 1,262 societies, 272 (21.6 percent) paid the minimum wage to both men and women workers, 69 (5.5 percent) paid the minimum to men alone, 281 (22.2 percent) did not pay it, and 640 (50.7 percent) had not even bothered to reply.[85] It is obvious from these statistics that a substantial majority of societies paid wages below the minimum wage demanded by the AUCE.[86] In time, the Co-operative Union even had to produce wage lists providing for advances according to trades and geographical location as many management committees adopting the minimum wage rate treated it as the standard to avoid paying more for experienced shopkeepers.[87] The unwillingness of the movement to pay living wages fostered a more militant approach. Already in 1908, the Oldham Industrial and Coventry branches had proposed a strike fund at the annual meeting of the AUCE, arguing "that in the ten years that the minimum had been Union policy 'we have done too much requesting ... we are at present held cheap.'"[88] While the strike at the CWS Avonmouth flour mill in 1912 constitutes the first stoppage organized by the AUCE, there were also disputes with retail societies in Grays (Essex), Warrington, Lincoln, and Leeds in 1913, and Coalburn (Scotland) in 1914. Agreements were reached before the strike at Grays and Warrington, and the cases of Lincoln and Leeds were resolved within a week of the strike. In Coalburn, a bitter strike ensued after two employees were sacked.

Things turned violent after the society advertised for new staff and brought in black-leg labour. The strike was ultimately called off by the AUCE and workers placed on out-of-work benefit.[89] Ongoing resistance among co-operative societies to pay a decent wage to their employees was a strong reminder that the ability of the movement to deliver cheap food – embodied as it was in the "divi" – was in no small way rooted in its willingness to maintain cheap labour among distributive workers.

MULTIPLE SHOPS

The impact of multiples on the organization and structures of retailing was profound. Fuelled by developments in food manufacturing, product innovations, new sources of supply, increased urban population, improvements in transportation and storage facilities, and enhanced consumer spending power and mobility, multiple stores contributed to the concentration of retailing through its rescaling at the international level.[90] Multiples were capital-intensive ventures with the sole objective of making profits, and they operated on an aggressive price-cutting policy of small profits and quick returns on high volume.[91] Like co-operative stores, multiples relied heavily on their ability to realize economies of scale by negotiating discounts with their suppliers on bulk turnover and by selling their own-brand goods through vertical diversification "into production to reduce costs and to ensure regularity and consistency of supply."[92] Thomas Lipton's rule of "abolishing, wherever possible, the middle-man or intermediary profiteer between the producer and the consumer" captured the importance of vertical integration in a competitive distributive environment.[93] Moreover, multiples' capacity to increase the velocity of distribution and cut labour costs, both through the introduction of more efficient methods and low wages, tended to heighten "the process of de-skilling the shop labour force as management practices standardised the work routines of most shop assistants."[94] Indeed, the adoption of formal structures of labour management in both co-ops and multiples was deeply affected by their development as networks of branch stores, which created a particular imperative for deskilling through the growing necessity to standardize work practises, normalize staff education and training, and define employees' roles and responsibilities.

To keep it simple, I follow James B. Jefferys' definition of a multiple shop organization "as a firm, other than a Co-operative Society, possessing 10 or more retail establishments."[95] Although somewhat arbitrary, this definition has the merit of differentiating between locally based, small-scale multiples with two to nine shops, and major firms operating in several different towns either regionally or nationally.[96] While providing a spatio-temporal demarcation for the emergence of major multiples, it also suggests that multiple-shop retailers owning several premises were far from being uncommon. "There is ample evidence of shopkeepers owning several premises in early nineteenth-century Britain. However, these early multiple-shop retailers … rarely had permanent branches in more than one or two neighbouring towns. Moreover, there was little to link this style of trading with the chain stores that appeared in the later nineteenth century. In this sense, large-scale multiple retailing can be seen as new – a Victorian retail revolution."[97] There were indeed numerous small multiple-shop retailers in large towns such as Cardiff, Glasgow, Liverpool, London, Manchester, and Newcastle owning several shops in the first half of the nineteenth century. Like the co-operative movement, however, what distinguishes major multiples is not only the scale and scope at which they operated but also and more fundamentally their systematic adoption of the branch system as the main vector through which their expansion was made possible. Multiples expanded either regionally by "opening branches in neighbouring towns and villages in response to local demand," such as the Newcastle-based Brough's grocery chain, or nationally by targeting large regional centres before moving into smaller towns, such as Lipton.[98]

According to historian Michael Winstanley, there were a certain number of constraints inhibiting the growth of large-scale retailers before 1880. To begin with, shopkeepers were by and large uninterested in expanding their operations, preferring instead the direct control afforded by a single fixed shop. As we saw in the last chapter, shopkeepers were important figures at the local level with symbiotic ties to the communities they served. Their economic interests and social status were better served by investing in the public life of where they lived, which would have been jeopardized by geographical expansion. Second, the growth of manufacturing goods and the development of a more extensive division of labour in the food trade after 1850 contributed to the decline of skilled shops. Lower barriers of entry into small-scale retailing contributed further to a highly competitive retail environment that was detrimental to amalgamation. Another key factor concerned important shortcomings in the

reliability and regularity of supply, especially in the context of an agricultural sector struggling to keep up with the pace of a growing urban
population. Finally, the limited and spatially fragmented nature of
purchasing power tended to undermine efforts towards concentration in food retailing.[99] One should also take into account the potential difficulties of management and supply created by expansion as yet
another constraint on the growth of large-scale retailing. All of these
limits were overcome following the mass imports of cheap food in
the 1870s as capital acquired the structural capacity to take advantage
of the new possibilities created by mass food transportation and rising real wages.

Table 5.2 shows estimates in the number of firms in the main food
trades between 1875 and 1915. Lipton's success in provision perhaps
best exemplifies the growing ability of multiples to exploit developments in transport technologies and storage facilities, a more reliable
and regular supply, and the scalar opportunities afforded by the stan-
dardization of production. Lipton opened his first shop in 1871 and
by 1878 his four shops had a combined weekly turnover of 6,000
hams, 16 tons of bacon, 16,000 dozen eggs, 10 tons of butter, and 200
blocks of cheese.[100] The introduction of tea in 1889 represented the
beginning of a highly dynamic decade of economic growth culmi-
nating with incorporation in 1898. By that time, the company had
over 400 shops (242 in Britain) and 10,000 employees worldwide.
Four million pounds of tea were sold the first year Lipton moved into
the trade and 6 million pounds the next year. At the end of the
decade, fifty tons of tea was moved out every day from the City Road
premises in London, which represented a staggering annual turnover
of over 40 million pounds. Despite some successes in the meat trade
in the United States between 1880 and 1902, Lipton's most important
diversification scheme remained its acquisition of tea plantations. In
1890, Lipton went to Ceylon and spent £20,000 on large warehouses
and offices in Colombo, and seven estates totalling over 3,000 acres
worked out by more than 3,000 coolies. More plantations were later
added, although they produced only a fraction of Lipton's total retail
sales of tea.

Lipton's rising economic empire rested on cheap food imports as
well as a complex and elaborate infrastructure of distribution, with
warehouses in Glasgow, Liverpool, London, and Dublin assuring
national distribution. High volume, fast turnover, growing vertical
integration, and aggressive advertising campaigns gave the company

Table 5.2
Number of multiple shop firms with ten or more branches, 1875–1915

	Grocery and provisions		Meat		Bread and flour		Milk		Chocolate and sugar	
	Firms	Branches	Firms	Branches	Firms	Branches	Firms	Branches	Firms	Branches
1875	6	108	–	–	–	–	–	–	–	–
1880	14	277	–	–	–	–	–	–	–	–
1885	31	688	5	200	–	–	–	–	–	–
1890	46	1265	8	564	–	–	–	–	–	–
1895	72	2239	11	1253	–	–	–	–	–	–
1900	80	3444	13	2058	8	105	8	101	–	–
1905	96	4429	17	2982	16	261	15	203	5	163
1910	114	5870	23	3828	21	451	20	324	10	308
1915	125	7130	27	3675	26	628	23	401	15	496

Source: Jefferys, *Retail trading in Britain*, 137, 187, 214, 232, 257.

an important competitive edge through rock-bottom prices. The tea sold by family grocers at 3 to 4 shillings per pound could hardly compete against Lipton's own blends at 1 shilling tuppence to one shilling nine pence. Butter, usually sold at one shilling eightpence per pound, retailed at 1 shilling, and bacon, ham, and jam were all half price. Lipton's commitment to vertical integration was nothing new. Already in the late 1870s he had drying and curing capacity for fifteen thousand hams and smoking rooms for bacon, to which were later added sausage and pie manufacturing as well as a large bakery to supply cakes and biscuits to his shops. Lipton carried this commitment with him when he moved the company headquarters from Glasgow to London in 1891, bringing with him coffee roasting, grinding and essence-making, sausage-making, and a bakery for pork pies and sausage rolls. Ham- and bacon-curing capacities were extended and diversification into production continued unabated. Jam production began in 1892, six plum farms were purchased in Kent in 1894, and a confectionery factory was opened in 1895. By 1898, shops were stocked with Lipton's manufactured cocoa, chocolate, confectionery, jams, marmalade, preserved fruits, pickles, preserved meats, sauces, biscuits, cakes, coffee and cocoa essence, beef extract and fluid beef.

Home and Colonial Stores also developed primarily in groceries.[101] It avoided co-operative competition by being a "southern phenomenon," with only ten branches in Lancashire in the 1910s compared to about two hundred in London and its suburban areas. Except for the establishment of a small factory for the production of custard, blancmange powder, jelly, and similar goods in 1912, as well as holdings in Albers Creameries Ltd in Dordrecht, Holland, to secure a cheap supply of margarine, Home and Colonial did not develop productive activities. Bulk orders were in the hands of a few large merchants until the development of integrated wholesale trade in its main lines in 1904. At the retail level, the company developed by combining a few large stores stocking a wide variety of lines and a larger number of smaller shops – known as "tea stores" – handling high turnovers in tea, sugar, butter, margarine, and cheese. Cheap imported butter soon replaced tea as the principal staple of trade, and by 1905 no less than seventy tons of margarine were sold weekly. Incorporated in 1888, continuous capitalization allowed the financial basis for expansion, with the number of shops rising from 107 to 500 between 1890 and 1903.[102] Annual profits reached £220,000 in 1901 before declining to £150,000 in 1908. Home and Colonial then moved into the provisions trade and widened the numbers of grocery lines stocked, the distinction between large and small stores increasingly vanishing as smaller shops stocked new commodities like cocoa essence, coffee, Worcester sauce, table jellies, custard, blancmange, baking powder, treacle, self-raising flour, tinned milk, jam, and many others. Annual profits jumped up to £300,000 in 1914.

Like other retail firms, the Maypole Dairy Company expanded through specialization in a narrow range of mainly imported commodities.[103] Its first margarine shop was opened in Wolverhampton in 1887, and by 1895 the company had sixty shops, eight creameries, and buying offices in Denmark and Sweden. Maypole amalgamated with George Jackson in 1898, who carried an extensive butter retailing business. At this point, the company claimed 185 shops, which almost exclusively dealt in butter, tea, and margarine. Capitalized at £923,000, the meteoric expansion of Maypole brought the number of shops to 958 in 1915. Its business model was fairly simple: providing a large part of the population with few basic essentials at rock-bottom prices. Strategically avoiding locking capital up in property, stores were usually located in high-density shopping areas of high streets on leasehold. Declining profits in butter ca. 1900 provided the basis to heighten further trade in more profitable commodities such as eggs, tea, and margarine. Maypole was still conducting an important trade in butter with an annual turnover of £1.5 million in 1906 (95 percent of which was imported from Denmark), although the rising popularity of margarine was undeniable. After substantial investments, Maypole produced about one thousand tons of margarine in 1913, about as much as its two closest competitors Jergens and Van der Berghs combined. During those years, Maypole was also developing oil-milling and oil refinery capacities to expand its control over the international oil and fat markets, with intent to establish groundnut operations in West Africa for margarine production. In 1913, the firm sold 1,445 tons of eggs, 3,450 tons of condensed milk, 9,550 tons of tea, 14,000 tons of butter, and, the following year, 48,000 tons of margarine. At that point, Maypole's share of the national market amounted to 7 percent in tea, 6.7 percent in butter, and 33 percent in margarine.

In contrast to the grocery and provisions trade, which expanded to secure supply, the growth of multiples in the frozen and chilled meat trade was the result of packing and shipping interests seeking to guarantee outlets for a rapidly expanding wave of supply at a time during which skilled butchers showed little desire to handle it.[104] Indeed, the National Federation of Meat Traders Association reported that over

80 percent of imported meat in the early 1900s "was sold by firms dealing exclusively with overseas producers."[105] Despite an important prejudice against frozen and chilled meat, which, like margarine, tended to be associated with a poverty-stricken diet, low prices and the growing quality of meat secured its popularity. Already in 1885, the Glasgow-based firm John Bell & Sons, which specialized in American dead meat imports, had over one hundred shops. Many wholesale butchers in Glasgow complained that, while they had to pay dues on every bullock taken into the dead meat market, private companies importing dead meat and stocking it in their refrigerators at Cheapside escaped these dues, thus bypassing entirely the dead meat market by selling into private shops. As it happened, the number of American carcasses brought to the dead meat market declined from 12,992 to 449 between 1880 and 1888.[106] Anxieties over the growing distributive role of multiples in the trade did not fade away with the amalgamation of John Bell with American firm T.C. and Joseph Eastman in 1889. The newly formed Eastman's controlled 1,400 shops in 1912, compared to the 1,500 owned by James Nelson and Sons, and both owned storage facilities, refrigerated ships, and packing plants.[107]

Retail shops in the meat trade were generally small and unsophisticated, and more often than not they were located in side streets to lower costs, some even consisting of a stall or barrow in the market. The whole retailing environment was geared towards low prices and high turnover, dealing exclusively in cash and offering no credit or delivery. Shops were particularly concentrated in and around London, the Midlands, and Lancashire, where the main ports and cold storage facilities were located. From the late 1890s onwards, these firms were facing an increasingly difficult conundrum: while their cheap meat was more and more appreciated by growing segments of the working class in the context of rising prices, it also put pressure on them to absorb at least part of the rising costs through lower profit margins in order to secure the loyalty of these new customers. The result was rationalization, first through the maintenance of fewer but larger shops to reduce overheads, and then through amalgamations. The acquisition of W. & R. Fletcher by Union Cold in 1911 was followed by the creation of the British and Argentine Meat Company in 1914, a merger between James Nelson and the River Plate.

The milk trade is an entirely different beast, so to speak.[108] While the slow development in the bread and flour trade was largely the result of excessive competition and dependence on imported flour,[109] the timid presence of large companies in the milk trade in the early 1910s must be understood both in relation to the lack of international competition and the demands of a highly perishable commodity. As increased imports of factory-made North American cheese and European butter lowered the price of both, many British farmers turned towards the more profitable production of liquid milk.[110] Before the 1860s, the supply of milk in large cities tended to be drawn from a circuit of up to ten miles within which urban and suburban producers supplied the bulk of the milk. With the slow disappearance of urban pastures and meadows in and around large towns, intra-urban milk producers either relocated on the periphery or moved into small cowsheds to cut costs. In the latter case, heightened dependency on the country to import bulky fodder, root crops, and meadow hay increased production costs. Already financially unstable, the outbreak of cattle plague in 1865 decimated upwards of one-half of a large town's milk cows. Moreover, the outbreak shed light on the lack of space and cleanliness, and the cramped and filthy state of many cowsheds.[111] Stricter regulations over ventilation, air space, lighting, water supply, and drainage to limit what was now perceived as a public nuisance further affected the economic viability of town dairies.[112] It was in this context that rail-borne liquid milk became prominent. The quantity of railway milk brought into London rose from 1.4 million to 93.2 million gallons between 1861 and 1914, which by then represented 97 percent of its supply.[113]

One key aspect of the expansion of the railway milk trade was its restructuring of the trade through a spatial division of labour between rural or peri-urban production and urban distribution. Given the perishable nature of milk and the lack of proper development in refrigeration technologies, however, the producer's proximity to the railway system was key to profitability. Firms such as the Aylesbury Dairy Company, which received between four and five thousand gallons of milk a day at the end of the 1870s, and the wholesale milk contractors Freeth and Pocock, which depended on some three hundred farmers in 1900, obliged their suppliers by contract to cool the milk down in order to slow down the souring process.[114] Yet these capital-intensive firms, however important, remained the exception in a trade in which pasteurization was still in its infancy and where the majority of farmers did not have cooling devices.[115] From the late 1870s onwards, wholesalers seeking to reduce wastage from the souring of milk in transit set up depots at country stations. These depots often offered cooling facilities and enabled the bulking of churns into vanloads, thus helping to lower the circulation time of milk in transit. Railway companies were often anxious to offer facilities, reliable schedules, and special freight rates to develop and capture the growing market in railway milk.[116] Furthermore, British farmers' proximities to railway lines fostered an environment within which railway companies enjoyed a comparatively low level of inter-district competition.

The transformation of large towns into places of consumption and the growing distance between spaces of production and consumption contributed to large firms concentrating their activities. That being said, this process was inhibited by the perishable nature of the commodity itself, which acted as a technological and organizational barrier to investments. By the early 1910s, the London milk trade had achieved "a stable pattern of semi-monopolistic competition" dominated by four or five wholesalers equipped with country depots, a huge supply of churns, regular contracts with the railways, and pasteurizing plants and cold stores in their town dairies.[117] Evidence suggests that there were at least 1,450 dairymen working for large firms in London in 1895. The vast majority were milk-carriers, with managers and foremen typical of large firms. Milk carriers in the retail trade earned from 20 to 26 shillings per week, and worked from 5:00 a.m. until 7:00 p.m. every day. While earning a relatively decent wage, milk carriers still worked over ninety hours per week to secure the right to a minimum of comfort.[118]

Working Conditions

While scholars interested in the so-called "retail revolution" have often stressed the capital-intensive nature of large firms to explain their successes, including the adoption of the branch system and rock-bottom prices through vertical integration and wholesale bargains on bulk purchases, very few (if any) have highlighted the key importance of cheap labour in this business model. As Mathias noted, the surviving records of large companies such as Lipton's and Home and Colonial tell us very little about working conditions, and no series of wage figures exist to document the working life of those attending to the shops and warehouses.[119] "This fact indicates something of the structure of employment offered by the multiple shop companies. The bulk of employees were not skilled persons and recruitment presented few problems ... They [shop assistants] worked very long hours for meagre returns, in common with equivalent categories of employment."[120] Available evidence nonetheless suggests that working conditions were in line with those in private shops. For example, even though he supported closing early once a week throughout his life, Thomas Lipton failed to implement this in order "to maintain the competitive position of his shops where no local agreement between everyone in the trade could be managed."[121] The competitive battle between large-scale retailers and small shopkeepers had the effect "of forcing down wages amongst the assistants of the private firms" and lengthening hours of work for all.[122]

Most male assistants' working hours ranged from 60 to 90, and their wages varied between 17 and 28 shillings, the average falling somewhere along the lines of 80 hours for 20 shillings. Unpaid overtime – incurred in order to prepare next morning's deliveries, clear the shop, and restock the shelves – was mandatory, running from one to three hours per day. Given that many multiple firms demanded a weekly return of sales and stocks to be delivered to the head office on Mondays, the staff frequently stayed after the closing of the shop at 11:00 or 12:00 p.m. on Saturday for stocktaking, with the manager often coming in on the Sunday to finish off his return. Similarly, even in firms where shopworkers were entitled to a weekly half-holiday (before it became mandatory in 1911), it was often forfeited to dress the window or for stocktaking, in accordance with demands from the head office.[123] Some evidence also suggests that wages were lower in multiples. For example, Hallsworth and Davies noted that, in private shops in the district of Canton in Cardiff, women in the fruit trade earned from 8 to 15 shillings a week, while junior assistants in the grocery trade obtained from 18 to 25 shillings and experienced assistants from 27 to 33 shillings. "The standard of wages in the multiple firms is rather lower," they argued, "an experienced man obtaining on the average 24s. to 28s."[124] In the absence of legislation to limit the number of hours and due to the lack of a strong union movement to agitate for higher wages, there is no reason to believe that large multiple-shop retailers were better employers than small shopkeepers, considering, for example, that they also followed the tendency to replace "old" assistants with younger (and cheaper) hands.

Examined before the Departmental Committee on the Truck Acts in July 1907, J. Aubrey Rees, appearing on behalf of the National Association of Grocers' Assistants, gave evidence on the basis of four large firms located in London and its suburbs, which he saw as "typical cases" of multiples where living-in existed: (1) private firm, 36 branches, opened 76 hours a week, early closing at 2:00 p.m. on Thursday, 50 minutes a day for meals, total of 71 working hours; (2) limited company, 34 branches, opened 75.5 hours a week, early closing at 2:00 p.m. on Thursday, 1.5 hours a day for meals, total of 66.5 working hours; (3) private firm, 40 branches, open 81.5 hours a week, no early closing, 1.25 hours a day for meals, total of 74 working hours; (4) limited company, over 100 branches, opened 73.5 hours a week, early closing at 2:00 p.m. on Wednesday, up to 2 hours a day for meals, total of 61.5 working hours.[125] If we factor in unpaid overtime of one hour per day, six days per week, and based on the questionable assumption that shopworkers enjoyed the totality of their meal times, we have a more realistic working week ranging from 67.5 hours to 80 hours. Rees does not specify which trade these firms represent, yet here again there is no reason to believe that working hours would have been different in other firms, especially among food retailers where opening hours were generally the longest. Moreover, the existence of two private firms testifies to the fact that family businesses, while attracting less attention than incorporated giants like Lipton and Home and Colonial, had developed important regionally based multiple chains, such as William Jackson in Hull, James Duckworth in Rochdale, T. D. Smith in Lancaster, and the Ludlow-based Gaius Smith and Co.[126]

With regard to the living arrangements, the vast majority of shop assistants who worked for multiples in the food trade did not live on the premises. They were thus "living-out" as it was referred to at the time.[127] Living-in was generally found among private retail traders in the grocery trade who emulated arrangements from the parent shop as they expanded by opening new branches, thus carrying with them the living-in system.[128] Having rented "a shop in a market or a busy thoroughfare," the private grocer then offered the living premises "to the manager for his own accommodation and that of his staff," with special arrangements being taken, depending on whether or not the manager was a married man. Although the Shop Assistants' Union's negotiations to abolish the living-in system was mostly limited to private shopkeepers, it was also successful in negotiating living-out arrangements for the employees of Peglers Stores in 1907, a multiple-shop retailer in South Wales with nineteen branches.[129] In contrast, the newly formed, capital-intensive multiple shop companies rejected from the outset the living-in system, preferring to let their employees make their own living arrangements. Indeed, the living-in system was economically onerous and administratively burden-some, especially in a food retailing industry characterized by a decen-tralized branch system designed to reach customers in their locali-ties.[130] As we saw in the case of Home and Colonial, the economic interest of large companies was tied to their ability to use their capi-tal to expand rapidly through the construction of a comprehensive network of retail outlets. In this context, most firms saw the burden of renting out and managing living premises as an unproductive use of their resources.

This was particularly visible in the fact that very few firms owned or built new shops, preferring instead to rent and improve premises according to their needs.[131] In the same way that renting or owning living premises represented a sterile investment, large firms such as Maypole equally saw no advantage in sinking capital to acquire prop-erty. As Winstanley's study of retail property ownership in Edwardian England demonstrates, most multiples entered into leases from seven to twenty-one years in length, with meat companies being the main exception as they preferred short-term tenancies of one year or less. Given the lack of interest for property ownership, multiples "may have preferred long leases because they stabilized rents, by preventing landlords from imposing substantial increases if business in the dis-trict improved. A lease of 7, 14 or 21 years, especially one that offered a sitting tenant first option of renewal on expiry, also provided the necessary security and opportunity to undertake substantial improve-ments to premises." In contrast, with a higher number of branches and a business model based on smaller shops located in working-class sub-urbs, short-term leases gave meat companies the spatial and temporal flexibility that they needed.[132]

Most if not all firms were hostile to organized labour, and many such as Lipton's fired employees if they found out that they were members of a union. Although such tactics aimed to intimidate other potential sympathizers, labour militancy among shopworkers was clearly on the rise, with numerous agreements taking place in the gro-cery trade from 1914 onwards.[133] One of the most important agree-ments at the time took place between the Shop Assistants' Union and Glasgow-based Galbraith's Stores in May 1914, which covered 130 shops and close to 1,000 employees. The agreement provided rates of up to 36 shillings for males at 25 years of age and up to 21 shillings for females at 24 years of age, as well as rates of 38 shillings for managers and 24 shillings for manageresses. Wages were paid in full for up to six weeks in case of sickness, in addition to ten days' holiday per year.[134] Another important campaign took place at the Home and Colonial Stores. The company was known for its problematic labour practices, such as imposing fines for being late, forcing its employees "to be searched at any time by an authorised official of the company,"[135] or dismissing shopworkers with a mere twenty-four-hour notice even though it required them to give a week's notice to resign. Managers were subjected to non-compete agreements (called a "radius clause" at the time), had to pay for all breakages of utensils in the shops, and were not allowed to leave the cash in the shop after closing, which led to cases of assault as they came home with cash. To add insult to injury, they had to pay up to thirty shillings a year to insure against potential loss. Some managers earned only thirty shillings a week, unpaid overtime was rampant, and many worked on Sundays, especially for stocktaking.

Some three hundred employees met at the Mildmay Radical Club in North London in March 1914 to fight for better working conditions. Parallel to the ongoing recruitment of union members over the following months, local conferences across the country took place to establish a program for negotiations, which was discussed at a national conference held in London in August, only few days after the First World War was declared. Although Home and Colonial refused to recognize the union, the company made some concessions, including the right to leave the cash in the shop after closing, the abandonment of the radius clause, increased commissions for managers and wages for shop assistants, and the suspension of the breakage deduction. Despite a successful vote for strike action, however, it was decided at the national conference held in February 1915 that, in light of the concessions won and in the context of the war, further actions would be postponed.[136] Other agreements were reached in 1915 with Cooper's Stores, Andrew Cochrane, and R. and J. Templeton.[137] There is very little evidence of labour struggles affecting multiple shop retailers before the war. The important breakthrough happened in the years following, through hundreds of separate bargaining meetings taking place with employees of large multiple firms such as Lipton's, Home and Colonial, Meadow Dairy, Peark's Dairies, and Pegrams. Occurring at single branches or in districts, these negotiations would eventually lead to a national agreement with large multiple firms, many of which came to recognize the benefits accruing from streamlining labour relations and establishing a comprehensive management system across the company. In towns such as Ammanford and Aberavon, all the shops – irrespective of the trade and including small shopkeepers and multiples alike – had agreed to a forty-eight-hour week and union rates.[138]

While public markets, street sellers, and shopkeepers remained essential to food distribution, the emergence of a new breed of large-scale competitors capable of taking full advantage of the possibilities that accrued from mass transportation technologies and the constitution of international food markets greatly affected the ways in which people gained access to their food. The trend towards increased concentration was unmistakable. By 1915, large-scale retailers accounted for 31 percent of groceries and provisions, 16.8 percent of the meat trade, and 11.8 percent of the bread and flour trade (table 5.1). The proportions would have been significantly higher in some areas, such as industrial towns. The retail environment started showing larger structural trends towards a capital-intensive food distribution system organized around mass consumption, high turnover, standardized manufactured products, organizational capacities in handling large volume of goods, and the deskilling of the labour force. Co-operative stores and multiples catered for the masses by offering low prices on items for which there was high demand, either through negotiated discounts with suppliers on bulk purchases or vertical diversification into production, something that smaller retailers could never achieve. Although more data are required, evidence suggests that labour relations in large-scale retailers before 1914 were not substantially better than in the rest of the food distribution sector. Multiple retailers were often identified as ungenerous employers when it came to matters of pay and they had a propensity, like shopkeepers, to dispense with workers as they grew older and required higher wages. Similarly, high consumer dividends within co-operative societies all too often were accomplished on the back of their distributive workers. Although offering comparatively better working conditions than their competitors, large-scale retailers were no less dependent on cheap labour, thus proving that capital-intensive business models and labour-intensive forms of exploitation were by no means incompatible.

Conclusion

The first objective of this book was to highlight the importance of distribution as a key sector of activity for social change and economic development. Through an analysis of the British system of food distribution between 1830 and 1914, I have shown the extent to which the latter was an active and dynamic structure mediating the space between farm and fork. Finding its origin in the separation of direct producers from their means of subsistence, the constitution of a properly capitalist sphere of distribution is crucial to bridge the gap between increasingly distant spaces and scales of production and consumption. This means that distribution is a fundamental dimension of capital accumulation as well as an essential moment in the production and reproduction of labour. In this increasingly complex geography of food relations, the rescaling of the value of labour-power through free trade policies and the shift from national to world agriculture must be understood through the growing role played by distribution. Far from being a residual moment of the political economy of food, the sphere of distribution was central in reconciling the imperatives of capital accumulation with those of social reproduction, thereby normalizing the dynamics of capital accumulation by providing the working class with the means of life. This came at a heavy cost, however, as most retailers came to absorb the price of cheap food through low wages, long hours, and degrading working conditions.

Key to this dynamic was the social, economic, and architectural restructuring of the public market towards capitalist imperatives. By no means an archaic institution, public markets, as capitalists recognized, were dynamic structures essential to how people obtained their food, and they initially provided the main interface to connect urban dwellers with producers. Municipal authorities were indeed extremely anxious over inadequate markets and therefore very active in their attempt to acquire market rights in order to provide adequate retail facilities. Subsequent investments towards market improvements, combined with market incentives, sought to increase the town's food supply by unlocking the new possibilities offered by railways in bringing distant producers into the market. In this regard, food distribution was not only shaped by a rapidly changing geography of food production; it also actively transformed the latter by rewarding competitive producers and suppliers. As we saw, the opening up of the distributive environment and the acceleration of the flow of food commodities everywhere proved to be essential to secure a reliable, abundant, and cheap food supply as well as to increase the quantity, quality, and variety of goods available. And as the growing army of street sellers, shopkeepers, co-operative stores, and multiple shops demonstrated, the reproductive life of the community was indeed based on an increasingly comprehensive and competitive system of food distribution.

In line with this, the second main objective of the book was to stress the central importance of adopting a more wide-ranging approach to the food distribution sector. This holistic approach has two key advantages. To begin with, it gives us a better appreciation of the specific developmental patterns emerging out of an otherwise common retail environment. Shopkeepers, for instance, represented an extremely diverse class of retailers divided by social status, economic achievements, trades, and individualistic tendencies. Despite the fact that some were very successful during those years, most shopkeepers between 1830 and 1870 survived through food adulteration, the use of false weights and measures, the establishment of long opening and working hours, and the granting of credit to trusted customers to secure a custom. Cheap food imports in the 1870s, the rise of large-scale retailers, and the development of stricter state regulations and enforcement capacities over food quality and integrity forced a shift in the reproductive strategies of most shopkeepers, who increasingly came to compete through heightened labour exploitation, including extended working hours, unpaid overtime, the introduction of child and female labour, and the use of the living-in system and family labour. Similarly, the spatial fixity of the public market in the context of rapid urbanization and demographic changes played no small part in the development of an important wholesaling function, which, in turned, supported the growth of those actors, like street sellers, who carried in space the marketplace's original function – retailing. Others, like co-ops and multiples, sought economic redemption through economies of scale and high turnover on low prices. There were therefore important differences as well as noticeable similarities in the ways in which the actors of the distributive sector responded to their changing economic environment.

Studying the food distributive sector as a whole also gives us the ability to see how tensions and contradictions emanating from the retail environment shaped structures of food distribution. For instance, street sellers' ability to sell cheaper than anybody else was closely linked to their precariousness, which was reinforced by municipal policies designed to uphold ideals of modernity and progress in urban development, or by shopkeepers' attempts to use municipal politics as a lever to advance their economic interests. It was precisely costermongers' political marginalization within the retail environment that underpinned the economic importance of this "dangerous class." Meanwhile, shopkeepers' political activism was often ambiguous and counter-productive. Limitations placed on market improvements or bylaws against street sellers often turned against their own economic interests, either by lowering the number of suppliers and wholesalers in town or by creating discontent among customers who resented them for chasing away street sellers. Similarly, shopkeepers who were willing to stall the development of local regulatory controls and the constitution of a proper inspectorate gave the co-operative movement a higher standing in guaranteeing pure food to its customers. At the same time, co-operative retail societies continuously entertained an ambiguous politics of consumption by obtaining most of their supplies from private traders and wholesalers, thus reinforcing the very structure that the movement sought to replace. Vertical integration further transformed the distributive environment by reinforcing the competitive nature of the sector and its ability to offer cheap food. Through economies of scale and high turnover on the few commodities bought on both national and international markets, co-operative retail stores and multiples dramatically changed the nature of food retailing.

Finally, the third main objective of this book was to recover the centrality of labour in the British system of food distribution. As I have argued, the rise in the standard of living at home for large segments of the working class was partly achieved through the subjection of the distributive sphere and those who worked in it. In this respect, the

ability of food retailers to live on very low profit margins and therefore to transfer the full benefits of cheap food imports directly to the
working class was accomplished by locking food distribution workers
into poverty and insecurity, and subordinating their material comfort
and well-being to the imperatives of competition in the retail environment. For the majority of street sellers, shop assistants, and family
relatives, shop life was hard. There is also no evidence to suggest that
large-scale retailers were model employers. Both co-operative stores
and multiple shops adopted highly exploitative labour practices,
including the employment of children and the dismissal of "old" shop
assistants as well as the ubiquitous long working hours and low
wages. Even though the co-operative movement and multiples were
highly profitable, their ability to offer low prices and high dividends
– either to customers or shareholders – was also rooted in employment relationships designed to lower the cost of labour.

   In demonstrating the critical role that the constitution of a food-
related underclass in the distributive sector played in rising real wages
and working-class living standards, the book also highlighted the
extent to which the sphere of distribution was deeply implicated in
the creation of more consumption capacity for the majority of working-class families through the cheapening of the value of labour-
power. Remarkably, this happened without any redistribution of
wealth, thus showing the central role played by cheap food in mediating the contradiction between capital and labour. This means that,
even in the absence of organized political movements and struggles
over wages and what constitutes a fair distribution of the social surplus, capitalism as a whole has a vested interest in the subordination
of food producers and distributors to food consumers. In other
words, most capitalists, as employers and producers of consumer
goods and services, have an economic interest in supporting a shift
from a commitment to the control of surpluses and high prices for
farmers to a commitment to growing surpluses and low prices for
consumers. As we have seen, however, the production of cheap food,
although strongly influenced by technologies and low wages in the
agricultural sector, is also the result of dynamics pertaining to the
food distributive sector.

   Taken together, these three main objectives support the view that
cheap food production was not merely the result of cheap food
imports but also the result of a highly competitive, dynamic, and
heterogenous sphere of distribution that was largely based on a

cheap, labour-intensive logic of reproduction. Cheap food was therefore realized through cheap labour in the retail environment – that is, through the active subordination of the sphere of distribution to the expanded reproduction of capital. As I draw this work to an end, I want to reflect on the contemporary relevance of some of the themes addressed in the previous chapters – themes that are likely to define the future of food distribution and food relations over the coming decades.

MARKET POWER AND CONCENTRATION IN FOOD RETAILING

Selling food is big business, with retail profits rising quickly among a handful of increasingly powerful players. In 2013, total food retailing revenue reached £95.9 billion in the United Kingdom, €152.7 billion in France, and €180.4 billion in Germany.[1] The largest four global retailers by retail revenue in 2016 were also food retailers: Wal-Mart ($US 485.9 billion), Costco ($US 118.7 billion), Kroger ($US 115.3 billion), and Schwarz Group ($US 99.3 billion), with Carrefour ($US 84.1 billion), Tesco ($US 72.4 billion), and Aeon ($US 70.9 billion) ranking ninth, eleventh, and twelfth, respectively.[2] In 2011 in the European Union, the largest five food retailers in every country had a combined market share of more than 60 percent in thirteen member states (Austria, Belgium, Finland, France, Germany, Ireland, Luxembourg, the Netherlands, Portugal, Sweden, and the United Kingdom), with market concentration exceeding 80 percent in both Denmark and Estonia.[3] In most countries, however, market concentration among two or three major retailers is the norm. Two supermarket chains – Coles and Woolworths – control over 70 percent of Australia's food retailing sector,[4] while Wal-Mart and Kroger made 43.2 percent of grocery store sales in the US in 2013.[5] In Canada, three retailers – Weston Group, Empire Company, and Metro – held 55.5 percent of the grocery and food retail sector in 2011.[6] Similar consolidation can be observed in South Korea, Brazil, and elsewhere.[7]

While concentration in the grocery market has tended to reinforce the interplay between cheap imports and the exploitation of cheap distributive labour, it has also resulted in an hourglass-shaped global food system as masses of farmers and small producers compete to supply a smaller number of processors, manufacturers, and wholesalers. These supply the handful of large retailers at the choke point, who sell

directly to the global population of consumers. Food retailers'
unprecedented power as buyers within national and global markets
gives them the ability to set the terms under which the food supply
chain operates. Their capacity to impose contracts and prices with
tough deadlines is key to understanding the growing demand for sub-
minimum wages and working standards in the food industry. In order
to meet their obligations, stay afloat financially, and weather the
efforts of retailers and processors to lower costs, producers and suppliers often subcontract labour and other low value-adding business
activities. These agencies may in turn outsource their activities to a
third party, either because they are unable to meet their obligations or
because they want to take advantage of a lower cost provider. Labour
supply chains operating through multiple intermediaries and stages
of subcontracting are particularly vulnerable to some of the worst
forms of labour exploitation.

THE ESSENTIAL ROLE OF CHEAP LABOUR
IN SHAPING ACCESS TO CHEAP FOOD

Retailers' hold over global food production and their ability to command low prices not only breeds cheap, flexible, and casual labour in
food production; it also creates the conditions of insecurity under
which cheap labour is produced. While the capitalization of the space
between farm and fork is unmistakable, the sector continues to rely
extensively on labour-intensive methods characterized by poor working conditions. In the United States, for example, more than 10 million restaurant workers feed the population daily, yet live economically precarious lives.[8] Indeed, the ability of the country to produce
cheap food is based on highly exploitative labour practices in the food
distributive sector, which is characterized by low wages, part-time
employment, temporary contracts, and limited social benefits and
opportunities for advancement. The maintenance of living standards
and purchasing power since the early 1980s has been accomplished
through the constitution of a food-related underclass. These workers
are systematically at the bottom of the wage scale. In the United
States, the median hourly wage of the 13 million workers employed
in food preparation and serving related occupations was $10.01 in
May 2016.[9] Out of the twenty occupations with the lowest median
wages in 2012, at least a third of them were directly related to food dis-

tribution, including cashiers; counter attendants in cafeterias, food concessions, and coffee shops; cooks in fast food restaurants; hosts and hostesses; and waitresses and waiters. With an average annual income of about $20,000 for full-time work, most of these workers are locked into poverty wages.[10]

The ascendency of neoliberal policy making dedicated to expanding the role of markets within society has also reshaped the nature, place, and dynamics of food consumption. More meals are prepared and eaten out of the home than ever before and food delivery is increasing. Even groceries and supermarkets have reconsidered their business model by offering a growing selection of ready-made food. The marketization of social reproduction has not only occurred in the formal sector of the economy but is also part and parcel of a vast and expansive network of informal street sellers in the global South, where millions of vendors ply the streets or attend unplanned markets selling prepared foods that are essential to the reproduction of urban populations. This not only suggests that the sphere of food distribution is expanding by taking on responsibilities that were traditionally the purview of private consumption but also that distribution continues to be central to gaining access to cheap food.

Today's cheap food basket depends on cheap labour in the distributive sector. One's ability to secure her or his physical integrity all too often come at the expense of someone else's growing inability to earn a decent wage and achieve adequate standards of living. Moreover, the capitalization of food retailing and the formation of large-scale retailers that are global in scope has tended to reinforce, rather than eliminate, labour-intensive methods of distribution, although more and more large grocery stores are seeking to cut (already low) labour costs by introducing self-checkout machines. While many small-scale retailers have been hit hard in recent decades by the growth of retail structures capable of enforcing a highly competitive environment characterized by low food prices, most survive through cost-cutting strategies aimed at lowering labour costs. These workers are part of the growing army of working poor without which cheap food would not be accessible under the capitalist system. Interestingly, working conditions for employees of earlier multiple retailers would have been comparable with the chronic poverty of most employees of today's large-scale retailers.

CHEAP FOOD AND THE RESILIENCE OF FOOD INSECURITY AMIDST PLENTY

In the United States, the social, political, and economic dislocation of the postwar class compromise was accomplished at the price of a deep recession, soaring rates of unemployment, poverty and homelessness, and the effective decline of the American standard of living. Yet, buried in the fact that average weekly earnings in private non-agricultural industries (in 1982–84 dollars) fell from $325.83 in 1974 to $266.43 in 1992, before reaching $310.63 in 2017, is an important restructuring of the household budget.[11] Indeed, the relative impor-tance of food (including meals out) and beverages as a share of dis-posable personal income declined from 24.8 percent in 1973 to 19 percent in 1982, dropping further still to 13.7 percent in 2010. According to the *Economist* food-price index, food prices in real terms declined from 100 in 1980 to about 30 in the early 2001, before increasing to slightly over 60 in 2010.[12] While the importance of cheap food under neoliberalism has often been overlooked because real wages have remained below the mark of their historical peak of 1973, the vital role that cheap food has played during this period lies precisely in its ability to mediate and, in some cases, counter-balance the structural effects of pay cuts, temporary unemployment, and eco-nomic uncertainty.

Despite their historical importance, however, plummeting food prices since 1980 have not been entirely successful at containing some of the worst effects of neoliberal labour market restructuring, includ-ing stagnant and declining real wages, unemployment and underem-ployment, and precarious forms of temporary and part-time work, piecework, and contractual employment. The growth of food banks and other forms of hunger-relief charities in recent years is a strong reminder that the 2008 financial crisis has not gone away. And as banks post record profits, another type of bank is thriving – the food bank. Indeed, over 13 million people in the United Kingdom (about one in five) live below the poverty line.[13] According to a recent survey for Tesco, the Trussell Trust, a charity dedicated to providing food in the United Kingdom, and FareShare, a national charity that redistrib-utes surplus food to local charities, a staggering 30 percent of adults have either skipped meals, gone without food to feed their family, or relied on relatives or friends for food during the last year, and 40 per-cent of United Kingdom households have grown more food insecure over that period. With growing numbers of people having to choose between heating and eating, food banks are reporting that increasing numbers of people are returning food items that need to be heated as they cannot afford the associated energy cost.

The Trussell Trust reported a 170 percent increase in the number of people who have turned to its food banks over the last twelve months. The number of unique users receiving a minimum of three days of emergency food increased from 61,468 in 2010–11 to 346,992 in 2012–13 to 666,476 in 2017–18. While the number of three-day emergency food supplies distributed is much greater, about a third of them went to children throughout those years. To keep up with demand, the charity is launching three new food banks every week, and now runs over four hundred food banks across the United Kingdom. By December 2013, the Sikh Federation UK estimated serving around five thousand meals to non-Sikhs each week.[14] FareShare is also rapidly growing. Between 1 April 2016 and 31 March 2017, the organization provided close to 1.2 million three-day emergency food supplies.[15] Rising food insecurity amidst plenty is likely to reinforce the role of large-scale retailers as cheap food distributors. Furthermore, their ability to provide everyday low prices will further entrench a competitive environment in which food distribution is increasingly an economic refuge from unemployment and austerity budgeting. Retailers' hold over global food production and their ability to command low prices gives them a particularly important role in this context. Given their market power and central role in shaping the conditions underpinning global food production, food retailers are already the prime mover of cheap food production globally.

Although unevenly developed, all of the themes identified above existed in the British food distribution system at the beginning of the twentieth century. Far from being something external to Britain, the ability of the system to produce cheap food required the emergence of a complex and multifarious system of food distribution capable of transferring the benefits of cheaper food imports into real gains for the working class. The acceleration of the movement of goods in space, the decrease of bottlenecks caused by inefficient retail and wholesale infrastructures, the ability to handle food commodities in bulk while preserving their integrity, the articulation of a class of retailers capable of adapting to the new exigencies of urban development, in short, the emergence of a system of mass food distribution was key to the creation of a highly competitive distributive environment geared towards cheap food. While today's food distribution has radically outgrown the scale and scope at which it operated in Victorian and Edwardian Britain, notably in terms of the power of large-scale retailers in the market, the resilience of the relationship between cheap food and cheap labour in the distributive sector is striking. As a result, it is my hope that this book will be understood not only as a historically informed intervention concerning the importance of the political economy of food distribution in Britain between 1830 and 1914 but also as a contribution to a wider reflection upon the continued relevance of the sphere of distribution for understanding labour market restructuring and the dynamics of social change and development under capitalism.

Money, Weights, and Measures

OLD BRITISH MONEY

1 farthing = ¼ penny or ¼*d*.
Half penny (ha'penny) = ½*d*.
1 penny (1*d*.) refers to a copper coin
Threepence or Thruppenny Bit = 3*d*.
Sixpence (a silver coin also called a "tanner") = 6*d*.
1 shilling (1*s*.) = 12*d*.
1 florin = 2*s*. or 24*d*.
1 pound (£1, also called a "sovereign") = 20*s*. = 240*d*.
1 crown = 5*s*. = ¼£
1 half-crown = 2*s*. 6*d*.

MASS

1 ounce (oz) = 1/16 pound
1 pound (lb) = 16 ounces
1 stone (st) = 14 pounds
1 quarter (qt) = 28 pounds
1 hundredweight (cwt) = 112 pounds
1 ton (t) = 2240 pounds = 20 hundredweights or 80 quarters or 160 stones
1 "quartern loaf" = approximately 4.33 pounds

VOLUME

1 fluid ounce (fl oz) = 1/20 pint
1 pint (pt) = 20 ounces
1 quart (qt) = 40 ounces = 2 pints
1 gallon (gal) = 160 ounces = 8 pints

Notes

1 Anon., "London Commissariat," 307, 308.
2 Webb, *Scandal of London's Markets*; Johnson, *Shop Life and Its Reform*; McCleary, *Municipalization of the Milk Supply*; McCleary, *Municipal Bakehouses*; Dodd, *Municipal Milk and Public Health*; Dale, *Child Labour under Capitalism*.
3 Abernathy et al., "Retailing and Supply Chains in the Information Age"; Bonacich and Wilson, "Global Production and Distribution"; Burch and Lawrence, *Supermarkets and Agri-Food Supply Chains*; Coe and Hess, "Internationalization of retailing"; Coe and Wrigley, *Globalization of Retailing*; Wrigley and Lowe, *Retailing, Consumption and Capital*; Wrigley and Lowe, *Reading Retail*; Wrigley and Lowe, "Globalization of Trade in Retail Services"; Wrigley, Coem and Currah, "Globalizing Retail."
4 Hobsbawm, *Industry and Empire*, 121.
5 Floud, *People and the British Economy*, 97–101; Allen, "Great Divergence in European Wages and Prices."
6 Feinstein, "New Look at the Cost of Living."
7 Easterlin, *Reluctant Economist*, chap. 7.
8 Assael, *London Restaurant*; Burnett, *Plenty and Want*; Burnett, *Liquid Pleasures*; Burnett, *England East Out*; Critchell and Raymond, *History of the Frozen Meat Trade*; Drummond and Wilbraham, *Englishman's Food*; Perren, *Meat Trade in Britain*; Perren, "Structural Change and Market Growth in the Food Industry"; Perren, *Taste, Trade and Technology*.
9 Jefferys, *Retail Trading in Britain*; Blackman, "Food Supply of an Industrial Town"; Davis, *History of Shopping*; Alexander, *Retailing in England*; Bucklin, *Competition and Evolution in the Distributive Trades*; Scola, "Food Markets

and Shops in Manchester"; Scola, *Feeding the Victorian City*; Benson and Shaw, *Evolution of Retail Systems*; Benson and Ugolini, *Nation of Shopkeepers*; Mitchell, *Tradition and Innovation in English Retailing*.

10 Shaw, "Changes in Consumer Demand"; Benson, *Rise of Consumer Society in Britain*; Purvis, "Societies of Consumers and Consumer societies"; Whitlock, *Crime, Gender and Consumer Culture*.

11 Wild and Shaw, "Locational Behaviour of Urban Retailing"; Wild and Shaw, "Population Distribution and Retail Provision"; Shaw and Wild, "Retail Patterns in the Victorian City"; Hall, "The Butcher, the Baker, the Candlestickmaker"; Shaw et al. "Structural and Spatial Trends in British Retailing"; Winstanley, "Retail Property Ownership in Edwardian England."

12 Winstanley, *Shopkeeper's World*; Crossick and Heinz-Gerhard, *Shopkeepers and Master Artisans*; Mui and H. Mui, *Shops and Shopkeeping*; Hosgood, "Pigmies of Commerce"; Osgood, "Brave and Daring Folk"; Horn, *Behind the Counter*.

13 Benson, *Penny Capitalists*; Jankiewicz, "Dangerous Class."

14 Blackman, "Food Supply of an Industrial Town"; Scola, *Feeding the Victorian City*; Forshaw and Bergström, *Smithfield*; Hodson, "Municipal Store"; Schmiechen and Carls, *British Market Hall*; Smith, "Wholesale and Retail Markets of London"; Metcalfe, *Meat, Commerce and the City*.

15 Cole, *Century of Co-operation*; Mathias, *Retailing Revolution*; Purvis, "Development of Co-operative Retailing"; Gurney, *Co-operative Culture and the Politics of Consumption*; Alexander, Shaw, and Hodson, "Regional Variations in the Development of Multiple Retailing"; Robertson, *Co-operative Movement and Communities*.

16 Whitaker, *Victorian and Edwardian Shopworkers*.

17 Hodson, "Municipal Store," 94.

18 Thompson, *Making of the English Working Class*, 12.

19 United States Government. "Economic Report of the President," 550.

20 *Economist*, "Malthusian Mouthfuls."

21 MacInnes, "Monitoring Poverty and Social Exclusion."

22 Badshah, "Gurdwaras-Turned-Food Banks."

23 Trussell Trust, "UK Foodbank Use Continues to Rise" and "Benefit Levels Must Keep Pace with Rising Cost of Essentials."

CHAPTER ONE

1 Floud, *People and the British Economy*, chap. 1.

2 Bailey, *Leisure and Class in Victorian England*; Benson, *Rise of Consumer Society in Britain*; Davies, *Leisure, Gender and Poverty*; Fraser, *Coming of the Mass*

Market; Mason, *Association Football and English Society*; Walton, "Towns and Consumerism."

3 Walvin, *Beside the Seaside*; Walton, *English Seaside Resort*.

4 Araghi, "Food Regimes and the Production of Value"; Friedmann, "World Market, State and Family Farm"; Friedmann and McMichael, "Agriculture and the State System"; McMichael, *Settlers and the Agrarian Question*; McMichael, *Food Regimes and Agrarian Questions*, 26–32; Mintz, *Sweetness and Power*; Tomich, *Through the Prism of Slavery*; Winders, "The Vanishing Free Market."

5 Rioux, "Rethinking Food Regime Analysis."

6 Moore, *Capitalism in the Web of Life*, 244.

7 Allen, "Economic Structure and Agricultural Productivity in England," 19–20; Allen, "English and Welsh Agriculture," 39.

8 Voth, "Longest Years."

9 Moore, *Capitalism in the Web of Life*, 246.

10 Thompson, "Second Agricultural Revolution," 64.

11 Anderson, *Calm Investigation*.

12 Foster, *Marx's Ecology*, 141–77. For critical views on the metabolic rift, see: Moore, "Environmental Crises and the Metabolic Rift"; Schneider and McMichael, "Deepening, and Repairing, the Metabolic Rift"; Moore, "Transcending the Metabolic Rift."

13 Thompson, "Second Agricultural Revolution," 75.

14 Moore, *Capitalism in the Web of Life*, 243, emphasis in original.

15 Deane and Cole, *British Economic Growth*; Holderness, "Prices, Productivity, and Output"; Mokyr, "Is There Still Life in the Pessimist Case?"

16 Polanyi, *Great Transformation*, 82.

17 Castel, *Les métamorphoses de la question sociale*.

18 On food adulteration, see: Accum, *Treatise on Adulterations of Food*; Atkins, "Sophistication Detected"; Burnett, *Plenty and Want*, 99–120, 240–67; Hassall, *Food and Its Adulterations*; Mitchell, *Treatise of the Falsifications of Food*; BPP 1856, "Select Committee Adulteration of Food"; Scott, "On food"; BPP 1872a, "Select Committee on Adulteration of Food Act"; BPP 1894, "Select Committee on Food Products Adulteration."

19 Hammond, "Industrial Revolution and Discontent"; Hobsbawm, "British Standard of Living"; Hobsbawm, "Standard of Living during the Industrial Revolution"; Thompson, *Making of the English Working Class*; Feinstein, "Pessimism Perpetuated."

20 Floud, Wachter, and Gregory, *Height, Health, and History*, 136–54.

21 Riggs, "Standard of Living in Scotland," 70–3; Nicholas and Oxley, "Living Standards of Women."

22 Johnson and Nicholas, "Male and Female Living Standards," 480. Other scholars have also documented stagnant and declining average adult heights: Haines, "Growing Incomes, Shrinking People"; Komlos, "Secular Trend"; Nicholas and Steckel, "Heights and Living Standards."

23 Wrigley and Schofield, *Population History of England*, 230–6, 529. See also Woods, "Effects of Population Redistribution," 650.

24 Szreter and Mooney, "Urbanization, Mortality, and the Standard of Living Debate," 88, 104, 106.

25 Armstrong, "Trend of Mortality in Carlisle"; Cage, "Standard of Living Debate"; Cage, *Working Class in Glasgow*; Neale, *Bath*, 79–94; Neale, "Standard of Living"; Szreter and Mooney, "Urbanization, Mortality, and the Standard of Living Debate"; BPP 1904b, "Physical Deterioration," 24.

26 Haines, "Inequality and Childhood Mortality"; Woods, Wattersonm and H. Woodward, "Causes of Rapid Infant Mortality Decline," pts. 1 and 2; Millward and Bell, "Infant Mortality in Victorian Britain." On the relation between childhood mortality and the quality of milk, see: Rioux, "Food Quality and the Circulation Time of Commodities"; Atkins, "Milk Consumption and Tuberculosis in Britain."

27 Huck, "Infant Mortality and Living Standards."

28 Brown, "Condition of England and the Standard of Living"; Walton, *Social History of Lancashire*, chap. 9; Fleischman, *Conditions of Life*.

29 Mitchell, *British Historical Statistics*, 709–11; Davis, *Industrial Revolution*, 45–6; Mokyr, "Is There Still Life"; Mokyr, "Has the Industrial Revolution Been Crowded Out?"

30 Burnett, *Liquid Pleasures*, 57–8.

31 Feinstein, "Pessimism Perpetuated"; Allen, "Great Divergence in European Wages and Prices."

32 Burnett, *Annals of Labour*, 23–6.

33 Johnston, *Hundred Years Eating*, 2.

34 Booth, *Darkest England and the Way Out*, 17–23.

35 Feinstein, "New Estimates," 603–4.

36 Greenhow, "Report on Murrain in Horned Cattle."

37 Booth, cited in Oddy, "Working-Class Diets," 321.

38 Giffen, "On the Fall of Prices," 38–9.

39 Burnett, *Plenty and Want*, 132; Johnston, *Hundred Years Eating*, 9; Perren, *Agriculture in Depression*, 9.

40 Mitchell, *British Historical Statistics*, 770.

41 Burnett, "Trends in Bread Consumption," 73, 72. See also Johnston, *Hundred Years Eating*, 23.

42 Roberts, *Classic Slum*, 108.

43 McNamee, "Trends in Meat Consumption," 83.

44 Mayhew, *London Labour*, 122.

45 McNamee, "Trends in Meat Consumption," 77.

46 Osborne and Winstanley, "Rural and Urban Poaching in Victorian England," 204–7.

47 BPP 1877, "Cattle Plague and Importation of Live Stock," Q. 3895 (Lambert).

48 Perren, *Meat Trade in Britain*, 3.

49 Barfoot-Saunt et al., "Production and Consumption of Meat and Milk, Second Report," 382.

50 Barfoot-Saunt et al., "Production and Consumption of Meat and Milk, Third Report," 391–2.

51 Rioux, "Capitalism and the Production of Uneven Bodies."

52 Brown, *Food of the People*, 22.

53 Burnett, *England Eats Out*.

54 Mitchell, *British Historical Statistics*, 709–11; Davis, *Industrial Revolution*, 45.

55 Fraser, *Coming of the Mass Market*, 31; Roberts, *Classic Slum*, 113.

56 Walton, *Fish and Chips*; Robinson, *Trawling*.

57 Mitchell, *British Historical Statistics*, 710. See also Mintz, *Sweetness and Power*, 161.

58 Mayhew, *London Labour*, 206–8.

59 Jam had a bitter taste for those who cheaply made it. In 1911, in Bermondsey, fifteen thousand women from over twenty factories spontaneously came out on strike. Most of the strikers were involved in food processing – many in jam making. These women were very poorly paid, on average 9 shillings per week. On this issue, see: Drake, *Women in Trade Unions*, 46ff; Cliff, *Class Struggle and Women's Liberation*; de la Mare, "Necessity and Rage."

60 Torode, "Trends in Fruit Consumption," 122–4.

61 Dodd, *Food of London*, 366.

62 Drummond and Wilbraham, *Englishman's Food*, 329–35; Nelson, "Social-Class Trends in British Diet," 102–4; Oddy, "Food, Drink and Nutrition," 267–73.

63 Mitchell, *British Historical Statistics*, 12–3, 25–9.

64 Drummond and Wilbraham, *Englishman's Food*, 403; Oddy, "Working-Class Diets," 314–23; Oddy, "Health of the People," 121–9; Oddy, *From Plain Fare to Fusion Food*.

65 Nelson, "Social-Class Trends in British Diet," 101. See also Dingle, "Drink and Working-Class Living Standards in Britain," 122.

66 Smith, *People's Health*, 117; Pember Reeves, *Round about a Pound a Week*, 168.

67 Walton, "Review." See also Chaloner, "Trends in Fish Consumption."

68 McMichael, "Food Regime Genealogy," 141.

69 Schlote, *British Overseas Trade*; Saul, *Studies in British Overseas Trade*; Crouzet, "Trade and Empire"; Cain, "Economics and Empire"; Davis, *Late Victorian Holocausts*.

70 Sussman, *Victorian Technology*; Bray, *Innovation and the Communications Revolution*; Perren, Taste, *Trade and Technology*; Critchell and Raymond, *History of the Frozen Meat Trade*; Ahvenainen, "Telegraphs, Trade, and Policy"; Jarvis, *Port and Harbour Engineering*.

71 Headrick, *Tools of Empire*.

72 Cain and Hopkins, *British Imperialism*, 161, 163.

73 Goetzmann and Ukhov, "British Investment Overseas," tables 1–3.

74 Hobsbawm, *Age of Capital*, 70.

75 Stone, "British Direct and Portfolio Investment in Latin America before 1914," 694–5.

76 Cited in Headrick, *Tools of Empire*, 182.

77 Habib, "Studying a Colonial Economy," 376.

78 Harvey, *Limits to Capital*; Lefebvre, *Production of Space*; Smith, *Uneven Development*.

79 Banaji, "Capitalist Domination and the Small Peasantry," 1,400.

80 Paish, "Great Britain's Capital Investments," 180.

81 Cited in Gallagher and Robinson, "Imperialism of Free Trade," 4–5.

82 Hurd, "Railways," 743. Naoroji (*Poverty and Un-British Rule in India*, 137) estimated the amount paid in railway interest to £51,133,987 for the 1858–75 period.

83 Naoroji, *Poverty and Un-British Rule in India*; Cain and Hopkins, *British Imperialism*, 293.

84 On the social and economic importance of ports, see: Gordon, *History and Archaeology of Ports*; Hyde, *Liverpool and the Mersey*; Jarvis, *Liverpool Dock Engineers*; Turnbull, Woolfson, and Kelly, *Dock Strike*; Ritchie-Noakes, *Liverpool's Historic Waterfront*; Pudney, *London's Docks*; Neale, *Port of Bristol*; Leng, *Welsh Dockers*; Harris, *Liverpool and the Merseyside*.

85 Graham, "Ascendency of the Sailing Ship," 75.

86 Shaw, "Changes in Consumer Demand and Food Supply," 289.

87 BPP 1906a, "Railway Rates," 4751–7, 4877 (Gardner).

88 Critchell and Raymond, *History of the Frozen Meat Trade*, 137, 127–8.

89 Ibid., 131.

90 McNamee, "Trends in Meat Consumption," 82.

91 Critchell and Raymond, *History of the Frozen Meat Trade*, 418–20.

92 Robinson, "Development of the British Distant-Water Trawling Industry," 150.

93 Wood, *North Sea Fishers and Fighters*, chap. 5, 67–8.

94 Ibid., 52–4.

95 Robinson, "Development of the British Distant-Water Trawling Industry," 155.

96 Wood, *North Sea Fishers and Fighters*, 158–60.

97 BPP 1881a, "Select Committee on Railways, Part 1," Q. 1621 (Forwood); Wood, *North Sea Fishers and Fighters*, 159.

98 Wood, *North Sea Fishers*, 153–5. See also BPP 1881a, "Select Committee on Railways, Part 1," Q. 10,088 (Bennett).

99 BPP 1914–16. "Annual Report on Sea Fisheries," 100.

100 Perren, *Agriculture in Depression*, 8.

101 Pollen, "Food Problem of Great Britain," 91.

102 Saul, *Studies in British Overseas Trade*, 27; BPP 1924, "Agricultural Tribunal of Investigation," 276.

103 Cited in McMichael, *Food Regimes and Agrarian Questions*, 30.

104 Hall, *Agriculture after the War*, 3.

CHAPTER TWO

1 Jefferys, *Retail Trading in Britain*, 39. See also Clapham, *Economic History of Modern Britain*, 219–28.

2 Daunton, *Cambridge Urban History of Britain*.

3 Scola, "Retailing in the Nineteenth Century," 154; Benson and Ugolini, *Nation of Shopkeepers*, 3; Schmiechen and Carls, *British Market Hall*; Mitchell, *Tradition and Innovation in English Retailing*, 1–4.

4 Thompson, "Moral Economy Reviewed," 273. See also: Phillips, "Evolution of Markets and Shops in Britain," 57; Bohstedt, *Politics of Provisions*, 4.

5 BPP 1890–91c, "Market Rights and Tolls," 2.

6 Alexander, *Retailing in England*, 30; BPP 1890–91d, "Market Rights and Tolls"; BPP 1890–91e, "Market Rights and Tolls"; BPP 1890–91f, "Market Rights and Tolls"; Schmiechen and Carls, *British Market Hall*, 166; Stobart, *Spend, Spend, Spend!*, 98–9, 123.

7 Alexander, Retailing in England, 34.

8 Cited in Benson, *Penny Capitalists*, 111. See also BPP 1888d, "Market Rights and Tolls," Q. 1837 (Mason).

9 BPP 1888a, "Market Rights and Tolls," 4.

10 Brown, *English Market Town*, 41.

11 McNally, *Bodies of Meaning*, 157. In the same way, the canal survived the age of railways by redeploying itself on a world stage (e.g., Suez Canal, Panama Canal).

12 Schlesinger, *Saunterings in and about London*, 64; Stobart, *Spend, Spend, Spend!*, 97.

13 Thompson, *Making of the English Working Class*; Bohstedt, *Riots and Community Politics in England and Wales*; Bohstedt, *Politics of Provisions*.

14 BPP 1888b, "Market Rights and Tolls," Q. 17 (Provis); BPP 1890–91c, "Market Rights and Tolls," 2.

15 BPP 1888a, "Market Rights and Tolls," 26.

16 Schmiechen and Carls, *British Market Hall*, 31.

17 Ibid., 129; BPP 1890–91a, "Market Rights and Tolls," QQ. 13,582-4 (Clare); BPP 1890–91c, "Market Rights and Tolls," 52.

18 Winstanley, *Shopkeeper's World*, 6; BPP 1890–91c, "Market Rights and Tolls," 54.

19 Schmiechen and Carls, *British Market Hall*, 274. See also Stobart, *Spend, Spend, Spend!*, 97–8.

20 Alexander, *Retailing in England*, 55.

21 BPP 1888d, "Market Rights and Tolls," 313.

22 Schmiechen and Carls, *The British Market Hall*, 21.

23 Rees, *St Michael*, 18.

24 Stobart, *Spend, Spend, Spend!*, 98; Mitchell, *Tradition and Innovation in English Retailing*, 155.

25 Stobart, *Spend, Spend, Spend!*, 122.

26 Hodson, "Civic Identity, Custom and Commerce," 40.

27 Davies, "Saturday Night Markets," 5.

28 Foley, *Bolton Childhood*, 26.

29 Hird, *Mirfield*, 63.

30 Schmiechen and Carls, *British Market Hall*, 39.

31 BPP 1890–91c, "Market Rights and Tolls," 9.

32 Ibid., 18. See also Mitchell, "Retail Markets in Northern and Midland England," table 1.

33 BPP 1888d, "Market Rights and Tolls," QQ. 3569 (Nalder); BPP 1888b, "Market Rights and Tolls," Q. 6098 (Fulford); BPP 1890–91a, "Market Rights and Tolls," QQ. 13,844-6 (Talbot).

34 BPP 1888d, "Market Rights and Tolls," 309. See also Q. 4985 (McGowen), QQ. 5066-7 (Dunwell and McGowen).

35 BPP 1890–91a, "Market Rights and Tolls," Q. 12,179 (Chapman).

36 BPP 1888b, "Market Rights and Tolls," QQ. 940-2 (Casson).

37 BPP 1890–91b, "Market Rights and Tolls," QQ. 14,206-8, 14,288 (Gaine), 14,454 (Birley).

38 BPP 1890–91a, "Market Rights and Tolls," Q. 15,095 (Stevenson).

39 Cunningham, *London in 1857*, 73.

40 BPP 1890–91c, "Market Rights and Tolls," 51–2.

41 Blackman, "Food Supply of an Industrial Town."

42 BPP 1888b, "Market Rights and Tolls," Q. 5239 (Ellison); BPP 1888d, "Market Rights and Tolls," 234. See also: BPP 1888b, "Market Rights and Tolls," QQ. 2556, 2575, 2643 (Bourne); BPP 1888d, "Market Rights and Tolls," 347, 434; BPP 1890–91a, "Market Rights and Tolls," Q. 13,592 (Clare).

43 On this issue, see: Webb, "Scandal of London's Markets," 3

44 BPP 1888b, "Market Rights and Tolls," QQ. 6,100, 6,104-7 (Fulford).

45 BPP 1888d, "Market Rights and Tolls," QQ. 131-3, 140-1 (Gray, Motum and Ellis)

46 BPP 1890–91b, "Market Rights and Tolls," Q. 14,456-8 (Birley).

47 Schmiechen and Carls, *British Market Hall*, 134.

48 Davies, "Saturday Night Markets," 3; Mitchell, "Retail Markets in Northern and Midland England," 17.

49 Rioux, "Food Quality and the Circulation Time of Commodities."

50 Lardner, *Railway Economy*, 13; Dodd, *Food of London*, 116.

51 Freeman, *Railways and the Victorian Imagination*.

52 BPP 1867, "Royal Commission of Railways," lxv; BPP 1881a, "Select Committee on Railways, Part 2," 262.

53 Gourvish, *Railways and the British Economy*, 29.

54 BPP 1844a, "Select Committee on Railways," 20.

55 Bagwell, *Railway Clearing House*, 295, 304–5.

56 Cited in Salt, *Facts and Figures*, 107.

57 Hawke and Reed, "Railway Capital," 270, 272.

58 Gourvish, *Railways and the British Economy*, 28.

59 BPP 1872b, "Railway Companies Amalgamation," xxvii; BPP 1906a, "Railway Rates," Q. 3857 (Andrew).

60 BPP 1867, "Royal Commission of Railways," lxv.

61 BPP 1907, "Royal Commission on Canals and Waterways," 2; BPP 1913a, "Railway returns," xxi.

62 BPP 1910a, "Royal Commission on Canals and Waterways," 49; BPP 1913a, "Railway returns," 58, 60.

63 Bradley, *Cadbury's Purple Reign*, 51; BPP 1888c, "Market Rights and Tolls," Q. 13,344 (Ward).

64 BPP 1910a, "Royal Commission on Canals and Waterways," 62. See also Dodd, *Food of London*, 169ff.

65 BPP 1882, "Railways (Rates and Fares)," QQ. 225 (Birt), QQ. 502-3 (Walker), Q. 1934 (Noble), Q. 2415 (Forbes); BPP 1906a, "Railway Rates," QQ. 3488-90

(Millar), Q. 4322 (Forbes); Q. 4891 (Gibb). On the cost structure of coastal shipping, see: Aldcroft, "Eclipse of British Coastal Shipping"; Aldcroft, "Depression in British Shipping"; Armstrong, "Role of Coastal Shipping"; Armstrong, "Freight Pricing Policy."

66 Armstrong, "Climax and Climacteric," 43–5.

67 BPP 1882, "Railways (Rates and Fares)," QQ. 1834-43 (Craze); BPP 1881a, "Select Committee on Railways, Part 1," QQ. 3412-8 (Taylor).

68 Dodd, *Food of London*, 266.

69 Ibid., 107–10; Smith, "Cattle Trade of Aberdeenshire"; Blackman, "Cattle Trade and Agrarian Change."

70 Anon., "London Commissariat," 287.

71 Smith, "Cattle Trade of Aberdeenshire," 114–15.

72 Channon, "Aberdeenshire Beef Trade with London," 23.

73 BPP 1888b, "Market Rights and Tolls," QQ. 6113-4 (Fulford). For a similar example in Stockton, see: BPP 1888d, "Market Rights and Tolls," QQ. 5487-8 (Creasor and Dodds).

74 BPP 1888d, "Market Rights and Tolls," QQ. 6823-9 (Morley and Leak).

75 BPP 1890–91b, "Market Rights and Tolls," 512; BPP 1890–91a, "Market Rights and Tolls," 576, 578, Q. 15,721 (Alderly); BPP 1888b, "Market Rights and Tolls," Q. 1712 (Matthews); BPP 1888b, "Market Rights and Tolls," Q. 1722 (Allen); BPP 1882, "Railways (Rates and Fares)," Q. 1897 (Craze).

76 BPP 1882, "Railways (Rates and Fares)," Q. 248 (Birt); BPP 1888b, "Market Rights and Tolls," Q. 2939 (Birt).

77 BPP 1882, "Railways (Rates and Fares)," Q. 191 (Birt); BPP 1888b, "Market Rights and Tolls," Q. 3117 (Birt).

78 BPP 1888b, "Market Rights and Tolls," QQ. 3032-7 (Birt).

79 Ibid., QQ. 3022-4, 3108 (Birt).

80 Page, "Sources of Supply," 478.

81 BPP 1888b, "Market Rights and Tolls," Q. 5107 (Bradnum).

82 Ibid., Q. 6145 (Fulford).

83 Beavington, "Development of Market Gardening in Bedfordshire," 36–7, 40–1.

84 Manby, "Cultivation of Early Potatoes," 101.

85 Anon., "London Commissariat," 296; Dodd, *Food of London*, 375; BPP 1882, "Railways (Rates and Fares)," QQ. 1762, 1764, 1795–6, 1844 (Craze); Page, "Sources of Supply," 476. On the food supply of Manchester, see: Bear, "Food Supply of Manchester, Part 1"; and Bear, "Food Supply of Manchester, Part 2"; Scola, *Feeding the Victorian City*.

86 Page, "Sources of Supply," 475.

87 BPP 1888b, "Market Rights and Tolls," Q. 2789 (Tallerman). See also QQ. 2835 (Tallerman), QQ. 3314-5 (Russell).

88 Smith, "Wholesale and Retail Markets of London," 43. See also: Blackman, "Food Supply of an Industrial Town," 84; BPP 1890–91a, "Market Rights and Tolls," QQ. 8984-90 (Little), QQ. 9021-4 (Mahony); BPP 1888b, "Market Rights and Tolls," Q. 1257-8 (Stephens).

89 BPP 1890–91a, "Market Rights and Tolls," QQ. 14,176-7 (Harris), QQ. 15,103-4 (Stevenson).

90 BPP 1890–91a, "Market Rights and Tolls," QQ. 13,881-2 (Talbot), Q. 13,126 (Kirkman).

91 Mayhew, *London Characters*, 334. For similar examples in Birmingham and the villages of Kent, see: BPP 1888b, "Market Rights and Tolls," Q. 6109 (Fulford); Winstanley, *Shopkeeper's World*, 208.

92 BPP 1888d, "Market Rights and Tolls," Q. 6695 (Hardwick). This was true in a great many cities, including Bacup, Stockton, and Newcastle: BPP 1890–91b, "Market Rights and Tolls," Q. 13,941 (Heyworth); BPP 1888d, "Market Rights and Tolls," 358, QQ. 5018-20, 5141-4 (McGowen and Dunwell), QQ. 565-8 (Gray, Smith and Motum).

93 BPP 1888b "Market Rights and Tolls," Q. 1232-3, 1253-7 (Stephens).

94 Lardner, *Railway Economy*, 141.

95 Anon., "London Commissariat," 287. See also Poole, *Statistics of British Commerce*, 225.

96 BPP 1870a, "Contagious Diseases (Animals) Act," 108.

97 Dodd, *Food of London*, 266.

98 BPP 1866b, "Second report on the cattle plague," QQ. 5165, 5170-3 (Benjamin).

99 Perren, "Meat and Livestock Trade in Britain," 390.

100 Blackman, "Food Supply of an Industrial Town," 85–92; Shaw, "Changes in Consumer Demand," 288–89; BPP 1890–91b, "Market Rights and Tolls," Q. 14,288 (Gaine), 491.

101 Anon., "Smithfield Cattle Market," 142.

102 On the political struggle to relocate the Smithfield cattle market, see: Metcalfe, *Meat, Commerce and the City*.

103 BPP 1866a, "First report on the cattle plague," xv.

104 Baxter, "Butchers and Fishmongers," 202.

105 Winstanley, *Shopkeeper's World*, 141.

106 BPP 1888d, "Market Rights and Tolls," 310. Q. 4990 (McGowen).

107 Ibid., QQ. 5018-20, 5141 (McGowen).

108 Ibid., Q. 6052 (Richardson).

109 BPP 1890–91b, "Market Rights and Tolls," Q. 14,259 (Hacking); BPP 1888b, "Market Rights and Tolls," Q. 6109 (Fulford).

110 BPP 1905, "Fruit Culture in Great Britain," Q. 5863 (Sinclair). See also Q. 6034 (Hodge).

111 BPP 1882, "Railways (Rates and Fares)," Q. 441 (Birt).

112 Cain, "Traders versus Railways."

113 BPP 1906a, "Railway Rates," QQ. 4888, 4912-5, 5016, 5022, 5045 (Gibb). The same was true from the agricultural district covered by the Great Eastern: QQ. 4753-4 (Gardner), QQ. 4613-7 (Hennell).

114 BPP 1972b, "Railway Companies Amalgamation," xxvii; BPP 1906a, "Railway Rates," QQ. 4212-4 (Bury).

115 Winstanley, "Retail Property Ownership in Edwardian England," 195.

116 Evans, *From Mouths of Men*, 33–4.

117 Hodson, "Civic Identity, Custom and Commerce," 40.

118 BPP 1888c, "Market Rights and Tolls," QQ. 467-520; Marsh, "Shopping in Denton," 75.

119 Winstanley, "Retail property ownership in Edwardian England," 195.

120 Mitchell, "Retail Markets in Northern and Midland England," 13–15; Hodson, "Civic Identity, Custom and Commerce," 41.

121 Rees, *St Michael*, 8–12, 17, 20.

122 BPP 1888b, "Market Rights and Tolls," QQ. 3855-9 (Hunt), Q. 4050 (Casson); Schmiechen and Carls, *British Market Hall*, 166.

123 BPP 1888b, "Market Rights and Tolls," Q. 3531 (Osmond).

124 Thomson and Smith, *Street Life in London*, 51–2; Grey, "Covent Garden Market," 331.

125 Grey, "Covent Garden Market," 333.

126 Ibid., 332–3.

127 BPP 1909a, "Poor Laws and Relief Distress," 99.

128 BPP 1888b, "Market Rights and Tolls," QQ. 2299-2304, Q. 2385 (Butler).

129 Horn, *Behind the Counter*, 14.

130 Schmiechen and Carls, *British Market Hall*, 170.

131 Rees, *St Michael*, 27, 36–7.

CHAPTER THREE

1 Dendy, "Industrial Residuum," 601, 606–7, 616.

2 Chesney, *Victorian Underworld*, 49.

3 Dodd, *Food of London*, 363.

4 Rogers, "Street Hawkers of London," 298.

5 Costers who inherited their trade from their fathers tended to do relatively better than those taking to the streets due to economic necessity. See: Cloete, "Boy and His Work," 133.

6 Benson, *Penny Capitalists*, 101. See also: Mayhew, *London Labour and the London Poor*, 324; BPP 1910c, "Employment of Children," Q. 1608 (Statham).

7 Johnson and Walker, *Dictionary of the English Language*, 162; Johnson, *Johnson's Dictionary*, 82.

8 Marlowe, *Works of Christopher Marlowe*, 168; Valpy, *Plays and Poems of Shakespeare*, 160. See also Shesgreen, *Criers and Hawkers of London*.

9 BPP 1890–91c, "Market Rights and Tolls," 60; BPP 1903, "Alien Immigration," QQ. 7792-3 (Blake). See also Scola, *Feeding the Victorian City*, 246–53.

10 Alexander, *Retailing in England*, 61.

11 BPP 1824, "Number of licences granted to hawkers and pedlars"; BPP 1844b, "Number of hawkers licenced"; Folio, *Hawkers and Street Dealers*, 13; Alexander, *Retailing in England*, 63; Ashby, *Joseph Ashby of Tysoe*, 202; Penn, *Manchester Fourteen Miles*, 173–5.

12 Mayhew, *London Labour*, 6; BPP 1852–53a, "Census of Great Britain 1851," 10, 14 (London). See also Horn, *Victorian Town Child*, 183–4.

13 BPP 1852–53a, "Census of Great Britain 1851," 648, 652 (Manchester, Salford, and Liverpool), 720, 724 (Leeds), 792, 796 (Newcastle), 834, 838 (South Wales), 1016, 1020 (Glasgow).

14 Hollingshead, *Ragged London*, 28.

15 Hardy, "Costers and Street Sellers," 259, 262–3. See also BPP 1906c, "London Traffic," 512–13 (Nott Bower).

16 Sherwell, *Life in West London*, 60–1. See also Cadbury, Matheson, and Shann, *Women's Work and Wages*, 330, 219.

17 Mayhew, *London Labour*, 6. See also: Greenwood, "Food Committee," 94; Phillips, "Evolution of Markets and Shops in Britain," 54.

18 BPP 1888d, "Market Rights and Tolls," Q. 6844 (Bradnum); BPP 1888c, "Market Rights and Tolls," Q. 10,934 (Pengelly). On the other hand, in places such as Hungerford, where many town's inhabitants "got very good gardens," the number of market gardeners driving their carts from neighbouring villages was more limited. See also BPP 1888d, "Market Rights and Tolls," Q. 3178 (Taylor), Q. 3291 (Major)

19 BPP 1888c, "Market Rights and Tolls," Q. 15,312 (Pepler). On the resilience of farmers killing their own stock and hawking butchers' meat in the streets, see: BPP 1890–91b, "Market Rights and Tolls," QQ. 13,222-6 (Waddington).

20 Stedman Jones, *Outcast London*, 61.

21 Ibid., 37.

22 Alexander, *Retailing in England*, 62; Benson, *Penny Capitalists*, 103.

23 Hardy, "Costers and Street Sellers," 260.

24 Smith, "Wholesale and Retail Markets of London," 45. See also Webb, *Scandal of London's Markets*.

25 Sullivan, *Markets for the People*, 224. For a comic song figuring a costermonger, see: Hindley, *Life and Adventures of a Cheap Jack*, 285–6.

26 Mayhew, *London Labour*, 9; BPP 1888b, "Market Rights and Tolls," Q. 3816 (Wood); Mayhew, *London Labour*, 13; Hardy, "Costers and Street Sellers," 260, 264; Sullivan, *Markets for the People*, 211–12; BPP 1902b, "Employment of School Children," Q. 4135 (Spencer); Kelley, "Streets for the People," 395–6; BPP, 1890–91b, QQ. 3560-90 (Denton).

27 Roberts, *Classic Slum*, 76n1; Foley, *Bolton Childhood*, 17.

28 BPP 1890–91a, "Market Rights and Tolls," Q. 13,126 (Kirkman); BPP 1890–91b, "Market Rights and Tolls," QQ. 13,693 (Radcliffe), QQ. 13,840-2 (Walker).

29 Williams, *36 Stewart Street Bolton*, 10; Alice Foley, *Bolton Childhood*, 17.

30 BPP 1890–91b, "Market Rights and Tolls," 312.

31 BPP 1888d, "Market Rights and Tolls," Q. 4194 (Walton and Culpan); BPP 1888b, "Market Rights and Tolls," QQ. 5851-2 (Tolon).

32 BPP 1888d, "Market Rights and Tolls," QQ. 3607 (Potts), Q. 3644 (Dugdale).

33 Phillips, "Evolution of Markets and Shops in Britain," 54–6.

34 BPP 1888c, "Market Rights and Tolls," Q 13,581 (Buckley), Q. 13,586 (Simpson).

35 Ibid., Q. 11,226 (Gibbs).

36 BPP 1888b, "Market Rights and Tolls," QQ. 1713-4 (Matthews). See also Dickens Jr., *Dickens's Dictionary of London*, 20.

37 BPP 1888b, "Market Rights and Tolls," QQ. 3562, 3571 (Denton). See also Hardy, "Costers and Street Sellers," 268.

38 Greenwood, "Food Committee," 92. See also Dickens Jr., *Dictionary of London*, 72.

39 Sullivan, *Markets for the People*, 227–8.

40 Folio, *Hawkers and Street Dealers*, 32; BPP 1888b, "Market Rights and Tolls," Q. 3711 (Shave).

41 BPP 1888d, "Market Rights and Tolls," Q. 2882 (Carter). See also Page, "Sources of Supply of the Manchester Fruit and Vegetable Markets," 485.

42 BPP 1888c, "Market Rights and Tolls," QQ. 11,053 (Shorto). See also QQ. 10,956, 11,018-9, 11,045 (Shorto); Q. 11,074 (Cornish), Q. 11,086 (Cane).

43 Poyntz, "Introduction," 50–1.

44 Greenwood, *In Strange Company*, 154.

45 BPP 1888b, "Market Rights and Tolls," Q. 1853 (Packer), QQ. 1607-8 (Horner). See also: Q. 525 (Goldney); Dodd, *Food of London*, 364; Thomson and Smith, *Street Life in London*, 59; Mayhew, *London Characters*, 340.

46 Hollingshead, *Ragged London*, 132; Hardy, "Costers and Street Sellers," 260.

47 Mayhew, *London Characters*, 341; BPP 1888b, "Market Rights and Tolls," Q. 1994 (Hanman), Q. 1884 (Le Poer Trench). See also: Dodd, *Food of London*, 349; BPP 1888b, "Market Rights and Tolls," Q. 525 (Goldney). According to the Royal Commission on Market Rights and Tolls, higglers also existed in Dover, Newcastle, Kidderminster, Aylesbury, and Canterbury, but it seems fair to say that they probably existed, in one form or another, in most market towns.

48 Dodd, *Food of London*, 349; BPP 1888b, "Market Rights and Tolls," Q. 3663 (Shave).

49 BPP 1888b, "Market Rights and Tolls," QQ. 3805-6 (Wood), QQ. 3540-58 (Denton).

50 Dodd, *Laboring Classes of England*, 29. See also Greenwood, *In Strange Company*, 18–34.

51 Briggs, *Victorian Cities*, 62.

52 Taylor, "Beyond the Bounds of Respectable Society."

53 Booth, *Life and Labour of the People in London*, 4:92.

54 Hollingshead, *Ragged London*, 28–9.

55 Romer, *Metropolitan Traffic Manual*, 36.

56 Ibid., 37.

57 Hardy, "Costers and Street Sellers," 264.

58 Chesney, *Victorian Underworld*, 38.

59 BPP 1906b, "London Traffic," QQ. 14,948-53 (Nott Bower).

60 Schmiechen and Carls, *British Market Hall*, 27.

61 BPP 1888d, "Market Rights and Tolls," Q. 5546-7 (Wade, Creasor, and Foster); BPP 1890–91b, "Market Rights and Tolls," QQ. 14,529-39 (Robinson, Birley, Satterthwaite, and Garlick); BPP 1888b, "Market Rights and Tolls," QQ. 5308-9 (Ellison).

62 BPP 1890-91b, "Market Rights and Tolls," Q. 11,143 (Mellor).

63 Roberts, *Classic Slum*, 76n1.

64 BPP 1888b, "Market Rights and Tolls," Q. 5846 (Tolon).

65 Mayhew, *London Labour*, 20.

66 Rogers, "Street Hawkers of London," 300.

67 Mayhew, *London Labour*, 20; Chesney, *Victorian Underworld*, 48.

68 *Times* (London), 2 September 1880, 10; *Times* (London), 28 December 1882, 10. See also: *Times* (London), 7 December 1880, 12; *Times* (London), 19 August 1913, 2.

69 Dale, *Child Labour under Capitalism*, 7.

70 BPP 1899a, "Elementary schools (children working for wages)," 4, 22, 44-6.

71 BPP 1902a, "Employment of School Children," 17.

72 BPP 1902b, "Employment of School Children," QQ. 4136, 4139, 4172 (Spencer).

73 BPP 1910b, "Employment of Children," 5.

74 Ibid.; Clopper, *Child Labor in City Streets*, 4.

75 BPP 1910b, "Employment of Children," 7.

76 BPP 1910c, "Employment of Children," 380, 390; BPP 1910b, "Employment of Children," 10.

77 BPP 1910c, "Employment of Children," Q. 1270, 1299 (Mulvany). See also Ibid., Q. 7663 (Pennington), 532.

78 BPP 1902b, "Employment of School Children," 415–16.

79 BPP 1910c, "Employment of Children," Q. 6745 (Rafter), QQ. 8751-4 (Jackson).

80 BPP 1902b, "Employment of School Children," 415–16; BPP 1910c, "Employment of Children," Q. 1612 (Statham), 523, 545; Pennybacker, *Vision for London*, 124.

81 BPP 1910b, "Employment of Children," 19. On the relation between poverty and children employed in street trading, see BPP 1910c, "Employment of Children," QQ. 494 (Smith), 3099 (Russell), 4432 (Allan), 6839-45, 6859 (Chadwick), 7214-27 (Commander), and 7669-71 (Pennington).

82 Folio, *Hawkers and Street Dealers*, 14.

83 BPP 1890–91b, "Market Rights and Tolls," QQ. 12,520, 12,522 (Foster). See also BPP 1904b, "Physical Deterioration," 3, 27, 34, 41.

84 Sykes and Neison, "State of the Inhabitants and Their Dwellings in Church Lane"; Dodd, *Food of London*, 363–4; Mayhew, *London Labour*, 1:109–13; Thomson and Smith, *Street Life in London*, 58; Hardy, "Costers and Street Sellers," 270; Booth, *Labour and Life of the People*, 2:46ff.

85 Mayhew, *London Labour*, 30; Malvery, *Soul Market*, 143.

86 Anon., "State of the Poorer Classes in St George's in the East," 205; Mayhew, *London Labour*, 68, 176; Greenwood, *In Strange Company*, 27.

87 Bosanquet, *Rich and Poor*, 56–7. The employment of children early on in the trade in part explains costermongering as a hereditary occupation, composed as it was of "poor but closely knit communities, living together and possessed of hereditary cultural ties." See Stedman Jones, *Outcast London*, 61–2.

88 BPP 1847–48a, "Third Report of the Metropolitan Sanitary Commission," 26.

89 Stedman Jones, *Outcast London*, 172.

90 Hollingshead, *Ragged London*, 111.

91 Greenwood, *In Strange Company*, 64.

92 BPP 1881b, "Artizans' and Labourers' Dwellings Improvement"; BPP 1884–85, "Housing of the working classes"; Bowmaker, *Housing of the Work-*

ing Classes; Howarth and Wilson, *West Ham*, bk. 1, chaps. 1–6; Gauldie, *Cruel Habitations*; Wohl, *Eternal Slum*; Burnett, *Social History of Housing*; Daunton, *House and Home in the Victorian City*.

93 This problem with model dwellings existed before the 1975 act, although at a much lower scale. See Hollingshead, *Ragged London*, 207. See also Marr, *Housing Conditions in Manchester and Salford*.

94 Stedman Jones, *Outcast London*, 199–214.

95 Hollingshead, *Ragged London*, 207; Stedman Jones, *Outcast London*, 184–5, 216; Hardy, "Costers and Street Sellers," 271.

96 Greenwood, *In Strange Company*, 152, 153, 155.

97 Ibid., 155–6. See also Edwards et al., *House Famine and How to Relieve It*, 16.

98 Holland, "Lowest Classes in Large Towns," 123–4.

99 London, *People of the Abyss*, 115–17. See also Steadman, *Overcrowding in London*.

100 Dickens, Jr, *Dickens's dictionary of London*, 20. See also Greenwood, "Food Committee," 94.

101 Greenwood, *In Strange Company*, 262.

102 BPP 1906d, "Sunday Trading," QQ. 3745-6 (Ailion).

103 Malvery, *Soul Market*, 139, 144.

104 Mayhew, *London Labour*, 8, 59. See also BPP 1902b, "Employment of School Children," Q. 4142 (Spencer).

105 Arlidge, Hygiene, Diseases and Mortality of Occupations, 132.

106 Mayhew, *London Labour*, 41.

107 Ibid., 537, 157–8.

108 Rogers, "Street hawkers of London," 304; BPP 1874, "Local Government Board," 227.

109 Tabor, "Elementary Education," 492. See also Whitehouse, "Street Trading by Children," 166.

110 Benson, *Penny Capitalists*, 113.

111 BPP 1904a, "Physical Deterioration," QQ. 436-7 (Eichholz).

112 Booth, *Life and Labour of the People in London*, 4:92.

113 BPP 1904a, "Physical Deterioration," Q. 440 (Eichholz).

114 Ibid., Q. 6290 (Niven).

115 Sponza, *Italian Immigrants in Nineteenth-Century Britain*, 94. See also de Felice, "Reconstructing Manchester's Little Italy," 58.

116 Sims, "Trips about Town," pt. 3," 511.

117 Sponza, *Italian Immigrants in Nineteenth-Century Britain*, 67; Colpi, *Italian Factor*, 60; Wilkins, "Traffic in Italian Children," 8. See also Wilkins, "Italian Aspect."

118 De Felice, "Reconstructing Manchester's Little Italy," 59.

119 Sponza, *Italian Immigrants in Nineteenth-Century Britain*, 99.
120 Anon., "Sanitary Condition of the Italian Quarter," 592; Sponza, *Italian Immigrants in Nineteenth-Century Britain*, 195–216, 224.
121 De Felice, "Reconstructing Manchester's Little Italy," 62
122 Sponza, *Italian Immigrants in Nineteenth-Century Britain*, 109.
123 Ibid., 109, 113.
124 Thomson and Smith, *Street Life in London*, 53–4; Anon., "Sanitary Condition of the Italian Quarter," 590; White, *Destitute Alien in Great Britain*; Wilkins, *Alien Invasion*.
125 BPP 1888b, "Market Rights and Tolls," QQ. 3818-28, 3949; Zangwill, *Children of the Ghetto*, 65; Anon., "London Commissariat," 301; Howarth and Wilson, *West Ham*, 56; Ó Tuathaigh, "Irish in Nineteenth-Century Britain," 17.
126 MacRaild, *Irish Migrants in Modern Britain*, 155–62; Hollingshead, *Ragged London*, 147.
127 Sims, "Trips about Town, part 2," 462. See also Zangwill, *Children of the Ghetto*, 234.
128 Ogle, "Supplement to the forty-fifth annual report of the Registrar-General," lxi.
129 Dunlop, "Occupation Mortalities," 54.
130 Arlidge, *Hygiene, Diseases and Mortality of Occupations*, 133.

CHAPTER FOUR

The expression is from Adam Smith: "To found a great empire for the sole purpose of raising up a people of customers may at first sight appear a project fit only for a nation of shopkeepers. It is, however, a project altogether unfit for a nation of shopkeepers; but extremely fit for a nation whose government is influenced by shopkeepers." See Smith, *Wealth of Nations*, 197.
1 Johnson, *Shop Life and Its Reform*, 2.
2 Anon., "Passing of the Grocer," 13.
3 Baxter, "Grocers, Oil and Colourmen, &c.," 220. On the history of the grocery trade, see: Rees, *Grocery Trade*; Stobart, *Sugar and Spice*.
4 Winstanley, *Shopkeeper's World*, 63–74.
5 Blackman, "Corner Shop," 149.
6 Winstanley, *Shopkeeper's World*, 9–15; Phillips, "Evolution of Markets and Shops in Britain," 63–4.
7 Williams, *36 Stewart Street Bolton*, 9, 11.
8 Norwood, *Victorian and Edwardian Hampshire*, photo, 123. See also Penn, *Manchester Fourteen Miles*, 53, 56–8.
9 Feinstein, "New Estimates of Average Earnings," 602.

10 Shaw, "Changes in Consumer Demand," 291, 293.

11 BPP 1888b, "Market Rights and Tolls," QQ. 1642-3 (Allen); BPP 1890–91a, "Market Rights and Tolls," Q. 13,661 (Clare); BPP 1888c, "Market Rights and Tolls," Q. 15,231 (Kidd).

12 Burnett, *England Eats Out*, chaps. 4–5; Walton, *Fish and Chips*, 5.

13 Roberts, *Woman's Place*, 159.

14 Williams, *Life in a Railway Factory*, 111; Roberts, *Classic Slum*, 107–8; Walton, *Fish and Chips*, 144–5.

15 Wild and Shaw, "Population Distribution and Retail Provision"; Shaw and Wild, "Retail Patterns in the Victorian City," 283–90; Scola, "Food Markets and Shops in Manchester," 167; Winstanley, "Concentration and Competition in the Retail Sector," 237.

16 BPP 1890–91a, "Market Rights and Tolls," Q. 14,175 (Harris). For similar evidence in Middlesbrough, Liverpool, London, and Newcastle, see: BPP 1888d, "Market Rights and Tolls," Q. 7,024 (Sanderson); BPP 1890–91a, "Market Rights and Tolls," Q. 13,685 (Holden); BPP 1888b, "Market Rights and Tolls," Q. 458 (Goldney); BPP 1888d, "Market Rights and Tolls," Q. 282 (Smith).

17 Shaw, "Changes in Consumer Demand," 293.

18 BPP 1888c, "Market Rights and Tolls," QQ. 467-520; BPP 1890-91b, "Market Rights and Tolls," Q. 14,604 (Ashcroft); Kelley, "Streets for the People," 406.

19 BPP 1888d, "Market Rights and Tolls," Q. 4094 (Kaye).

20 BPP 1890–91b, "Market Rights and Tolls," QQ. 14,305-12 (Hacking and Gaine).

21 Hosgood, "Pigmies of Commerce."

22 Foley, *Bolton Childhood*, 3; Thomas, *Shop Boy*, 21.

23 Hosgood, "Pigmies of Commerce," 442.

24 Roberts, *Classic Slum*, 81; Foley, *Bolton Childhood*, 19.

25 This symbiotic role was finally put to rest as new welfare provisions in the early 1900s "transferred the control of welfare from the community to the state." See Hosgood, "Pigmies of Commerce," 444.

26 BPP 1877, "Cattle Plague and Importation of Live Stock," QQ. 967-72 (Brown), QQ. 6177-81, 6181-94, 6313-5, 6335-7 (Burkett).

27 Winstanley, *Shopkeeper's World*, 45; Hosgood, "Pigmies of Commerce," 450–1; Hosgood, "Brave and Daring Folk," 296.

28 BPP 1890–91c, "Market Rights and Tolls," 107.

29 Walton, *Social History of Lancashire*, 229–33.

30 BPP 1888b, "Market Rights and Tolls," QQ. 833-4 (Casson). On shopkeepers regulating the markets in Bolton and legislating according to their interests since the 1860s, see BPP 1890–91a, "Market Rights and Tolls," Q. 13,105 (Kirkman).

31 BPP 1890–91a, "Market Rights and Tolls," Q. 15,359 (Kirkwood). The master butchers of Edinburgh made the same point: Q. 14,413 (Smith).

32 Sullivan, *Markets for the People*, 216.

33 Mayhew, *London Labour*, 59–60.

34 Sullivan, *Markets for the People*, 212–13. See also: Greenwood, "Food Committee," 92; Hardy, "Costers and Street Sellers," 262; Howarth and Wilson, *West Ham*, 34–5.

35 BPP 1888c, "Market Rights and Tolls," Q. 14,420 (King); Williams, *36 Stewart Street Bolton*, 9.

36 BPP 1888b, "Market Rights and Tolls," Q. 4,685 (Mellor). See also BPP 1890–91b, "Market Rights and Tolls," Q. 11,144 (Mellor).

37 BPP 1890–91b, "Market Rights and Tolls," QQ. 11,141, 11,143 (Mellor); BPP 1888b, "Market Rights and Tolls," QQ. 5844, 5887-8 (Tolon).

38 Anon., "Live and Let Live," 5.

39 Macrosty, *Trust Movement in British Industry*, 209.

40 Hosgood, "Brave and Daring Folk," 290–91.

41 Crossick, "Petite Bourgeoisie in Nineteenth-Century Britain"; Crossick, "Shopkeepers and the State in Britain"; Hosgood, "Brave and Daring Folk," 285.

42 Hosgood, "Brave and Daring Folk," 293.

43 Ibid., 290.

44 BPP 1881a, "Select Committee on Railways, part 2," 227.

45 BPP 1881a, "Select Committee on Railways, part 1," QQ. 3329-489 (Taylor).

46 Booth, "Shopkeepers and General Dealers"; Ford, "Excessive Competition in the Retail Trades"; Ford, "Decentralisation and Changes in the Number of Shops"; Ford and White, "Trends in Retail Distribution in Yorkshire (West Riding)"; Crossick, "Shopkeepers and the State," 240; Winstanley, *Shopkeeper's World*, 75–93, 126; Winstanley, "Concentration and Competition in the Retail Sector," 247–55; Shaw, "Evolution and Impact of Large-Scale Retailing in Britain," 163.

47 Greenwood, *Seven Curses of London*, 168.

48 Accum, *Treatise on Adulterations of Food*, 3–4; Mitchell, *Treatise of the Falsifications of Food*, viii; Hassall, *Food and Its Adulterations*, iii; Scott, "On Food," 154; Atkins, "Sophistication Detected," 318.

49 BPP 1856, "Adulteration of Food." See also Scott, "On Food," 156–7.

50 BPP 1863b, "Medical Officer of the Privy Council," 22.

51 For a review of the literature on food adulteration in Great Britain, see: French and Phillips, *Cheated Not Poisoned*; Rioux, "Food Quality and the Circulation Time of Commodities"; Rioux, "Capitalist Food Production and the Rise of Legal Adulteration."

52 BPP 1856, "Adulteration of Food," xv–xvi.

53 Hassall, "Adulteration, and Its Remedy," 91. See also: Anon., "Food and Its Adulterations."

54 Perren, *Meat Trade in Britain*, 64.

55 Greenwood, *Seven Curses of London*, 152.

56 BPP 1872a, "Adulteration of Food," viii (emphasis in original). On the low quality of milk, see Atkins, "White Poison?"

57 Burnett, *Plenty and Want*, 260–67.

58 BPP 1878, "Local Government Board," xcii–iv. See also Rioux, "Food Quality and the Circulation Time of Commodities."

59 BPP 1883, "Local Government Board," cvi; BPP 1889, "Local Government Board," cxlix.

60 BPP 1883, "Local Government Board"; BPP 1899b, "Local Government Board," cxxxiii.

61 Roberts, *Classic Slum*, 113; Waddington, *Bovine Scourge*.

62 BPP 1872a, "Adulteration of Food," iii; BPP 1889, "Local Government Board," clii–iii; BPP 1894, "Food Products Adulteration," Q. 257 (Preston-Thomas).

63 BPP 1870b, "Inspection of Weights and Measures," 112–13, 379.

64 BPP 1870b, "Inspection of Weights and Measures," 405.

65 Greenwood, *Seven Curses of London*, 152, 153.

66 Ibid., 154.

67 BPP 1870b, "Inspection of Weights and Measures," vi.

68 Pennybacker, *Vision for London*, 124, 127.

69 Mayhew, *London Labour*, 202; Folio, *Hawkers and Street Dealers*, 125; BPP 1888c, "Market Rights and Tolls," Q. 13,586 (Simpson); Folio, *Hawkers and Street Dealers*, 129.

70 Horn, *Behind the Counter*, 126–7.

71 Morrison, cited in Hoffman, *They Also Serve*, vi.

72 On the condition of shop assistants, see: Sutherst, *Death and Disease behind the Counter*; Anderson, *Counter Exposed*; Paine, *Shop Slavery and Emancipation*; Hallsworth and Davies, *Working Life of Shop Assistants*; Hoffman, *They Also Serve*; Bondfield, *Socialism for Shop Assistants*; BPP 1892, "Shop Hours Bill," app. 10.

73 Cox and Hobley, *Shopgirls*, 7.

74 Ibid., 34.

75 Sanders, *Consuming Fantasies*, 24; Cox and Hobley, *Shopgirls*, 11–2; Cadbury, Matheson, and Shann, *Women's Work and Wages*, 107.

76 Cox and Hobley, *Shopgirls*, 135.

77 Hallsworth and Davies, *Working Life of Shop Assistants*, 65, 68–70. See also Black, *Sweated Industry and the Minimum Wage*, 66.

78 Hallsworth and Davies, *Working Life of Shop Assistants*, 36.

79 On the issue of child labour, see: Russell, *Manchester Boys*; Urwick, *Studies of Boy Life in Our Cities*; Sherard, *Child Slaves of Britain*; Alden, *Child Life and Labour*; Clopper, *Child Labor in City Streets*; Bray, *Boy Labour and Apprenticeship*; Rose, *Erosion of Childhood*, chap. 11; Tuckwell, *State and Its Children*.

80 Bondfield, "Conditions Under Which Shop Assistants Work," 277; Johnson, *Shop Life and Its Reform*, 10; Anderson, *Counter Exposed*, 20; Hallsworth and Davies, *Working Life of Shop Assistants*, 114; Hosgood, "Mercantile Monasteries," 337; Cross, *Quest for Time*, 91.

81 BPP 1893–94, "Employment of Women," 85, 287–8.

82 Pennybacker, *Vision for London*, 124. See also Bray, *Boy Labour and Apprenticeship*, 122–3.

83 BPP 1910c, "Employment of Children," Q. 9021 (Chamings).

84 BPP 1910b, "Employment of School Children," 422. See also: BPP 1909b, "Poor Laws and Relief Distress," 193–204, 210; BPP 1902b, "Employment of School Children," 265, 274; Walton, *Fish and Chips*, 16, 82–3; Foley, *Bolton Childhood*, 49.

85 Davies, *Autobiography of a Super-Tramp*, 10; Evans, *From Mouths of Men*, 47; Morrison, cited in Hoffman, *They Also Serve*, v–vi; Penn, *Manchester Fourteen Miles*, 4, 197–8, 211–17; Williams, *36 Stewart Street Bolton*, 28.

86 BPP 1909c, "Poor Laws and Relief Distress," 326, §141 (Majority report).

87 Cloete, "Boy and His Work," 125; Foley, *Bolton Childhood*, 49.

88 BPP 1909b, "Poor Laws and Relief Distress," 4; Tawney, "Economics of Boy Labour," 32.

89 Greenwood, "Blind-Alley Labour," 309. See also Gibb, "Boy Labour," 58–9.

90 Paine, *Shop Slavery and Emancipation*, 83.

91 BPP 1917–18, "Census of England and Wales 1911," 139–40.

92 Thomas, *Shop Boy*, 90, 97–8.

93 Gibb, "Boy Labour," 70.

94 Williams, *36 Stewart Street Bolton*, 28; Hallsworth and Davies, *Working Life of Shop Assistants*, 29.

95 Alden, *Child Life and Labour*, 115–16.

96 BPP 1902b, "Employment of School Children," Q. 6796 (Christie).

97 BPP 1909b, "Poor Laws and Relief Distress," 54, 165, 211; Greenwood, "Blind-Alley Labour," 310–11.

98 BPP 1909b, "Poor Laws and Relief Distress," 165; Greenwood, "Blind-Alley Labour," 311.

99 Tawney, "Economics of Boy Labour," 26.

100 Davies, *Essay on the Evils Which are Produced by Late hours of Business*; Flower, *Hours of Business*; King, *System of Late Hours in Business*.

101 Grindrod, *Wrongs of our Youth*, 2–4; Honiborne, *Word for Early Closing*; Landels, *English Slavery and Early Closing*; Smeeton, *Necessity of Early Closing*; Wallace, *British Slavery*; Vincent, *Early Closing Movement*, 2; Hallsworth and Davies, *Working Life of Shop Assistants*, 60, 121.

102 BPP 1895, "Shops (Early Closing) Bill," QQ. 3930-2 (Robinson), QQ. 4107-8 (Wilson); BPP 1901b, "Early Closing of Shops," QQ. 114, 119 (Rees); Anderson, *Counter Exposed*, 37–8; Cross, *Quest for Time*, 86. On Sunday trading, see: Lilwall, *Half-Holiday Questions*, 20-1; BPP 1886, "Shop Hours Regulation Bill," Q. 1710 (Noel); Hoffman, *They Also Serve*, 6; Hallsworth and Davies, *Working Life of Shop Assistants*, 65.

103 Hallsworth and Davies, *Working Life of Shop Assistants*, 62–3. See also: BPP 1901b, "Early Closing of Shops," xiii; Hoffman, *They Also Serve*, 5.

104 Thomas, *Shop Boy*, 157–9; Anderson, *Counter Exposed*, 46.

105 BPP 1886, "Shop Hours Regulation Bill," iv. See also Anon., *Sunday Trading in London*, 6.

106 Johnson, *Shop Life and Its Reform*, 12–13.

107 BPP 1901b, "Early Closing of Shops," Q. 275 (Spencer).

108 Hoffman, *They Also Serve*, 8-10.

109 Horn, *Behind the Counter*, 135. See also Cross, *Quest for Time*, 89–90.

110 Hosgood, "Brave and Daring Folk," 300–01; Sanders, *Consuming Fantasies*, 39–40.

111 Hoffman, *They Also Serve*, 12–13.

112 BPP 1908, "Truck Acts, vol. 3," QQ. 13,107-10, 13,261-4, 13,372 (Bondfield), Q. 13,862 (Seddon), Q. 18,286 (Maddison); Cole, *Century of Co-operation*, 340; Hosgood, "Mercantile Monasteries," 332n47.

113 Cox and Hobley, *Shopgirls*, 121.

114 BPP 1908, "Truck Acts, vol. 3," QQ. 13,484-7.

115 Sanders, *Consuming Fantasies*, 34–5.

116 Cox and Hobley, *Shopgirls*, 37.

117 Bondfield, "Conditions Under Which Shop Assistants Work," 278–9; Black, *Sweated Industry and the Minimum Wage*, 49, 54–5. For an extensive overview of shops' rules and regulations, see BPP 1909e, "Truck Acts, vol. 4," 174–80 (app. XI).

118 Sanders, *Consuming Fantasies*, 34–5.

119 Harrods Ltd., *Story of British Achievement*, 29.

120 Bondfield, "Conditions Under Which Shop Assistants Work," 279–86; BPP 1893–94, "Employment of Women," 3, 87.

121 Thomas, *Shop Boy*, 162.

122 BPP 1886, "Shop Hours Regulation Bill," Q. 535 (Sutherst).

123 BPP 1893–94, "Employment of Women," 89, 287 (Edmistoun), 318 (Service); Tuckwell and Smith, *Worker's Handbook*, 153.

124 BPP 1893–94, "Employment of Women," 314; Hosgood, "Mercantile Monasteries," 328.

125 BPP 1908, "Truck Acts, vol. 3," Q. 13,451 (Bondfield). The lack of a closet for living-in employees was also common, the water supply often being cut off because shopkeepers were assessed for it. See: BPP 1893–94, "Employment of Women," 314.

126 Hoffman, *They Also Serve*, 24; BPP 1892, "Shop Hours Bill," QQ. 3960-1 (Jones); BPP 1908, "Truck Acts, vol. 3," Q. 13,613 (Tilley).

127 Bondfield, "Conditions Under Which Shop Assistants Work," 283.

128 Richardson, *Union of Many Trades*, 16. On the difficulty of organizing distributive workers, see: Johnson, *Shop Life and Its Reform*, 11; Hallsworth and Davies, *Working Life of Shop Assistants*, 7; Whitaker, *Victorian and Edwardian Shop Workers*, 25–6.

129 Anderson, *Counter Exposed*, 68; Horn, *Behind the Counter*, 136; Hoffman, *They Also Serve*, 2; Cox and Hobley, *Shopgirls*, 99; Whitaker, *Victorian and Edwardian Shop Workers*, 21.

130 McIvor, *History of Work in Britain*, 202; Hosgood, "Mercantile Monasteries," 347.

131 Johnson, *Shop Life and Its Reform*, 3. See also: BPP 1893–94, "Employment of Women," 4, 87–8; Bondfield, "Conditions Under Which Shop Assistants Work," 282; Whitaker, *Victorian and Edwardian Shop Workers*, 24.

132 Johnson, *Shop Life and Its Reform*, 12. See also BPP 1892, "Shop Hours Bill," Q. 3950 (Jones); Hoffman, *They Also Serve*, 17; Hosgood, "Mercantile Monasteries," 326.

133 Hosgood, "Mercantile Monasteries," 347; Horn, *Behind the Counter*, 138; Winstanley, *Shopkeeper's World*, 72–3.

134 Hoffman, *They Also Serve*, 51, 53, 59.

135 Harrods Ltd., *Story of British Achievement*, 17.

136 Hallsworth and Davies, *Working Life of Shop Assistants*, 21–2, 25, 26–8.

137 Ibid., 29. See also BPP 1893–94, "Employment of Women," 3–4; Black, *Sweated Industry and the Minimum Wage*, 58–60; Baxter, "Grocers, Oil and Colourmen, &c.," 200–1, 226–7.

138 Hoffman, *They Also Serve*, 85–6.

139 Ibid., 79, 81, 85–6.

140 How-to books on the proper management of a shop rarely (if ever) men-

tioned the issue of labour: Philp, *Shopkeeper's Guide*; Anon., *Business Life*; U., *Hints for Country Shopkeepers*.

141 Jefferys, *Retail Trading in Britain*, 15. See also: Winstanley, *Shopkeeper's World*, 216–17; Winstanley, "Retail Property Ownership in Edwardian England," 199; Stobart, *Spend, Spend, Spend!*, 151.

142 BPP 1901b, "Early Closing of Shops," Q. 631 (Blundell Maple).

143 BPP 1895, "Shops (Early Closing) Bill," Q. 4146 (Wilson); Winstanley, *Shopkeeper's World*, 200; Vigne and Howkins, "Small Shopkeeper in Industrial and Market Towns," 186.

144 Greig, *My Life and Times*, 3–10, 19.

145 Cadbury, Matheson, and Shann, *Women's Work and Wages*, 179, 177.

146 Roberts, *Ragged Schooling*, 8–9, 142.

147 Cadbury, Matheson, and Shann, *Women's Work and Wages*, 178–9; Marsh, "Shopping in Denton," 71; Vigne and Howkins, "Small Shopkeeper in Industrial and Market Towns," 188; BPP 1886, "Shop Hours Regulation Bill," Q. 1718 (Noel); Winstanley, "Retail Property Ownership in Edwardian England," 185.

148 Vigne and Howkins, "Small Shopkeeper in Industrial and Market Towns," 200, 205; Winstanley, *Shopkeeper's World*, 155–6.

149 Vigne and Howkins, "Small Shopkeeper in Industrial and Market Towns," 200. See also Roberts, *Ragged Schooling*, 3.

150 Winstanley, *Shopkeeper's World*, 158.

151 BPP 1886, "Shop Hours Regulation Bill," Q. 3305 (Cushen); BPP 1895, "Shops (Early Closing) Bill," QQ. 3555, 3571, 3582, 3585-6 (Parker), QQ. 3620, 3628, 3674-6 (Coggan); BPP 1901b, "Early Closing of Shops," Q. 2157 (Parker).

152 Vigne and Howkins, "Small Shopkeeper in Industrial and Market Towns," 203.

153 Ibid., 188. See also: Roberts, *Ragged Schooling*, 3, 16, 19; Cadbury, Matheson, and Shann, *Women's Work and Wages*, 176; UU, *Hints for Country Shopkeepers*, 40–1.

154 Marsh, "Shopping in Denton," 71.

155 Cadbury, Matheson, and Shann, *Women's Work and Wages*, 176; Greig, *My Life and Times*, 23; Vigne and Howkins, "Small Shopkeeper in Industrial and Market Towns," 199; Winstanley, *Shopkeeper's World*, 157, 160.

156 Winstanley, *Shopkeeper's World*, 147, 161; Greig, *My Life and Times*, 6; Roberts, *Ragged Schooling*, 27, 38–42; Vigne and Howkins, "Small Shopkeeper in Industrial and Market Towns," 199, 205.

157 Winstanley, *Shopkeeper's World*, 163.

158 Ibid., 164. See also: Penn, *Manchester Fourteen Miles*, 53; Foley, *Bolton Childhood*, 19.
159 BPP 1886, "Shop Hours Regulation Bill," QQ. 1692-1701, Q. 1718 (Noel).
160 BPP 1895, "Shops (Early Closing) Bill," QQ. 3618, 3632 (Parker).
161 Roberts, *Ragged Schooling*, 8, 26. See also Williams, *36 Stewart Street Bolton*, 22.
162 Roberts, *Ragged Schooling*, 12. See also Greig, *My Life and Times*, 23.
163 Winstanley, *Shopkeeper's World*, 66.
164 BPP 1886, "Shop Hours Regulation Bill," Q. 429 (Sutherst).
165 Ibid., Q. 3301 (Cushen).
166 Ibid., QQ. 5507-21 (Gradwell), Q. 1705 (Noel); Winstanley, *Shopkeeper's World*, 94–5.
167 BPP 1895, "Shops (Early Closing) Bill," Q. 3565 (Parker).
168 Ibid., Q. 3930-2 (Robinson); BPP 1895, "Shops (Early Closing) Bill," Q. 4107-8 (Wilson); Winstanley, *Shopkeeper's World*, 98, 91.
169 Wells, *History of Mr Polly*, 184.

CHAPTER FIVE

1 BPP 1909c, "Poor Laws and Relief Distress," 316.
2 Gurney, *Co-operative Culture and the Politics of Consumption*; Yeo, *New Views of Co-operation*; Clarke and Purvis, "Dialectics, Difference, and the Geographies of Consumption"; Purvis, "Societies of Consumers and Consumer Societies"; Gurney, "Labor's Great Arch," 135, 143.
3 Birchall, *International Co-operative Movement*, chap. 1; Cole, *Century of Co-operation*; Purvis, "Co-operative Retailing in Britain."
4 Molesworth, "Co-operative Trading Associations at Rochdale"; Potter, *Co-operative Movement in Great Britain*; Webb and Webb, *Problems of Modern Industry*, chaps. 8 and 9; Webb and Webb, *Consumers' Co-operative Movement*; Holyoake, *History of Co-operation in England*, vols. 1 and 2; Pollard, "Nineteenth-Century Co-operation"; Birchall, *Co-op*, chaps. 1–2; Cole, *Century of Co-operation*; Harrison, *Robert Owen and the Owenites*; Backstrom, *Christian Socialism and Co-operation*.
5 Aves, *Co-operative Industry*, 47–9.
6 Bonner, *British Co-operation*, 97; Stobart, *Spend, Spend, Spend!*, 137. On food adulteration, see Accum, *Treatise on Adulterations of Food*; Hassall, *Food and Its Adulterations*; Burnett, *Plenty and Want*; French and Phillips, *Cheated Not Poisoned?*; Rioux, "Food Quality and the Circulation Time of Commodities"; Rioux, "Capitalist Food Production and the Rise of Legal Adulteration."

7 Holyoake, *History of Co-operation in England*, 2:38–9.

8 Gurney, "Labor's Great Arch," 141.

9 Stobart, *Spend, Spend, Spend!*, 134.

10 Gurney, *Co-operative Culture and the Politics of Consumption in England*, 18; Jefferys, *Retail Trading in Britain*, 17.

11 Holyoake, *History of Co-operation in England*, 2:32; Aves, *Co-operative Industry*; Stedman Jones, *Outcast London*; Sullivan, *Markets for the People*, 217––1; Bonner, *British Co-operation*, 98–99.

12 BPP 1909c, "Poor Laws and Relief Distress," 316. See also Hird, *Mirfield*, 59.

13 Stobart, *Spend, Spend, Spend!*, 135.

14 Cole, *Century of Co-operation*, 371; Co-operative Wholesale Society, *Annual*, viii.

15 Birchall, *Co-op*, 47.

16 Jefferys, *Retail Trading in Britain*, 17.

17 Winstanley, *Shopkeeper's World*, 38.

18 Macrosty, *Trust Movement in British Industry*, 216.

19 Jackson, *Study in Democracy*, 475. The Bristol Society was formed in 1906 as a result of the amalgamation between the Bedminster, Briston and District, Shirehampton and Avonmouth, and Keynsham societies.

20 Gide, *Consumers Co-operative Societies*, 258; Wilson, Webster, and Vorberg-Rugh, *Building Co-operation*, 137–42.

21 Stobart, *Spend, Spend, Spend!*, 136.

22 Winstanley, "Retail Property Ownership in Edwardian England," 185.

23 Jones, "Consumers' Co-operation in Victorian Edinburgh," 303–4. See also Hird, *Mirfield*, 61.

24 Wilson, Webster, and Vorberg-Rugh, *Building Co-operation*, 59–66.

25 Cole, *Century of Co-operation*, 371.

26 Jones, "Consumers' Co-Operation in Victorian Edinburgh," 295, 301.

27 Jackson, *Study in Democracy*, 318, 350, 353.

28 Gurney, "Labor's Great Arch," 139.

29 Marx, "Inaugural Address."

30 Jennings, "Co-operative Wholesale Society Ltd," 31; Kinloch and Butt, *History of the Scottish Co-operative Wholesale Society Limited*, 377.

31 Bonner, *British Co-operation*, 110.

32 This amount, however impressive, represented only 0.14 percent of the £14 million necessary for the construction of the canal.

33 The SS *Plover* (1876), resold in 1880; the SS *Pioneer* (1879), the first merchant vessel to reach Manchester from overseas through the Manchester Ship Canal; the SS *Cambrian* (1881); the SS *Unity* (1883), which ran down and sunk in the River Seine in October 1895; the SS *Progress* (1884); the SS *Feder-*

ation (1886); the ss *Equity* (1888); the ss *Unity II* (1902); the ss *Fraternity* (1903); and the ss *New Pioneer* (1905).

34 BPP 1909c, "Poor Laws and Relief Distress," 315–16.

35 Bonner, *British Co-operation*, 97.

36 Redfern, *Story of the CWS*, chap. 21.

37 Ibid., 207–14; Co-operative Union, *General Co-operative Survey*, 167–7; 172.

38 Redfern, *Story of the CWS*, 223. For a thorough discussion on the contradictions between socialism and co-operation, see Gurney, *Co-operative Culture and the Politics of Consumption*, chap. 7.

39 Holyoake, *History of Co-operation in England*, 2:9 (emphasis in original).

40 Pollard, "Nineteenth-Century Co-operation," 98.

41 BPP 1909d, "Poor Laws and Relief Distress," Q. 57,766ff.

42 Gurney, "Labor's Great Arch," 154.

43 Pollard, "Nineteenth-Century Co-operation," 77–83.

44 Gurney, *Co-operative Culture and the Politics of Consumption*, 22–3; Purvis, "Stocking the Store," 55.

45 Wilson, Webster, and Vorberg-Rugh, *Building Co-operation*, 59–66.

46 Purvis, "Stocking the Store," 67–8. See also: Redfern, *Story of the CWS*, 74; Holyoake, *History of Co-operation in England*, 2:154.

47 Holyoake, *History of Co-operation in England*, 2:103.

48 Purvis, "Stocking the Store," 70.

49 Bonner, *British Co-operation*, 126.

50 Co-operative Wholesale Society, *Annual*, xvi.

51 Jackson, *Study in Democracy*, 586–7.

52 Aves, *Co-operative Industry*, 66–9.

53 Cole, *Century of Co-operation*, 374.

54 Aves, *Co-operative Industry*, 63–4, 176. See also Gurney, "Labor's Great Arch," 156.

55 Davies, *Life as We Have Known It*, ix–xi.

56 Benson, *Penny Capitalists*, 124.

57 BPP 1890–91a, "Market Rights and Tolls," Q. 13,130 (Kirkman); Gloucester: BPP 1888c, "Market Rights and Tolls," QQ. 13,357-8 (Ward).

58 BPP 1909c, "Poor Laws and Relief Distress," 316.

59 Webb, *Industrial Co-operation*, 100; Richardson, *Union of Many Trades*, 10.

60 Horn, *Behind the Counter*, 60–1.

61 Thompson, cited in Horn, *Behind the Counter*, 62. See also: Hallsworth and Davies, *Working Life of Shop Assistants*, 108; Gide, *Consumers Co-operative Societies*, 245.

62 Richardson, *Union of Many Trades*, 9.

63 Kinloch and Butt, *History of the Scottish Co-operative Wholesale Society*, 110. See also Webb, *Industrial Co-operation*, 102.

64 Hallsworth and Davies, *Working Life of Shop Assistants*, 42–5; Richardson, *Union of Many Trades*, 11.

65 BPP 1908, "Truck Acts, vol. 3," Q. 13,100 (Bondfield); Cole, *Century of Co-operation*, 338; Kinloch and Butt, *History of the Scottish Co-operative Wholesale Society*, 168; Hallsworth and Davies, *Working Life of Shop Assistants*, 117.

66 Gurney, "Labor's Great Arch," 136.

67 Kinloch and Butt, *History of the Scottish Co-operative Wholesale Society*, 125.

68 Richardson, *Union of Many Trades*, 33.

69 Ibid., 17–19, 23–4.

70 Richardson, *Union of Many Trades*, 24; Cole, *Century of Co-operation*, 337; Horn, *Behind the Counter*, 138–9.

71 Cole, *Century of Co-operation*, 336; Richardson, *Union of Many Trades*, 40–1, 47, 52–3; Gurney, "Labor's Great Arch," 168n103; Horn, *Behind the Counter*, 141; Co-operative Union, *General Co-operative Survey*, 311–12.

72 Cole, *Century of Co-operation*, 339–40; Hallsworth and Davies, *Working Life of Shop Assistants*, 78.

73 Richardson, *Union of Many Trades*, 25.

74 Hallsworth and Davies, *Working Life of Shop Assistants*, 76–77, 83.

75 Webb, *Industrial Co-operation*, 262 ; Hallsworth and Davies, *Working Life of Shop Assistants*, 79, 82.

76 Cole, *Century of Co-operation*, 338. See also Horn, *Behind the Counter*, 65.

77 Richardson, *Union of Many Trades*, 36–7.

78 Hallsworth and Davies, *Working Life of Shop Assistants*, 46–9, 52.

79 Co-operative Union, *General Co-operative Survey*, 313.

80 Richardson, *Union of Many Trades*, 37–8. See also Hallsworth and Davies, *Working Life of Shop Assistants*, 52–3.

81 Horn, *Behind the Counter*, 65.

82 Cole, *Century of Co-operation*, 340–1.

83 Richardson, *Union of Many Trades*, 43 (emphasis in original).

84 Ibid.

85 Horn, *Behind the Counter*, 139. See also Drake, *Women in Trade Unions*, 56.

86 Kinloch and Butt, *History of the Scottish Co-operative Wholesale Society*, 166–7.

87 Hallsworth and Davies, *Working Life of Shop Assistants*, 134–8.

88 Richardson, *Union of Many Trades*, 45. See also: Kinloch and Butt, *History of the Scottish Co-operative Wholesale Society*, 129; Cole, *Century of Co-operation*, 341.

89 Richardson, *Union of Many Trades*, 46.

90 Winstanley, "Concentration and Competition in the Retail Sector," 243.

91 Shaw, "Evolution and Impact of Large-Scale Retailing in Britain," 153.

92 Winstanley, *Shopkeeper's World*, 244. See also: Jefferys, *Retail Trading in Britain*, 129; Stobart, *Spend, Spend, Spend!*, 143.

93 Lipton cited in Mathias, *Retailing Revolution*, 328. See also: Paine, *Shop Slavery and Emancipation*, 80–1.

94 Shaw, "Evolution and Impact of Large-Scale Retailing in Britain," 159.

95 Jefferys, *Retail Trading in Britain*, 465.

96 On Jefferys' method of calculation, see: Stobart, *Spend, Spend, Spend!*, 138; Alexander, Shaw, and Hodson, "Regional Variations in the Development of Multiple Retailing," 129–30.

97 Stobart, *Spend, Spend, Spend!*, 138.

98 Ibid., 139.

99 Winstanley, "Concentration and Competition in the Retail Sector," 253–4.

100 Mathias, *Retailing Revolution*, 96–124, 328–52.

101 Ibid., 125–47.

102 Macrosty, *Trust Movement in British Industry*, 201.

103 Mathias, *Retailing Revolution*, 165–91.

104 On large-scale retailing in the meat trade, see: Bear, "Food Supply of Manchester, Part 2," 490–2; Duncan, "Demand for Frozen Beef"; Hooker, "Meat Supply of the United Kingdom."

105 Shaw, "Changes in Consumer Demand and Food Supply," 289.

106 BPP 1890–91a, "Market Rights and Tolls," QQ. 12,446-62 (Hetherington, McIntyre, and Mahony).

107 Critchell and Raymond, *History of the Frozen Meat Trade*, 208–10. Other important companies included the River Plate Fresh Meat Company, the London Central Meat Company, W. & R. Fletcher, the Argenta Meat Company, the New Zealand Mutton Company, and the Direct Supply Meat Company.

108 This discussion draws on: Rioux, "Food Quality and the Circulation Time of Commodities."

109 BPP 1847–48b, "Baking trade"; BPP 1862, "Grievances complained of by the journeymen bakers"; BPP 1863c, "Grievances complained of by the journeymen bakers"; Booth and Fox, "Bakers and Confectioners"; Perren, "Structural Change and Market Growth in the Food Industry"; Rioux, "Rethinking Food Regime Analysis."

110 Whetham, "London Milk Trade, 1860–1900," 373–5, 379; Barnes, "Milk Production and Distribution in England and Wales."

111 Anon., "London Commissariat," 293; BPP 1866a, "First report on the cattle plague"; BPP 1866b, "First report on the cattle plague"; BPP 1866c, "First

report on the cattle plague"; BPP 1873c, "Contagious Diseases (Animals)";
Rew, "Production and Consumption of Milk," 263.

112 Dudfield, "Milk Supply of the Metropolis," 345.

113 Atkins, "London's Railway Milk Trade," 209–10; Atkins, "London's Intra-Urban Milk Supply," 387. See also Taylor, "London's Milk Supply."

114 BPP 1877, "Cattle Plague and Importation of Live Stock," QQ. 4841-5 (Wilson); BPP 1901a, "Milk and Cream Regulations," Q. 1256 (Pocock).

115 Atkins, "Pasteurization of milk in England."

116 BPP 1906a, "Railway Rates," Q. 5067 (Gibb), QQ. 5579, 5602 (Malby).

117 Whetham, "London Milk Trade, 1900–1930," 66.

118 Baxter, "Milksellers."

119 Mathias, *Retail Revolution*, 123, 143.

120 Ibid., 143.

121 Ibid., 123.

122 Paine, *Shop Slavery and Emancipation*, 51.

123 Ibid., 36–8.

124 Hallsworth and Davies, *Working Life of Shop Assistants*, 31.

125 BPP 1909e, "Truck Acts, vol. 4," 180-1 (app. XII).

126 Winstanley, *Shopkeeper's World*, 124; Wilkinson, *From Corner Shop to Corner Shop*.

127 BPP 1908, "Truck Acts, vol. 3," Q. 13,620 (Tilley).

128 Ibid., QQ. 14,191, 14,202 (Rees).

129 Hoffman, *They Also Serve*, 53.

130 BPP 1908, "Truck Acts, vol. 3," QQ. 14,193, 14,189 (Rees).

131 Stobart, *Spend, Spend, Spend!*, 141.

132 Winstanley, "Retail Property Ownership in Edwardian England," 190.

133 Horn, *Behind the Counter*, 79.

134 Hoffman, *They Also Serve*, 88.

135 Mathias, *Retail Revolution*, 143; Horn, *Behind the Counter*, 79.

136 Hoffman, *They Also Serve*, 88-91.

137 For a detailed presentation of the betterment of working conditions after 1914, see Hoffman, *They Also Serve*, 97–103.

138 Ibid., 97–8.

CONCLUSION

1 Office for National Statistics, "Consumer Trends," Table 01.CN; FranceAgriMer, "La dépense alimentaire," 2; GTAI, "Food and Beverage Industry in Germany," 3.

2 Deloitte, "Global Powers of Retailing 2018," 19.

3 European Commission, "Economic Impact of Modern Retail," 50.
4 Bariacto and Nunzio, "Market Power in the Australian Food System."
5 Economic Research Service, "Retail Trends."
6 Office of Consumer Affairs, "Canada's Changing Retail Market," 14.
7 Stiegert and Kim, *Structural Changes in Food Retailing*.
8 Jayaraman, *Behind the Kitchen Door*.
9 Bureau of Labor Statistics, "National Occupational Employment and Wage Estimates."
10 Ibid., "Occupations with the Lowest Median Wage."
11 United States Government, "Economic Report of the President," 550.
12 *Economist*, "Malthusian Mouthfuls."
13 MacInnes, "Monitoring Poverty and Social Exclusion."
14 Badshah, "Gurdwaras-Turned-Food Banks."
15 Trussell Trust, "UK Foodbank Use Continues to Rise" and "Benefit Levels Must Keep Pace with Rising Cost of Essentials."

Bibliography

Abernathy, Frederick H., John T. Dunlop, Janice H. Hammond, and David Weil. "Retailing and Supply Chains in the Information Age." *Technology in Society* 22, 1 (2000): 5–31.

Accum, Fredrick. *A Treatise on Adulterations of Food, and Culinary Poisons.* London: Longman, Hurt, Rees, Orme and Brown, 1820.

Ahvenainen, Jorma. "Telegraphs, Trade, and Policy: The Role of the International Telegraphs in the Years 1870–1914." In *The Emergence of a World Economy, 1500–1914.* Part 2: *1850–1914,* edited by Wolfram Fischer, R. Marvin McInnis, and Juergen Schneider, 505–18. Wiesbaden, West Germany: Franz Stiner Verlag, 1986.

Aldcroft, Derek H. "The Eclipse of British Coastal Shipping, 1913–21." *Journal of Transport History* 6, 1 (1963): 24–38.

– "The Depression in British Shipping, 1901–1911." *Journal of Transport History* 7, 1 (1965): 14–23.

Alden, Margaret. *Child Life and Labour.* London: Headley Brothers, 1908.

Alexander, Andrew, Gareth Shaw, and Deborah Hodson. "Regional Variations in the Development of Multiple Retailing in England, 1890–1939." In *A Nation of Shopkeepers: Five Centuries of British Retailing,* edited by John Benson and Laura Ugolini, 127–54. London: I.B. Tauris, 2003.

Alexander, David G. *Retailing in England during the Industrial Revolution.* London: Athlone Press, 1970.

Allen, Robert C. "Economic Structure and Agricultural Productivity in Europe, 1300–1800." *European Review of Economic History* 4, 1 (2000): 1–26.

– "The Great Divergence in European Wages and Prices from the Middle Ages to the First World War." *Explorations in Economic History* 38, 4 (2001): 411–47.

- "English and Welsh Agriculture, 1300–1850: Output, Inputs, and Income." Unpublished manuscript 2005: http://piketty.pse.ens.fr/files/ Allen2005.pdf.

Anderson, James. *A Calm Investigation of the Circumstances that Have Led to the Present Scarcity of Grain in Britain.* London: John Cumming, 1801.

Anderson, Will. *The Counter Exposed.* London: Klene, 1896.

Anon., "Report into the State of the Poorer Classes in St. George's in the East." *Journal of the Statistical Society of London* 11, 3 (1848): 193–249.

- "Smithfield Cattle Market." *Farmer's Magazine* 19, 2 (1849): 142–3.
- "The London Commissariat." *Quarterly Review* 95, 190 (1854): 271–308,
- "Food and Its Adulterations." *Dublin Review* 39, 77 (1855): 60–75.
- *Sunday Trading in London.* London: Rivingtons, 1856.
- *Business Life: The Experience of a London Tradesman.* London: Houlston and Wright, 1861.
- "Sanitary Condition of the Italian Quarter." *Lancet*, 18 October 1879, 590–2.
- "Live and Let Live." *Star* (London) 17 November 1894, 5.
- "The Passing of the Grocer." *Times* (London), 18 August 1902, 13.

Araghi, Farshad. "Food Regimes and the Production of Value: Some Methodological Issues." *Journal of Peasant Studies* 30, 2 (2003): 337–68.

Arlidge, John Thomas. *The Hygiene, Diseases and Mortality of Occupations.* London: Percival, 1892.

Armstrong, John. "The Role of Coastal Shipping in UK Transport: An Estimate of Comparative Traffic Movements in 1910." *Journal of Transport History* 8, 2 (1987): 164–78.

- "Freight Pricing Policy in Coastal Liner Companies before the First World War." *Journal of Transport History* 10, 2 (1989): 180–97.
- "Climax and Climacteric: The British Coastal Trade, 1870-1930." In *Exploiting the Sea: Aspects of Britain's Maritime Economy since 1870*, edited by David J. Starkey and Alan G. Jamieson. 37–58. Exeter: University of Exeter Press, 1998.

Armstrong, W. Alan. "The Trend of Mortality in Carlisle between the 1780s and the 1840s: A Demographic Contribution to the Standard of Living Debate." *Economic History Review* 34, 1 (1981): 94–114.

Ashby, M.K. *Joseph Ashby of Tysoe, 1859–1919: A Study of English Village Life.* London: Merlin Press, 1974.

Assael, B. *The London Restaurant, 1840–1940.* Oxford: Oxford University Press, 2018.

Atkins, Peter J. "London's Intra-Urban Milk Supply, circa 1790–1914." *Transactions of the Institute of British Geographers* 2, 3 (1977): 383–99.

- "The Growth of London's Railway Milk Trade, c. 1845–1914." *Journal of Transport History* 4, 4 (1978): 208–26.
- "Sophistication Detected: Or, the Adulteration of the Milk Supply, 1850–1914." *Social History* 16, 3 (1991): 317–39.
- "White Poison? The Social Consequences of Milk Consumption, 1850–1930." *Social History of Medicine* 5, 2 (1992): 207–27.
- "Milk Consumption and Tuberculosis in Britain, 1850–1950." In *Order and Disorder: The Health Implications of Eating and Drinking in the Nineteenth and Twentieth Centuries*, edited by Alexander Fenton, 83–95. East Linton: Tuckwell Press, 2000.
- "The Pasteurization of Milk in England: The Science, Culture and Health Implications of Milk Processing, 1900–1950." In *Food, Science, Policy and Regulation in the 20th Century*, edited by David F. Smith and Jim Phillips, 37–51. New York: Routledge, 2000.

Aves, Ernest. *Co-operative Industry*. London: Methuen, 1907.

Backstrom, Philip N. *Christian Socialism and Co-operation in Victorian England*. London: Croom Helm, 1974.

Badshah, Nadeem. "Gurdwaras-Turned-Food Banks: Sikh Temples Are Catering for Rise in Britain's Hungry." *Independent*, 8 December 2013.

Bagwell, Philip S. *The Railway Clearing House in the British Economy, 1842–1922*. London: Allen and Unwin, 1968.

Bailey, Peter. *Leisure and Class in Victorian England: Rational Recreation and the Contest for Control, 1830–1885*. Toronto: University of Toronto Press, 1978.

Banaji, Jairus. "Capitalist Domination and the Small Peasantry: Deccan Districts in the Late Nineteenth Century." *Economic and Political Weekly* 12, 33/34 (1977): 1375–404.

Barfoot-Saunt, W.H., Sir James Blyth, Major Craigie, R.F. Crawford, A. Wilson Fox, W.

Bariacto, Natazsa, and Jack Di Nunzio. "Market Power in the Australian Food System." Dalkeith, WA, Future Directions International, 2014. http://futuredirections.org.au/wp-content/uploads/2014/07/Market_Power_in_Australian_Food_System.pdf.

Barnes, F.A. "The Evolution of the Salient Patters of Milk Production and Distribution in England and Wales." *Transactions of the Institute of British Geographers* 25 (1958): 167–95.

Baxter, Arthur. "Milksellers." In *Life and Labour of the People in London*. Vol. 7: *Population Classified by Trades*, edited by Charles Booth, 172–87. London: Macmillan, 1896.
- "Butchers and Fishmongers." In *Life and Labour of the People in London*.

Vol. 7: *Population Classified by Trades*, edited by Charles Booth, 189–213. London: Macmillan, 1896.

– "Grocers, Oil and Colourmen, &c." In *Life and Labour of the People in London*. Vol. 7: *Population Classified by Trades*, edited by Charles Booth, 214–29. London: Macmillan, 1896.

Bear, William E. "The Food Supply of Manchester, Part 1: Vegetable Produce." *Journal of the Royal Agricultural Society of England* 8 (1897): 205–28.

– "The Food Supply of Manchester, Part 2: Animal Produce." *Journal of the Royal Agricultural Society of England* 8 (1897): 490–515.

Beavington, F. "The Development of Market Gardening in Bedfordshire, 1799–1939." *Agricultural History Review* 23, 1 (1975): 23–47.

Benson, John. *The Penny Capitalists: A Study of Nineteenth-Century Working-Class Entrepreneurs*. Dublin: Gregg Revivals, 1983.

– *The Rise of Consumer Society in Britain, 1880–1980*. London: Longman, 1994.

Benson, John, and Gareth Shaw. *The Evolution of Retail Systems, c. 1800–1914*. Leicester: Leicester University Press, 1992.

Benson, John, and Laura Ugolini, eds. *A Nation of Shopkeepers: Five Centuries of British Retailing*. London: I.B. Tauris, 2003.

Birchall, Johnston. *Co-op: The People's Business*. Manchester: Manchester University Press, 1994.

– *The International Co-operative Movement*. Manchester: Manchester University Press, 1997.

Black, Clementina. *Sweated Industry and the Minimum Wage*. London: Duckworth, 1907.

Blackman, Janet. "The Food Supply of an Industrial Town." *Business History* 5, 2 (1963): 83–97.

– "The Cattle Trade and Agrarian Change on the Eve of the Railway Age." *Agricultural istory Review* 23, 1 (1975): 48–62.

– "The Corner Shop: The Development of the Grocery and General Provisions Trade." In *The Making of the Modern British Diet*, edited by Derek J. Oddy and Derek S. Miller, 148–60. London: Croom Helm, 1976.

Bohstedt, John. *Riots and Community Politics in England and Wales, 1790–1810*. Cambridge, MA: Harvard University Press, 1983.

– *The Politics of Provisions: Food Riots, Moral Economy, and Market Transition in England, c. 1550–1850*. Farnham: Ashgate, 2010.

Bonacich, Edna, and Jake Wilson, "Global Production and Distribution: Wal-Mart's Global Logistics Empire." In *Wal-Mart World: The World's*

Biggest Corporation in the Global Economy, edited by Stanley D. Brunn, 227–42. New York, Routledge, 2006.

Bondfield, Margaret G. "Conditions Under Which Shop Assistants Work." *Economic Journal* 9, 34 (1899): 277–86.

– *Socialism for Shop Assistants*. London: The Clarion Press, 1909.

Bonner, Arnold. *British Co-operation: The History, Principles, and Organisation of the Co-operative Movement*. Manchester: Co-operative Union, 1970.

Booth, Charles, ed. *Labour and Life of the People*. Vol. 2. London: Williams and Norgate, 1891.

– ed. *Life and Labour of the People in London*. Vol. 4, *Inner South London*. London: Macmillan, 1902.

– "Shopkeepers and General Dealers." In *Life and Labour of the People in London*, vol. 7, *Population Classified by Trades*, edited by Charles Booth, 247–58. London: Macmillan, 1896.

Booth, Charles, and Stephen N. Fox. "Bakers and Confectioners." In *Life and Labour of the People in London*, vol. 7, *Population Classified by Trades*, edited by Charles Booth, 143–71. London: Macmillan, 1896.

Booth, William. *In Darkest England and the Way Out*. London: Funk & Wagnalls, 1890.

Bosanquet, Helen. *Rich and Poor*. London: Macmillan, 1908.

Bowmaker, Edward. *The Housing of the Working Classes*. London: Methuen, 1895.

BPP (British Parliamentary Papers). 1824. "An account of the number of licences granted to hawkers and pedlars, 1817–23." In *BPP* XVIII.225.

– 1844a. "Fifth report from the Select Committee on Railways; together with the minutes of evidence, appendix and index." In *BPP* XI.

– 1844b. "Return of the number of hawkers licensed in England, Ireland and Scotland, 1830–43." In *BPP* XXXII.377.

– 1847–48a. "Third Report of the Metropolitan Sanitary Commission." In *BPP* XXXII.339.

– 1847–48b. "Baking trade. Copy of the evidence given by Dr Guy before the Sanitary Commission, in reference to the persons employed in the trade." In *BPP* LI.

– 1852–53a. "Census of Great Britain 1851, Population tables 2, vol. 1." In *BPP* LXXXVIII, pt. I.1.

– 1852–53b. "Census of Great Britain 1851, Population tables 2, vol. 2." In *BPP* LXXXVIII, pt. II.1.

– 1856. "Report from the Select Committee on Adulteration of Food, &c." In *BPP* VIII.

– 1862. "Report addressed to Her Majesty's Principal Secretary of State for the Home Department, relative to the grievances complained of by the journeymen bakers; with appendix of evidence." In *BPP* XLVII.

– 1863a. "Census of England and Wales 1861, General Report." In *BPP* LIII, pt. I.1.

– 1863b. "Fifth Report of the Medical Officer of the Privy Council." In *BPP* XXV.

– 1863c. "Second report addressed to Her Majesty's Principal Secretary of State for the Home Department, relative to the grievances complained of by the journeymen bakers." In *BPP* XXVIII.

– 1864. "Census of Scotland 1861, vol. 2." In *BPP* LI.49.

– 1866a. "First report of the commissioners appointed to inquire into the origin and nature of the cattle plague." In *BPP* XXII.1.

– 1866b. "Second report of the commissioners appointed to inquire into the origin and nature of the cattle plague." In *BPP* XXII.227.

– 1866c. "Third report of the commissioners appointed to inquire into the origin and nature of the cattle plague." In *BPP* XXII.321.

– 1867. "Report of the Royal Commission of Railways." In *BPP* XXXVIII, pt. 1.

– 1870a. "Report from the committee on the Contagious Diseases (Animals) Act, 1869, together with the minutes of evidence and appendix." In *BPP* LXI.1.

– 1870b. "Fourth Report of the Royal Commission on Inspection of Weights and Measures." In *BPP* XXVII.249.

– 1872a. "Report for the Select Committee on Adulteration of Food Act (1872); together with the proceedings of the minutes of evidence, and appendix." In *BPP* VI.

– 1872b. "Report from the Joint Select Committee of the House of Lords and the House of Commons, on railway companies amalgamation." In *BPP* XIII, pt.1.

– 1873a. "Census of England and Wales 1871, vol. 3." In *BPP* LXXI, pt. 1.1.

– 1873b. "Census of Scotland 1871, vol. 2." In *BPP* LXXIII.1.

– 1873c. "Report from the Select Committee on Contagious Diseases (Animals)." In *BPP* XI.189.

– 1874. "Third Annual Report of the Local Government Board." In *BPP* XXV.

– 1877. "Report from the Select Committee on Cattle Plague and Importation of Live Stock; together with the proceedings of the committee, Minutes of evidence, and appendix." In *BPP* IX.1.

– 1878. "Seventh Annual Report of the Local Government Board." In *BPP* XXXVII, pt. 1.

– 1881a. "Report from the Select Committee on Railways." In *BPP* XIII–IV, pts. 1 and 2.
– 1881b. "Report from the Select Committee on Artizans' and Labourers' Dwellings Improvement; together with the proceedings of the committee, minutes of evidence, and appendix." In *BPP* VII.395.
– 1882. "Report from the Select Committee on Railways (Rates and Fares)." In *BPP* XIII.1.
– 1883. "Twelfth Annual Report of the Local Government Board." In *BPP* XXVIII.
– 1884–85. "First Report from the Royal Commission for inquiring into the housing of the working classes." *BPP* XXX.1.
– 1886. "Report from the Select Committee on Shop Hours Regulation Bill." In *BPP* XII.1.
– 1888a. "Royal Commission on Market Rights and Tolls, vol. 1." In *BPP* LIII.1.
– 1888b. "Royal Commission on Market Rights and Tolls, vol. 2." In *BPP* LIII.237.
– 1888c. "Royal Commission on Market Rights and Tolls, vol. 3." In *BPP* LIV.1.
– 1888d. "Royal Commission on Market Rights and Tolls, vol. 4." In *BPP* LV.
– 1889. "Eighteenth Annual Report of the Local Government Board." In *BPP* XXXV.
– 1890–91a. "Royal Commission on Market Rights and Tolls, vol. 7." In *BPP* XXXVII.243.
– 1890–91b. "Royal Commission on Market Rights and Tolls, vol. 9." In *BPP* XXXVIII.225.
– 1890–91c. "Royal Commission on Market Rights and Tolls, vol. 11: Final Report." In *BPP* XXXVII.1.
– 1890–91d. "Royal Commission on Market Rights and Tolls, vol. 13, part 1." In *BPP* XXXIX.665.
– 1890–91e. "Royal Commission on Market Rights and Tolls, vol. 13, part 2." In *BPP* XL.1.
– 1890–91f. "Royal Commission on Market Rights and Tolls, vol. 13, part 3." In *BPP* XLI.1.
– 1892. "Report and Special Report from the Select Committee on the Shop Hours Bill." In *BPP* XVII.387.
– 1893–94. "Royal Commission on Labour, The Employment of Women." In *BPP* XXXVII, pt. 1.545
– 1894. "Report from the Select Committee on Food Products Adulteration." In *BPP* XII.1.

- 1895. "Report from the Select Committee on Shops (Early Closing) Bill." In *BPP* XII.635.
- 1899a. "Elementary schools (children working for wages)." In *BPP* LXXV.433.
- 1899b. "Twenty-Eighth Annual Report of the Local Government Board." In *BPP* XXXVII.
- 1901a. "Report from the Departmental Committee on Milk and Cream Regulations." In *BPP* XXX.371.
- 1901b. "Report from the Select Committee of the House of Lords on Early Closing of Shops." In *BPP* VI.1.
- 1902a. "Inter-Departmental Committee on Employment of School Children, Report." In *BPP* XXV.261.
- 1902b. "Inter-Departmental Committee on the Employment of School Children, Minutes of Evidence." In *BPP* XXV.287.
- 1903. "Royal Commission on Alien Immigration, vol. 2, Minutes of Evidence." In *BPP* IX.61.
- 1904a. "Inter-Departmental Committee on Physical Deterioration, vol. 2." In *BPP* XXXII.145.
- 1904b. "Inter-Departmental Committee on Physical Deterioration, vol. 3." In *BPP* XXXII.655.
- 1904c. "Census of England and Wales 1901, General Report." In *BPP* CVIII.1.
- 1905. "Report of the Departmental Committee on Fruit Culture in Great Britain." In *BPP* XXIV.
- 1906a. "Departmental Committee on Railway Rates (preferential treatment), Minutes of Evidence." In *BPP* LV.
- 1906b. "Royal Commission on London Traffic, vol. 2." In *BPP*, XI.
- 1906c. "Royal Commission on London Traffic, vol. 3." In *BPP* XLI.
- 1906d. "Report from the Joint Select Committee on Sunday Trading." In *BPP* XIII.29.
- 1907. "Report of the Royal Commission on Canals and Waterways, vol. 4." In *BPP* XXXIII.1.
- 1908. "Departmental Committee on the Truck Acts, vol. 3." In *BPP* LIX.533.
- 1909a. "Royal Commission of the Poor Laws and Relief Distress, vol. 16." In *BPP* XLIII.1.
- 1909b. "Royal Commission of the Poor Laws and Relief Distress, vol. 20." In *BPP* XLIV.921.
- 1909c. "Royal Commission on the Poor Laws and Relief of Distress, Report." In *BPP* XXXVII.1.

- 1909d. "Royal Commission of the Poor Laws and Relief Distress, vol. 6." In *BPP* XLVI.1.
- 1909e. "Departmental Committee on the Truck Acts, vol. 4." In *BPP* XLIX.177.
- 1910a. "Fourth and Final Report of the Royal Commission on Canals and Waterways, vol. 7." In *BPP* XII.
- 1910b. "Departmental Committee on the Employment of Children Act, 1903, Report." In *BPP* XXVIII.1.
- 1910c. "Departmental Committee on the Employment of Children Act, 1903, Minutes of Evidence." In *BPP* XXVIII.25.
- 1913a. "Railway Returns: Returns of the Capital, Traffic, Receipts, and Working Expenditure of the Railway Companies of the United Kingdom for the Year 1912." In *BPP* LXXV.1.
- 1913b. "Census of Scotland 1911, vol. 2." In *BPP* LXXX.45.
- 1914–16. "Annual Report on Sea Fisheries for the Year 1914." In *BPP* XXII.1.
- 1917–18. "Census of England and Wales 1911, General Report." In *BPP* XXXV.483.
- 1924. "Agricultural Tribunal of Investigation, Final Report." In *BPP* VII.45.
Bradley, John. *Cadbury's Purple Reign: The Story Behind Chocolate's Best-Loved Brand*. West Sussex: John Wiley and Sons, 2008.
Bray, John. *Innovation and the Communications Revolution: From the Victorian Pioneers to Broadband Internet*. Stevenage: The Institution of Electrical Engineers, 2002.
Bray, Reginald A. *Boy Labour and Apprenticeship*. London: Constable, 1912.
Briggs, Asa. *Victorian Cities*. London: Penguin, 1990.
Brown, John C. "The Condition of England and the Standard of Living: Cotton Textiles in the Northwest, 1806–1850." *Journal of Economic History* 50, 3 (1990): 591–614.
Brown, Jonathan. *The English Market Town: A Social and Economic History, 1750–1914*. Marlborough: Crowood Press, 1986.
Brown, Joseph. *The Food of the People: A Letter to Henry Fenwick*. London: Longman, Green, Longman, Roberts & Green, 1865.
Bucklin, Louis P. *Competition and Evolution in the Distributive Trades*. Englewood Cliffs, NJ: Prentice Hall, 1972.
Burch, David, and Geoffrey Lawrence, eds. *Supermarkets and Agri-Food Supply Chain: Transformations in the Production and Consumption of Foods*. Cheltenham: Edward Elgar, 2007.
Bureau of Labor Statistics. "Occupations with the Lowest Median Wage, May 2012." United States Department of Labor, 2012. https://www.bls .gov/oes/2012/may/high_low_paying.htm.

- "May 2016 National Occupational Employment and Wage Estimates."
  United States Department of Labor, 2016. https://www.bls.gov/oes
  /current/oes_nat.htm#35-0000.

Burnett, John. "Trends in Bread Consumption." In *Our Changing Fare: Two
  Hundred Years of British Food Habits*, edited by Theodore C. Barker, John
  C. McKenzie, and John Yudkin, 61–75. London: MacGibbon and Kee
  1966.

- *The Annals of Labour: Autobiographies of British Working-Class People,
  1820–1920*. Bloomington: Indiana University Press, 1974.

- *Plenty and Want: A Social History of Diet in England from 1815 to the
  Present Day*. London: Scolar Press, 1979.

- *A Social History of Housing, 1815–1985*. London: Methuen, 1986.

- *Liquid Pleasures: A Social History of Drinks in Modern Britain*. London:
  Routledge, 1999.

- *England East Out: A Social History of Eating Out in England from 1830 to
  the Present*. London: Longman, 2004.

Cadbury, Edward, Cécile Matheson, and George Shann. *Women's Work and
  Wages: Phase of Life in an Industrial City*. London: T. Fisher Unwin, 1907.

Cage, R.A. "The Standard of Living Debate: Glasgow, 1800–1850." *Journal of
  Economic History* 43, 1 (1983): 175–82.

Cage, R.A., ed. *The Working Class in Glasgow, 1750–1914*. Beckenham:
  Croom Helm, 1987.

Cain, Peter J. "Traders versus Railways: The Genesis of the Railway and
  Canal Traffic Act of 1894." *Journal of Transport History* 2, 2 (1973): 65–84.

- "Economics and Empire: The Metropolitan Context." In *The Oxford
  History of the British Empire*. Vol. 3: *The Nineteenth Century*, edited by
  Andrew Porter, 31–52. Oxford: Oxford University Press, 1999.

Cain, Peter J., and Anthony G. Hopkins. *British Imperialism, 1688–2000*.
  London: Longman, 2002.

Castel, Robert. *Les métamorphoses de la question sociale: Une chronique du
  salariat*. Paris: Gallimard, 1995.

Chaloner, William Henry. "Trends in Fish Consumption." In *Our Changing
  Fare: Two Hundred Years of British Food Habits*, edited by Theodore C.
  Barker, John C. McKenzie, and John Yudkin, 94–114. London:
  MacGibbon and Kee, 1966.

Channon, Geoffrey. "The Aberdeenshire Beef Trade with London: A Study
  in Steamship and Railway Competition, 1850–69." *Journal of Transport
  History* 2, 1 (1969): 1–24.

Chesney, Kellow. *The Victorian Underworld*. London: Maurice Temple Smith,
  1970.

Clapham, J.H. *An Economic History of Modern Britain.* Vol. 1: *The Railway Age*. Cambridge: Cambridge University Press, 1926.

Clarke, David B., and Martin Purvis. "Dialectics, Difference, and the Geographies of Consumption." *Environment and Planning A* 26 (1994): 1091–109.

Cliff, Tony. *Class Struggle and Women's Liberation, 1840 to the Present Day*. London: Bookmarks, 1984.

Cloete, J. G. "The Boy and His Work." In *Studies of Boy Life in Our Cities*, edited by E.J. Urwick, 102–38. London: J.M. Dent, 1904.

Clopper, Edward N. *Child Labor in City Streets*. New York: Macmillan, 1913.

Coe, Neil M., and Martin Hess. "The Internationalization of Retailing: Implications for Supply Network Restructuring in East Asia and Eastern Europe." *Journal of Economic Geography* 5, 4 (2005): 449–73.

Coe, Neil M., and Neil Wrigley, eds. *Globalization of Retailing*, 2 vols. Cheltenham: Edward Elgar, 2009.

Cole, George Douglas Howard. *A Century of Co-operation*. London: Allen and Unwin, 1945.

Colpi, Terri. *The Italian Factor: The Italian Community in Great Britain*. Edinburgh: Mainstream, 1991.

Co-operative Union. *General Co-operative Survey*. Manchester: Co-operative Union, 1919.

Co-operative Wholesale Society (CWS). *Annual*. Manchester: Co-operative Wholesale Society, 1918.

Cox, Pamela, and Annabel Hobley. *Shopgirls: The True Story of Life behind the Counter*. London: Hutchinson, 2014.

Critchell, James Troubridge, and Joseph Raymond. *A History of the Frozen Meat Trade: An Account of the Development and Present Day Methods of Preparation, Transportation, and Marketing of Frozen and Chilled Meats*. London: Constable and Company, 1912.

Cross, Gary. *A Quest for Time: The Reduction of Work in Britain and France, 1840–1940*. Berkeley: University of California Press, 1989.

Crossick, Geoffrey. "The Petite Bourgeoisie in Nineteenth-Century Britain: The Urban and Liberal Case." In *Shopkeepers and Master Artisans in Nineteenth-Century Europe*, edited by Geoffrey Crossick and Heinz-Gerhard Haupt, 62–94. London: Methuen, 1984.

– "Shopkeepers and the State in Britain, 1870–1914." In *Shopkeepers and Master Artisans in Nineteenth-Century Europe*, edited by Geoffrey Crossick and Heinz-Gerhard Haupt, 239–69. London: Methuen, 1984.

Crossick, Geoffrey, and Heinz-Gerhard Haupt, edited by *Shopkeepers and Master Artisans in Nineteenth-Century Europe*. London: Methuen, 1984.

Crouzet, François. "Trade and Empire: The British Experience from the Establishment of Free Trade until the First World War." In *Great Britain and Her World: Essays in Honour of W.H. Henderson*, edited by Barrie M. Ratcliffe, 290–35. Manchester: Manchester University Press, 1975.

Cunningham, Peter. *London in 1857*. London: John Murray, 1857.

Dale, Mrs Hylton. *Child Labour under Capitalism*. Fabian Tract No. 140. London: The Fabian Society, 1908.

Davies, Andrew. "Saturday Night Markets in Manchester and Salford, 1840–1939." *Manchester Region History Review* 1, 2 (1987): 3–12.

– *Leisure, Gender and Poverty: Working-Class Culture in Salford and Manchester, 1900–1939*. Buckingham: Open University Press, 1992.

Davies, Margaret Llewelyn, edited by *Life as We Have Known It*. London: W.W. Norton, 1975.

Davies, Thomas. *Essay on the Evils Which are Produced by Late hours of Business*. London: James Nisbet, 1843.

Davies, William Henry. *The Autobiography of a Super-Tramp*. Cardigan: Parthian, 2013.

Davis, Dorothy. *A History of Shopping*. London: Routledge and Kegan Paul, 1966.

Davis, Mike. *Late Victorian Holocausts: El Niño Famines and the Making of the Third World*. London: Verso, 2001.

Davis, Ralph. *The Industrial Revolution and British Overseas Trade*. Leicester: Leicester University Press, 1979.

Daunton, Martin J. *House and Home in the Victorian City: Working-Class Housing, 1850–1914*. London: Arnold, 1983.

Daunton, Martin, edited by *The Cambridge Urban History of Britain*. Vol. 3: *1840–1950*. Cambridge: Cambridge University Press, 2000.

Deane, Phyllis, and W.A. Cole. *British Economic Growth, 1688–1959: Trends and Structure*. Cambridge: Cambridge University Press, 1967.

de Felice, Paul. "Reconstructing Manchester's Little Italy." *Manchester Region History Review* 5 (1997): 54–65.

de la Mare, Ursula. "Necessity and Rage: The Factory Women's Strikes in Bermondsey, 1911." *History Workshop Journal* 66, 1 (2008): 62–80.

Deloitte. "Global Powers of Retailing 2018: Transformative Change, Reinvigorated Commerce." 2018. https://www2.deloitte.com/content/dam/Deloitte/global/Documents/consumer-industrial-products/cip-2018-global-powers-retailing.pdf.

Dendy, Helen. "The Industrial Residuum." *Economic Journal* 3, 12 (1893): 600–16.

Dickens Jr., Charles. *Dickens's dictionary of London, 1879.* London: Charles Dickens, 1882.

Dingle, Anthony E. "Drink and Working-Class Living Standards in Britain, 1870–1914." In *The Making of the Modern British Diet*, edited by Derek J. Oddy and Derek S. Miller, 117–34. London: Croom Helm, 1976.

Dodd, F. Lawson. *Municipal Milk and Public Health.* Fabian Tract No. 122. London: The Fabian Society, 1905.

Dodd, George. *The Food of London.* London: Longman, Brown, Green, and Longmans, 1856.

Dodd, William. *The Laboring Classes of England.* Boston: John Putnam, 1848.

Drake, Barbara. *Women in Trade Unions.* London: Labour Research Department and George Allen and Unwin, 1920.

Drummond, Jack C., and Anne Wilbraham, *The Englishman's Food: Five Centuries of English Diet.* London: Pimlico, 1991.

Dudfield, Reginald. "The Milk Supply of the Metropolis." *Public Health* 16 (1904): 345–54.

Duncan, R. "The Demand for Frozen Beef in the United Kingdom, 1880–1940." *Journal of Agricultural Economics* 12, 1 (1956): 82–8.

Dunlop, James Craufurd. "Occupation Mortalities." *Transactions of the Faculty of Actuaries* 5, 45 (1909–11): 1–86.

Easterlin, Richard. *The Reluctant Economist: Perspectives on Economics, Economic History, and Demography.* Cambridge: Cambridge University Press, 2004.

Economic Research Service. "Retail Trends." United States Department of Agriculture, 2016. http://www.ers.usda.gov/topics/food-markets-prices/retailing-wholesaling/retail-trends.aspx.

The *Economist.* "Malthusian Mouthfuls." 2010. https://www.economist.com/blogs/dailychart/2010/11/economist_food-price_index.

Edwards, Clement, Constance Cochrane, Edward Bowmaker, R.C. Phillimore, W. Thompson, H.C. Lander, F. Lawson Dodd, and Sidney Webb. *The House Famine and How to Relieve It.* Fabian Tract No. 101. London: The Fabian Society, 1900.

European Commission. "The Economic Impact of Modern Retail on Choice and Innovation in the EU Food Sector, Final Report." Luxembourg: Publications Office of the European Union 2014. http://ec.europa.eu/competition/publications/KD0214955ENN.pdf.

Evans, George Ewart. *From Mouths of Men.* London: Faber and Faber, 1976.

Feinstein, Charles. "New Estimates of Average Earnings in the United Kingdom, 1880–1913." *Economic History Review* 43, 4 (1990): 595–632.

– "A New Look at the Cost of Living, 1870–1914." In *New Perspectives on the*

Late Victorian Economy: Essays in Quantitative Economic History, 1860–1914, edited by James Foreman-Peck, 151–79. Cambridge: Cambridge University Press, 1991.

– "Pessimism Perpetuated: Real Wages and the Standard of Living in Britain during and after the Industrial Revolution." *Journal of Economic History* 58, 3 (1998): 625–58.

Fleischman, Richard K. *Conditions of Life among the Cotton Workers of Southeastern Lancashire, 1780–1850*. New York: Garland, 1985.

Floud, Roderick. *The People and the British Economy, 1830–1914*. Oxford: Oxford University Press, 2003.

Floud, Roderick, Kenneth Wachter, and Annabel Gregory. *Height, Health and History: Nutritional Status in the United Kingdom, 1750–1980*. Cambridge: Cambridge University Press, 1990.

Flower, Edward. *Hours of Business: A Glance at the Present System of Business Among Shopkeepers, and the Effect of that System Upon the Young Men Engaged in Retail Trades, as Well as Upon Society at Large*. Liverpool: Smith, Rogerson and Co., 1843.

Foley, Alice. *A Bolton Childhood*. Bolton: Workers' Educational Association Bolton Branch, 1990.

Folio, Felix. *The Hawkers and Street Dealers of the North of England Manufacturing Districts*. Manchester: Abel Heywood, 1859.

Ford, P. "Excessive Competition in the Retail Trades: Changes in the Numbers of Shops, 1901–1931." *Economic Journal* 45, 179 (1935): 501–8.

– "Decentralisation and Changes in the Number of Shops, 1901–1931." *Economic Journal* 46, 182 (1936): 359–63.

Ford, P., and G.V. White. "Trends in Retail Distribution in Yorkshire (West Riding), 1901–1927." *Manchester School* 7, 2 (1936): 119–25.

Forshaw, Alec, and Theo Bergström. *Smithfield: Past and Present*. London: Robert Hale, 1990.

Foster, John Bellamy. *Marx's Ecology: Materialism and Nature*. New York: Monthly Review Press, 2000.

FranceAgriMer. "La dépense alimentaire des ménages français résiste à la crise." FranceAgriMer 2014: http://www.franceagrimer.fr/content/down load/33722/305888/file/A4-Les%20d%C3%A9penses%20alimentaire %20des%20m%C3%A9nage%20fran%C3%A7ais.pdf.

Fraser, W. Hamish. *The Coming of the Mass Market, 1850–1914*. London: Macmillan, 1981.

Fream, George Goodsir, R. Henry Row, H. Llewellyn Smith, W. Somerville, and G. Udny Yule. "Production and Consumption of Meat and Milk, Second Report from the Committee Appointed to Inquire into the Statistics Available as a Basis for Estimating the Production and Consumption of Meat and Milk in the United Kingdom." *Journal of the Royal Statistical Society* 67, 3 (1904): 368–84.

– "Production and Consumption of Meat and Milk, Third Report." *Journal of the Royal Statistical Society* 67, 3 (1904): 385–93.

Freeman, Michael. *Railways and the Victorian Imagination*. New Haven, CT: Yale University Press, 1999.

French, Michael, and Jim Phillips. *Cheated Not Poisoned? Food Regulation in the United Kingdom, 1875–1938*. Manchester: Manchester University Press, 2009.

Friedmann, Harriett. "World Market, State and Family Farm: Social Bases of Household Production in the Era of Wage Labor." *Comparative Studies in Society and History* 20, 4 (1978): 545–86.

Friedmann, Harriet, and Philip McMichael. "Agriculture and the State System: The Rise and Decline of National Agricultures, 1870 to the Present." *Sociologia Ruralis* 29, 2 (1989): 93–117.

Gallagher, John, and Ronald Robinson. "The Imperialism of Free Trade." *Economic History Review* 6, 1 (1953): 1–15.

Gauldie, Enid. *Cruel Habitations: A History of Working-Class Housing, 1780–1918*. London: Allen and Unwin, 1974.

Gibb, Spencer J. "Boy Labour: Some Studies in Detail." In *Problems of Boy Life*, edited by John Howard Whitehouse, 52–78. London: P.S. King and Son, 1912.

Gide, Charles. *Consumers Co-operative Societies*. New York: Alfred A. Knopf, 1922.

Giffen, Robert. "On the Fall of Prices of Commodities in Recent Years." *Journal of the Statistical Society of London* 42, 1 (1879): 36–78.

Goetzmann, W.N., and A.D. Ukhov. "British Investment Overseas, 1870–1913: A Modern Portfolio Theory Approach." Working Paper No. 11266. Cambridge, MA: National Bureau of Economic Research. http://scholarship.sha.cornell.edu/articles/369.

Gordon, Jackson. *The History and Archaeology of Ports*. Tadworth, Surrey: World's Work, 1983.

Gourvish, Terence R. *Railways and the British Economy, 1830–1914*. London: Macmillan, 1989.

Graham, Gerald S. "The Ascendency of the Sailing Ship, 1850–85." *Economic History Review* 9, 1 (1956): 74–88.

Greenhow, E. Headlam. "Report on Murrain in Horned Cattle, the Public Sale of Diseases Animals, and the Effects of the Consumption of their Flesh on Human Health." In *BPP* XX (1857).

Greenwood, Arthur. "Blind-Alley Labour." *Economic Journal* 22, 86 (1912): 309–14.

Greenwood, James. "Food Committee." *Journal of the Society of Arts* 16, 788 (1867): 91–5.

– *The Seven Curses of London.* London: Stanley Rivers and Co., 1869.

– *In Strange Company: Being the Experiences of a Roving Correspondent.* London: Vizetelly & Co., 1883.

Greig, Mrs David. *My Life and Times: Being the Personal Reminiscences of Mrs David Greig.* Bungay: Richard Clay, 1939.

Grey, E.C. "Covent Garden Market." In *Labour and Life of the People*, vol. 2, edited by Charles Booth, 322–34. London: Williams and Norgate, 1891.

Grindrod, Ralph Barnes. *The Wrongs of our Youth; An Essay on the Evils of the Late-Hour System.* London: William Brittain and Charles Gilpin, 1843.

GTAI. "The Food and Beverage Industry in Germany." Germany Trade and Investment 2016–17. http://www.gtai.de/GTAI/Content/EN/Invest/_SharedDocs/Downloads/GTAI/Industry-overviews/industry-overview-food-beverage-industry-en.pdf.

Gurney, Peter. *Co-operative Culture and the Politics of Consumption in England, 1870–1930.* Manchester: Manchester University Press, 1996.

– "Labor's Great Arch: Cooperation and Culture Revolution in Britain, 1795–1926." In *Consumers against Capitalism? Consumer Cooperation in Europe, North America, and Japan, 1840-1990*, edited by Ellen Furlough and Clark Strikwerda, 135–71. Lanham, MD: Rowman and Littlefield, 1999.

Habib, Irfan. "Studying a Colonial Economy – Without Perceiving Colonialism." *Modern Asian Studies* 19, 3 (1985): 355–81.

Haines, Michael. "Inequality and Childhood Mortality: A Comparison of England and Wales, 1911, and the United States, 1900." *Journal of Economic History* 45, 4 (1985): 885–912.

– "Growing Incomes, Shrinking People – Can Economic Development Be Hazardous to Your Health?" *Social Science History* 28, 2 (2004): 249–70.

Hall, Alfred Daniel. *Agriculture after the War.* London: Murray, 1916.

Hall, Catherine. "The Butcher, the Baker, the Candlestickmaker: The Shop and Family in the Industrial Revolution." In *The Victorian City: A Reader in British Urban History, 1820–1914*, edited by Robert John Morris and Richard Rodger, 307–21. London: Longman, 1993.

Hallsworth, Joseph, and Rhys T. Davies, *The Working Life of Shop Assistants: A Study of Conditions of Labour in the Distributive Trades*. Manchester: Published by the Authors, 1910.

Hammond, John L. "The Industrial Revolution and Discontent." *Economic History Review* 2, 2 (1930): 215–28.

Hardy, Harold. "Costers and Street Sellers." In *Life and Labour of the People in London*. Vol. 7: *Population Classified by Trades*, edited by Charles Booth, 259–71. London: Macmillan, 1896.

Harris, John Raymond. *Liverpool and the Merseyside: Essays in the Economic and Social History of the Port and Its Hinterland.* London: Routledge, 1968.

Harrison, John F.C. *Robert Owen and the Owenites in Britain and America: The Quest for the New Moral World*. London: Routledge and Kegan Paul, 1969.

Harrods Ltd. *A Story of British Achievement, 1849–1949*. London: Harrods, 1949.

Harvey, David. *The Limits to Capital*. London: Verso, 2006.

Hassall, Arthur Hill. *Food and Its Adulterations*. London: Longman, Brown, Green and Longmans, 1855.

– "Adulteration, and Its Remedy." *Cornhill Magazine* 2, 1 (1860): 86–96.

Hawke, G.R., and M.C. Reed. "Railway Capital in the United Kingdom in the Nineteenth Century." *Economic History Review* 22, 2 (1969): 269–86.

Headrick, Daniel R. *The Tools of Empire: Technology and European Imperialism in the Nineteenth Century*. New York: Oxford University Press, 1981.

Hindley, Charles, edited by *The Life and Adventures of A Cheap Jack*. London: Tinsley Brothers, 1876.

Hird, Joseph H. *Mirfield: Life in a West Riding Village, 1900–1914*. Huddersfield: Kirklees Metropolitan Council, 1984.

Hobsbawm, Eric J. "The British Standard of Living, 1790–1850." *Economic History Review* 10, 1 (1957): 46–68.

– "The Standard of Living during the Industrial Revolution: A Discussion." *Economic History Review* 16, 1 (1963): 119–34.

– *The Age of Capital, 1848–1875*. London: Abacus, 2009.

– *Industry and Empire: The Birth of the Industrial Revolution*. New York: The New Press, 1999.

Hodson, Deborah. "'The Municipal Store': Adaptation and Development in the Retail Markets of Nineteenth-Century Urban Lancashire." *Business History* 40, 4 (1998): 94–114.

– "Civic Identity, Custom and Commerce: Victorian Market Halls in the Manchester Region," *Manchester Region History Review* 12 (1998): 34–43.

Hoffman, Philip C. *They Also Serve: The Story of the Shop Worker*. London: Porcupine Press, 1949.

Holderness, B.A. "Prices, Productivity, and Output." In *The Agrarian History of England and Wales, Volume VI: 1750-1850*, edited by G.E. Mingay, 84–189. Cambridge: Cambridge University Press, 1989.

Holland, Rev H.W. "The Lowest Classes in Large Towns." *Wesleyan Methodist Magazine* 8 (1884): 123–31.

Hollingshead, John. *Ragged London in 1861*. London: Smith, Elder and Co., 1861.

Holyoake, George Jacob. *The History of Co-operation in England: Its Literature and its Advocate*. Vol. 1: *The Pioneer Period. 1812 to 1844*. London: Trübner & Co., 1875.

– *The History of Co-operation in England: Its Literature and its Advocates*. Vol. 2: *The Constructive Period*, 1845 to 1878. London: Trübner & Co., 1885.

Honiborne, Thomas. *A Word for Early Closing: Embracing a View of the Evils Connected with the Late Hour System of Business*. London: David Bicknell, 1843.

Hooker, R.H. "The Meat Supply of the United Kingdom." *Journal of the Royal Statistical Society* 72, 2 (1909): 304–86.

Horn, Pamela. *Behind the Counter: Shop Lives from Market Stall to Supermarket*. Stroud: Sutton Publishing, 2006.

– *The Victorian Town Child*. Stroud: Sutton Publishing, 1997.

Hosgood, Christopher P. "The 'Pigmies of Commerce' and the Working-Class Community: Small Shopkeepers in England, 1870–1914." *Journal of Social History* 22, 3 (1989): 439–60.

– "A 'Brave and Daring Folk'? Shopkeepers and Trade Associational Life in Victorian and Edwardian England." *Journal of Social History* 26, 2 (1992): 285–308.

– "'Mercantile Monasteries': Shops, Shop Assistants, and Shop Life in Late-Victorian and Edwardian Britain." *Journal of British Studies* 38, 3 (1999): 322–52.

Howarth, Edward G., and Mona Wilson. *West Ham: A Study in Social and Industrial Problems*. London: J.M. Dent and Co., 1907.

Huck, Paul. "Infant Mortality and Living Standards of English Workers during the Industrial Revolution." *Journal of Economic History* 55, 3 (1995): 528–50.

Hurd, John. "Railways." In *Cambridge Economic History of India*, vol. 2, edited by Dharma Kumar. Cambridge: Cambridge University Press, 1983.

Hyde, Francis Edwin. *Liverpool and the Mersey: An Economic History of a Port, 1700–1970*. Newton Abbott: David and Charles, 1971.

Jackson, Edward. *A Study in Democracy: Being an Account of the Rise and Progress of Industrial Co-operation in Bristol.* Manchester: Co-operative Wholesale Society's Printing Works, 1911.

Jankiewicz, Stephen. "A Dangerous Class: The Street Sellers of Nineteenth-Century London." *Journal of Social History: Societies and Cultures* 46, 2 (2012): 391–415.

Jarvis, Adrian. *The Liverpool Dock Engineers.* Stroud: Alan Sutton, 1996.

Jarvis, Adrian, ed. *Port and Harbour Engineering.* Farnham: Ashgate, 1998.

Jayaraman, Saru. *Behind the Kitchen Door.* Ithaca, NY: Cornell University Press.

Jefferys, James B. *Retail Trading in Britain, 1850–1950: A Study of Trends in Retailing with Special Reference to the Development of Co-Operative, Multiple Shop and Department Store Methods of Trading.* Cambridge: Cambridge University Press, 1954.

Jennings, H. Lincoln. "The Co-operative Wholesale Society Ltd." *Annals of Public and Cooperative Economics* 20, 1 (1949): 25–43.

Johnson, Paul, and Stephen Nicholas. "Male and Female Living Standards in England and Wales, 1812-1857: Evidence from Criminal Height Records." *Economic History Review* 48, 3 (1995): 470–81.

Johnson, Samuel. *Johnson's Dictionary.* Boston, MA: Charles J. Hendee, 1836.

Johnson, Samuel, and John Walker. *Dictionary of the English Language.* London: William Pickering, 1828.

Johnson, William. *Shop Life and Its Reform.* Fabian Tract No. 80. London: The Fabian Society, 1897.

Johnston, James P. *A Hundred Years Eating: Food, Drink and the Daily Diet in Britain since the late Nineteenth Century.* Montreal and Kingston: McGill-Queen's University Press, 1977.

Jones, Ronald. "Consumers' Co-operation in Victorian Edinburgh: The Evolution of a Location Pattern." *Transactions of the Institute of British Geographers* 4, 2 (1979): 292–305.

Kelley, Victoria. "The Streets for the People: London's Street Markets, 1850–1939." *Urban History* 43, 3 (2016): 391–411.

King, Arthur J. *The System of Late Hours in Business: Its Evils, Its Causes, and Its Cure.* London: William Aylott, 1843.

Kinloch, James, and John Butt. *History of the Scottish Co-operative Wholesale Society Limited.* Glasgow: Co-operative Wholesale Society, 1981.

Komlos, John. "The Secular Trend in the Biological Standard of Living in the United Kingdom, 1730–1860." *Economic History Review* 46, 1 (1993): 115–44.

Landels, Rev. William. *English Slavery and Early Closing*. London: s.n., 1856.

Lardner, Dionysius. *Railway Economy: A Treatise on the New Art of Transport*. London: Taylor, Walton, and Maberly, 1850.

Leng, Philip J. *The Welsh Dockers*. Ormskirk: G.W. and A. Hesketh, 1981.

Lilwall, John. *The Half-Holiday Questions*. London: Kent, 1856.

London, Jack. *The People of the Abyss*. London: Pluto Press, 2001.

MacInnes, Tom, Hannah Aldridge, Sabrina Bushe, Peter Kenway, and Adam Tinson. "Monitoring Poverty and Social Exclusion 2013." Joseph Rowntree Foundation, 2013. https://www.jrf.org.uk/report/monitoring-poverty-and-social-exclusion-2013.

MacRaild, Donald M. *Irish Migrants in Modern Britain, 1750–1922*. Houndmills: Palgrave, 1999.

Macrosty, Henry W. *The Trust Movement in British Industry: A Study of Business Organisation*. Kitchener: Batoche Books, 2001.

Malvery, Olive Christian. *The Soul Market*. London: Hutchinson and Co., 1907.

Manby, E.F. "Cultivation of Early Potatoes" *Journal of the Royal Agricultural Society of England* 18 (1857): 98–111.

Marlowe, Christopher. *The Works of Christopher Marlowe*, vol. 2. London: William Pickering, 1826.

Marr, T. R. *Housing Conditions in Manchester and Salford*. Manchester: Sherratt and Hughes, 1904.

Marsh, Myra. "Shopping in Denton in the Early Years of the Twentieth Century." In *Looking Back at Denton*, edited by Alice Lock, 70–82. Ashton: Libraries and Arts Committee, 1985.

Marx, Karl. "Inaugural Address and Provisional Rules of the International Working Men's Association". London, 1864. http://www.marxists.org/archive/marx/works/1864/10/27.htm.

Mason, Tony. *Association Football and English Society, 1863–1915*. Atlantic Highlands, NJ: Humanities Press, 1980.

Mathias, Peter. *Retailing Revolution: A History of Multiple Retailing in the Food Trades Based upon the Allied Suppliers Group of Companies*. London: Longmans, Green and Co., 1967

Mayhew, Henry. *London Labour and the London Poor*, vol. 1. London: Griffin, Bohn & Co., 1861.

– *London characters: Illustrations of the humour, pathos, and peculiarities of London life*. London: Chatto and Windus, 1881.

McCleary, George F. *The Municipalization of the Milk Supply*. Fabian Tract No. 90. London: The Fabian Society, 1899

– *Municipal Bakehouses*. Fabian Tract No. 94. London: The Fabian Society, 1900.

McIvor, Arthur. *A History of Work in Britain, 1880–1950*. London: Palgrave, 2001.

McMichael, Philip. *Settlers and the Agrarian Question: Foundations of Capitalism in Colonial Australia*. Cambridge: Cambridge University Press, 1984.

– "A Food Regime Genealogy." *Journal of Peasant Studies* 36, 1 (2009): 139–69.

– *Food Regimes and Agrarian Questions*. Halifax: Fernwood, 2013.

McNally, David. *Bodies of Meaning: Studies on Language, Labor, and Liberation*. New York: State University of New York Press, 2001.

McNamee, Betty. "Trends in Meat Consumption." In *Our Changing Fare: Two Hundred Years of British Food Habits*, edited by Theodore C. Barker, John C. McKenzie, and John Yudkin, 77–93. London: MacGibbon and Kee, 1966.

Metcalfe, Robyn S. *Meat, Commerce and the City: The London Food Market, 1800–1855*. London: Pickering and Chatto, 2012.

Millward, Robert and Frances Bell. "Infant Mortality in Victorian Britain: The Mother as Medium." *Economic History Review* 54, 4 (2001): 699–733.

Mintz, Sidney. *Sweetness and Power: The Place of Sugar in Modern History*. London: Penguin, 1986.

Mitchell, Brian R. *British Historical Statistics*. Cambridge: Cambridge University Press, 1990.

Mitchell, Ian. *Tradition and Innovation in English Retailing, 1700 to 1850: Narratives of Consumption*. Farnham: Ashgate, 2014.

– "Retail Markets in Northern and Midland England, 1870–1914: Civic Icon, Municipal White Elephant, or Consumer Paradise?" *Economic History Review* (forthcoming).

Mitchell, John. *Treatise of the Falsifications of Food, and the Chemical Means Employed to Detect Them*. London, Hippolyte Bailliere, 1848.

Mokyr, Joel. "Has the Industrial Revolution Been Crowded Out? Some Reflections on Crafts and Williamson." *Explorations in Economic History* 24, 3 (1987): 293–319.

– "Is There Still Life in the Pessimist Case? Consumption during the Industrial Revolution, 1790–1850." *Journal of Economic History* 48, 1 (1988): 69–92.

Molesworth, W.N. "On the Extent and Results of Co-operative Trading Associations at Rochdale." *Journal of the Statistical Society of London* 24, 4 (1861): 507–14.

Moore, Jason W. "Environmental Crises and the Metabolic Rift in World-Historical Perspectives." *Organization and Environment* 13, 2 (2000): 123–57.

- "Transcending the Metabolic Rift." *Journal of Peasant Studies* 38, 1 (2011): 1–46.
- *Capitalism in the Web of Life: Ecology and the Accumulation of Capital.* London: Verso, 2015.
Mui, Hoh-Cheung, and Lorna H. Mui. *Shops and Shopkeeping in Eighteenth-Century England.* Montreal and Kingston: McGill-Queen's University Press, 1989.
Naoroji, Dadabhai. *Poverty and Un-British Rule in India.* London: Swan Sonnenschein and Co., 1901.
Neale, R.S. "The Standard of Living, 1780-1844: a Regional and Class Study." *Economic History Review* 19, 3 (1966): 590–606.
- *Bath: A Social History 1680-1850, or A Valley of Pleasure, Yet a Sink of Iniquity.* London: Routledge and Kegan Paul, 1981.
Neale, W.G. *At the Port of Bristol*, vols. 1 and 2. Bristol: The Port of Bristol Authority, 1970.
Nelson, Michael. "Social-Class Trends in British Diet, 1860–1980." In *Food, Diet and Economic Change Past and Present*, edited by Catherine Geissler and Derek J. Oddy, 101–20. Leicester: Leicester University Press, 1993.
Nicholas, Stephen, and Deborah Oxley. "The Living Standards of Women during the Industrial Revolution, 1795–1820." *Economic History Review* 46, 4 (1993): 723–49.
Nicholas, Stephen, and Richard H. Steckel. "Heights and Living Standards of English Workers during the Early Years of Industrialization, 1770–1815." *Journal of Economic History* 51, 4 (1991): 937–57.
Norwood, John. *Victorian and Edwardian Hampshire and the Isle of Wight from Old Photographs.* London: Batsford, 1973.
Oddy, Derek J. "Working-Class Diets in Late Nineteenth-Century Britain." *Economic History Review* 23, 2 (1970): 314–23.
- "The Health of the People." In *Population and Society in Britain, 1850–1980*, edited by Theo Barker and Michael Drake, 121–9. New York: New York University Press, 1982.
- "Food, Drink and Nutrition." In *The Cambridge Social History of Britain, 1750-1950*, vol. 2, edited by Francis M. L. Thompson, 251–78. Cambridge: Cambridge University Press, 1990.
- *From Plain Fare to Fusion Food: British Diet from the 1890s to the 1990s.* Woodbridge: Boydell Press, 2003.
Office for National Statistics. "Consumer Trends Statistical Bulletin." http://www.ons.gov.uk/ons/rel/consumer-trends/consumer-trends /index.html.
Office of Consumer Affairs. "Canada's Changing Retail Market." Industry

Canada, 2013. https://www.ic.gc.ca/eic/site/oca-bc.nsf/vwapj/CTU-2013
_Q2_Canadas_Changing_Retail_Market-eng.pdf/$file/CTU-2013_Q2_
Canadas_Changing_Retail_Market-eng.pdf.

Ogle, William. "Supplement to the forty-fifth annual report of the Registrar-General of Births, Deaths, and Marriages in England." In *BPP* XVII:iii-lxiv, 1884–85.

Osborne, Harvey, and Michael Winstanley. "Rural and Urban Poaching in Victorian England." *Rural History* 17, 2 (2006): 187–212.

Ó Tuathaigh, M.A. Gearóid. "The Irish in Nineteenth-Century Britain: Problems of Integration." In *The Irish in the Victorian City,* edited by Roger Swift and Sheridan Gilley, 13–36. London: Croom Helm, 1985.

Page, John. "The Sources of Supply of the Manchester Fruit and Vegetable Markets." *Journal of the Royal Agricultural Society of England* 16 (1880): 475–85.

Paine, William. *Shop Slavery and Emancipation: A Revolutionary Appeal to the Educated Young Mend of the Middle Class.* London: P.S. King and Son, 1912.

Paish, George. "Great Britain's Capital Investments in Individual Colonial and Foreign Countries." *Journal of the Royal Statistical Society* 74, 2 (1911): 167–200.

Pember Reeves, Maud. *Round about a Pound a Week.* London: G. Bell and Sons, 1914.

Penn, Margaret. *Manchester Fourteen Miles.* Cambridge: Cambridge University Press, 1947.

Pennybacker, Susan D. *A Vision for London, 1889-1914: Labour, Everyday Life and the LCC Experiment.* London: Routledge, 1995.

Perren, Richard. "The Meat and Livestock Trade in Britain, 1850–70." *Economic History Review* 28, 3 (1975): 385–400.

– *The Meat Trade in Britain, 1840–1914.* London: Routledge and Kegan Paul, 1978.

– "Structural Change and Market Growth in the Food Industry: Flour Milling in Britain, Europe, and America, 1850–1914." *Economic History Review* 43, 3 (1990): 420–37.

– *Agriculture in Depression, 1870–1940.* Cambridge: Cambridge University Press, 1995.

– *Taste, Trade and Technology: The Development of the International Meat Industry since 1840.* Farnham: Ashgate, 2006.

Phillips, Martin. "The Evolution of Markets and Shops in Britain." In *The Evolution of Retail Systems, c. 1800–1914,* edited by John Benson and Gareth Shaw, 53–75. Leicester: Leicester University Press, 1992.

Philp, Robert Kemp. *The Shopkeeper's Guide*. London: Houlston and Stoneman, 1853.

Polanyi, Karl. *The Great Transformation: The Political and Economic Origins of Our Time*. Boston, MA: Beacon Press, 2001.

Pollard, Sidney. "Nineteenth-Century Co-operation: From Community Building to Shopkeeping." In *Essays in Labour History*, edited by Asa Briggs and John Saville, 74–112. London: Macmillan, 1960.

Pollen, Arthur. "The Food Problem of Great Britain: The Shipping Problem of the World." *Annals of the American Academy of Political and Social Science* 74 (1917): 91–4.

Poole, Braithwaite. *Statistics of British Commerce*. London: W.H. Smith & Son, 1852.

Potter, Beatrice. *The Co-operative Movement in Great Britain*. London: Swan Sonnenschein, 1891.

Poyntz, Juliet Stuart. "Introduction: Seasonal Trades." In *Seasonal Trades*, edited by Sidney Webb and Arnold Freeman, 1–69. London: Constable and Co., 1912.

Pudney, John. *London's Docks*. London: Thames and Hudson, 1975.

Purvis, Martin. "The Development of Co-operative Retailing in England and Wales, 1851–1901: A Geographical Study." *Journal of Historical Geography* 16, 3 (1990): 314–31.

– "Co-operative Retailing in Britain." In *The Evolution of Retail Systems, c. 1800–1914*, edited by John Benson and Gareth Shaw, 107–34. Leicester: Leicester University Press, 1992.

– "Societies of Consumers and Consumer Societies: Co-operation, Consumption and Politics in Britain and Continental Europe, c. 1850–1920." *Journal of Historical Geography* 24, 2 (1998): 147–69.

– "Stocking the Store: Co-operative Retailers in North-East England and Systems of Wholesale Supply, circa 1860–77." *Business History* 40, 4 (1998): 55–78.

Redfern, Percy. *The Story of the CWS, 1863–1913*. Manchester: The Co-operative Wholesale Society, 1913.

Rees, Goronwy. *St Michael: A History of Marks and Spencer*. London: Pan Books, 1973.

Rees, Joseph Aubrey. *The Grocery Trade: Its History and Romance*, 2 vols. London: Duckworth, 1910.

Rew, R. Henry. "An Inquiry into the Statistics of the Production and Consumption of Milk and Milk Products in Great Britain." *Journal of the Royal Statistical Society* 55, 2 (1892): 244–86.

Richardson, William. *A Union of Many Trades: The History of* USDAW. Manchester: USDAW, 1979.

Riggs, Paul. "The Standard of Living in Scotland, 1800–1850." In *Stature, Living Standards and Economic Development: Essays in Anthropometric History*, edited by John Komlos, 60–75. Chicago: Chicago University Press, 1995.

Rioux, Sébastien. "Food Quality and the Circulation Time of Commodities: Lessons from the British Milk Trade ,1845-1914." *Journal of Transport Geography* 38 (2014): 114–21.

– "Capitalism and the Production of Uneven Bodies: Women, Motherhood and Food Distribution in Britain, c.1850–1914." *Transactions of the Institute of British Geographers* 40, 1 (2015): 1–13.

– "Rethinking Food Regime Analysis: An Essay on the Temporal, Spatial and Scalar Dimensions of the First Food Regime." *Journal of Peasant Studies* 45, 4 (2018): 715–38.

– "Capitalist Food Production and the Rise of Legal Adulteration: Regulating Food Standards in 19th-Century Britain." *Journal of Agrarian Change* 19, 1 (2019): 64–81.

Ritchie-Noakes, Nancy. *Liverpool's Historic Waterfront: The World's First Mercantile Dock System*. London: HMSO, 1984.

Roberts, Elizabeth. *A Woman's Place: An Oral History of Working-Class Women, 1890–1940*. Oxford: Wiley-Blackwell, 1995.

Roberts, Robert. *The Classic Slum: Salford Life in the First Quarter of the Century*. London: Penguin, 1990.

– *A Ragged Schooling: Growing Up in the Classic Slum*. Manchester: Mandolin, 1997.

Robertson, Nicole. 2010. *The Co-operative Movement and Communities in Britain, 1914–1960*. Farnham: Ashgate, 2010.

Robinson, Robb. *Trawling: The Rise and Fall of the British Trawl Fishery*. Exeter: University of Exeter Press, 1996.

– "The Development of the British Distant-Water Trawling Industry, 1880–1939." In *Exploiting the Sea: Aspects of Britain's Maritime Economy since 1870*, edited by David J. Starkey and Alan G. Jamieson, 148–66. Exeter: University of Exeter Press, 1998.

Rogers, W. "On the trade, habits, and education of the street hawkers of London." *Journal of the Society of Arts* 5, 228 (1857): 298–304.

Romer, Carrol. *The Metropolitan Traffic Manual, containing the Law Relating to Road, River and Air Traffic in London and Elsewhere*. London: His Majesty's Stationery Office, 1922.

Rose, Lionel. *The Erosion of Childhood: Child Oppression in Britain*. London: Routledge, 1991.

Russell, Charles E.B. *Manchester Boys: Sketches of Manchester Lads at Work and Play*. Manchester: Manchester University Press, 1905.

Salt, Samuel. *Facts and Figures, principally relating to Railways and Commerce*. London: Longman, Brown, Green, and Longmans, 1848.

Sanders, Lise Shapiro. *Consuming Fantasies: Labor, Leisure, and the London Shopgirl, 1880–1920*. Columbus: Ohio State University Press, 2006.

Saul, S. B. *Studies in British Overseas Trade, 1870–1914*. Liverpool: Liverpool University Press, 1960.

Schlesinger, Max. *Saunterings in and about London*. London: Nathaniel Cooke, 1853.

Schlote, Werner. *British Overseas Trade: From 1700 to the 1930s*. Oxford: Basil Blackwell, 1952.

Schmiechen, James, and Kenneth Carls. *The British Market Hall: A Social and Architectural History*. New Haven, CT: Yale University Press, 1999.

Schneider, Mindi, and Philip McMichael. "Deepening, and Repairing, the Metabolic Rift." *Journal of Peasant Studies* 37, 3 (2010): 461–84.

Scola, Roger. "Food Markets and Shops in Manchester, 1770–1870." *Journal of Historical Geography* 1, 2 (1975): 153–68.

– "Retailing in the Nineteenth-Century Town: Some Problems and Possibilities." In *The Structure of Nineteenth-Century Cities*, edited by James H. Johnson and Colin G. Pooley, 153–69. London: Croom Helm, 1982.

– *Feeding the Victorian City: The Food Supply of Manchester, 1770–1870*. Manchester: Manchester University Press, 1992.

Scott, Wentworth Lascelles. "On Food: Its Adulterations, and Methods of Detecting Them." *Journal of the Society of Arts* 9, 428 (1861): 153–62.

Shaw, Gareth. "Changes in Consumer Demand and Food Supply in Nineteenth-Century British Cities." *Journal of Historical Geography* 11, 3 (1985): 280–96.

– "The Evolution and Impact of Large-Scale Retailing in Britain." In *The Evolution of Retail Systems, c. 1800–1914*, edited by John Benson and Gareth Shaw, 135–65. Leicester: Leicester University Press, 1992.

Shaw, Gareth, and M. Trevor Wild. "Retail Patterns in the Victorian City." *Transactions of the Institute of British Geographers* 4, 2 (1979): 278–91.

Shaw, Gareth, Andrew Alexander, John Benson, and John Jones. "Structural and Spatial Trends in British Retailing: The Importance of Firm-Level Studies." *Business History* 40, 4 (1998): 79–93.

Sherard, Robert Harborough. *The Child-Slaves of Britain*. London: Hurst and Blackett, 1905.

Sherwell, Arthur. *Life in West London: A Study and a Contrast*. London: Methuen, 1901.

Shesgreen, Sean. *The Criers and Hawkers of London*. London: Scolar Press, 1990.

Sims, George R. "Trips about Town, part 2." *Strand Magazine* 29, 172 (1905): 462–8.

– "Trips About Town, part 3." *Strand Magazine* 29, 173 (1905): 510–16.

Smeeton, William. *The Necessity of Early Closing to Self-Culture*. Leicester: J. Burton, 1855.

Smith, Adam. *The Wealth of Nations*, Books 4–5. London: Penguin, 1999.

Smith, Colin. "The Wholesale and Retail Markets of London, 1660–1840." *Economic History Review* 55, 1 (2002): 31–50.

Smith, Francis B. *The People's Health, 1830–1910*. New York: Holmes and Meier, 1979.

Smith, J.H. "The Cattle Trade of Aberdeenshire in the Nineteenth Century." *Agricultural History Review* 3, 2 (1955): 114–8.

Smith, Neil. *Uneven Development: Nature, Capital, and the Production of Space*. Athens: GA: University of Georgia Press, 2008.

Sponza Lucio. *Italian Immigrants in Nineteenth-Century Britain: Realities and Images*. Leicester: Leicester University Press, 1988.

Steadman, W.C. *Overcrowding in London and Its Remedy*. Fabian Tract No. 103. London: The Fabian Society, 1900.

Stedman Jones, Gareth. *Outcast London: A Study in the Relationship between Classes in Victorian Society*. Oxford: Clarendon Press, 1971.

Stiegert, Kyle W., and Dong Hwan Kim, eds. *Structural Changes in Food Retailing: Six Country Case Studies*. Madison: Food System Research Group, University of Wisconsin-Madison, 2009.

Stobart, Jon. *Spend, Spend, Spend! A History of Shopping*. Stroud: History Press, 2008.

– *Sugar and Spice: Grocers and Groceries in Provincial England, 1650–1830*. Oxford: Oxford University Press, 2013.

Stone, Irving. "British Direct and Portfolio Investment in Latin America Before 1914." *Journal of Economic History* 37, 3 (1977): 690–722.

Sullivan, James William. *Markets for the People: The Consumer's Part*. New York: Macmillan. 1913.

Sussman, Herbert L. *Victorian Technology: Invention, Innovation, and the Rise of the Machine*. Santa Barbara, CA: Praeger, 2009.

Sutherst, Thomas. *Death and Disease behind the Counter*. London: Kegan Paul and Trench, 1884.

Sykes, W.H., Dr Guy, and F.G.P. Neison, "Report on the State of the

Inhabitants and their Dwellings in Church Lane, St. Giles's." *Journal of the Statistical Society of London* 11, 1 (1848): 1–18.

Szreter, Simon, and Graham Mooney. "Urbanization, Mortality, and the Standard of Living Debate: New Estimates of the Expectation of Life at Birth in Nineteenth-Century British Cities." *Economic History Review* 51, 1 (1998): 84–112.

Tabor, Mary C. "Elementary Education." In *Labour and Life of the People*, vol. 2, edited by Charles Booth, 486–526. London: Williams and Norgate, 1891.

Tawney, R.H. "The Economics of Boy Labour." In *Problems of Boy Life*, edited by John Howard Whitehouse, 17–51. London: P.S. King and Son, 1912.

Taylor, David. "London's Milk Supply, 1850–1900: A Reinterpretation." *Agricultural History* 45, 1 (1971): 33–8.

– "Beyond the Bounds of Respectable Society: The 'Dangerous Classes' in Victorian and Edwardian England." In *Criminal Conversations: Victorian Crimes, Social Panic, and Moral Outrage*, edited by Judith Rowbotham and Kim Stevenson, 3–22. Columbus: Ohio State University Press, 2005.

Thomas, John Birch. *Shop Boy: An Autobiography*. London: Routledge and Kegan Paul, 1983.

Thompson, Edward P. *The Making of the English Working Class*. London: Penguin, 1991.

– "The Moral Economy Reviewed." In *Customs in Common: Studies in Traditional Popular Culture*, 259–351. New York: The New Press, 1993.

Thompson, F.M.L. "The Second Agricultural Revolution, 1815–1880." *Economic History Review* 21, 1 (1968): 62–77.

Thomson, J., and Adolphe Smith. *Street Life in London*. London: Sampson Low, Marston, Searle & Rivington, 1877.

Tomich, Dale. *Through the Prism of Slavery: Labor, Capital and the World Economy*. Lanham, MD: Rowman and Littlefield, 2004.

Torode, Angeliki. "Trends in Fruit Consumption." In *Our Changing Fare: Two Hundred Years of British Food Habits*, edited by Theodore C. Barker, John C. McKenzie and John Yudkin, 115–34. London: MacGibbon and Kee, 1966.

Trussell Trust. "UK Foodbank Use Continues to Rise." The Trussell Trust, 25 April 2017. https://www.trusselltrust.org/2017/04/25/uk-foodbank-use-continues-rise/.

– "Benefit Levels Must Keep Pace With Rising Cost of Essentials As Record Increase in Foodbank Figures is Revealed." The Trussell Trust, 24 April 2018. https://www.trusselltrust.org/2018/04/24/benefit-levels-must-keep-pace-rising-cost-essentials-record-increase-foodbank-figures-revealed/.

Tuckwell, Gertrude M. *The State and its Children*. London: Methuen, 1894.

Tuckwell, Gertrude M., and Constance Smith. *The Worker's Handbook*. London: Duckworth and Co., 1908.

Turnbull, Peter, Charles Woolfson, and John E. Kelly. *Dock Strike: Conflict and Restructuring in Britain's Ports*. Aldershot: Avebury, 1992.

U., H.U. *Hints for Country Shopkeepers; Or, How to Attract Customers*. n.p.: Moulton, 1847.

United States Government. "Economic Report of the President." United States Government Printing Office, Washington, 2018. https://www.gov info.gov/content/pkg/ERP-2018/pdf/ERP-2018.pdf.

Urwick, E.J. *Studies of Boy Life in Our Cities*. London: J.M. Dent, 1904.

Valpy, Abraham J. edited by *The Plays and Poems of Shakespeare*, vol. 7. London: Henry G. Bohn, 1857.

Vigne, Thea, and Alun Howkins. "The Small Shopkeeper in Industrial and Market Towns." In *The Lower Middle Class in Britain*, edited by Geoffrey Crossick, 184–209. London: Croom Helm, 1977.

Vincent, Henry. *Early Closing Movement*. London: James Paul, 1847.

Voth, Hans-Joachim. "The Longest Years: New Estimates of Labor Input in England, 1760–1830." *Journal of Economic History* 61, 4 (2001): 1065–82.

Waddington, Keir. *The Bovine Scourge: Meat, Tuberculosis and Public Health, 1850–1914*. Woodbridge: The Boydell Press, 2006.

Wallace, Rev. Thomas. *British Slavery, An Appeal to the Women of England*. London: W.F. Ramsay, 1850.

Walton, John K. *The English Seaside Resort: A Social History, 1750–1914*. Leicester: Leicester University Press, 1983.

– *A Social History of Lancashire, 1558–1939*. Manchester: Manchester University Press, 1987.

– *Fish and Chips and the British Working Class, 1870–1940*. Leicester: Leicester University Press, 1992.

– "Towns and Consumerism." In *The Cambridge Urban History of Britain*. Vol. 3: *1840–1950*, edited by Martin Daunton. Cambridge, 715–44, Cambridge University Press, 2000.

– "Review of *From Plain Fare to Fusion Food: British Diet from the 1890s to the 1990s*." Review no. 350. http://www.history.ac.uk/reviews/review/350.

Walvin, James. *Beside the Seaside: Social History of the Popular Seaside Holiday*. London: Viking, 1978.

Webb, Catherine. *Industrial Co-operation: The Story of a Peaceful Revolution*. Manchester: Co-operative Union, 1912.

Webb, Sidney. *The Scandal of London's Markets*. Fabian Tract No. 36. London: The Fabian Society, 1891.

Webb, Sidney, and Beatrice Webb. *Problems of Modern Industry*. London: Longmans, Green and Co., 1920.

– *The Consumers' Co-operative Movement*. London: Longman, Green and
    Co., 1921.
Wells, Herbert George. *The History of Mr.. Polly*. New York: Grosset and
    Dunlap, 1909.
Whetham, E.H. "The London Milk Trade, 1860–1900." *Economic History
    Review* 17, 2 (1964): 369–80.
– "The London Milk Trade, 1900–1930." In *The Making of the Modern British
    Diet*, edited by Derek J. Oddy and Derek S. Miller, 65–76. London:
    Croom Helm, 1976.
Whitaker, Wilfred B. *Victorian and Edwardian Shopworkers: The Struggle to
    Obtain Better Conditions and a Half-Holiday*. Newton Abbot: David and
    Charles, 1973.
White, Arnold, edited by *The Destitute Alien in Great Britain*. London: Swan
    Sonnenschein, 1892.
Whitehouse, John Howard. "Street Trading by Children." In *Problems of Boy
    Life*, edited by J.H. Whitehouse, 163–9. London: P.S. King and Son, 1912.
Whitlock, Tammy C. *Crime, Gender and Consumer Culture in Nineteenth-
    Century England*. Farnham: Ashgate, 2005.
Wild, M. Trevor, and Gareth Shaw. "Locational Behaviour of Urban
    Retailing during the Nineteenth Century: The Example of Kingston
    upon Hull." *Transactions of the Institute of British Geographers* 61 (1974):
    101–17.
– "Population Distribution and Retail Provision: The Case of the Halifax-
    Calder Valley Area of West Yorkshire during the Second Half of the
    Nineteenth Century." *Journal of Historical Geography* 1, 2 (1975): 193–210.
Wilkins, W.H. "The Traffic in Italian Children." *Times* (London), 23 August
    1890.
– "The Italian Aspect." In *The Destitute Alien in Great Britain: A Series of
    Papers Dealing with the Subject of Foreign Pauper Immigration*, edited by
    Arnold White, 146–67. London: Swan Sonnenschein, 1892.
– *The Alien Invasion*. London: Methuen, 1892.
Wilkinson, Alan. *From Corner Shop to Corner Shop in Five Generations: A
    History of William Jackson & Son*. Beverley: Hutton Press, 1994.
Williams, Albert. *36 Stewart Street Bolton: An Exercise in Nostalgia,
    1901–1914*. Manchester: Neil Richardson, 1983.
Williams, Alfred. *Life in a Railway Factory*. London: Duckworth and Co.,
    1920.
Wilson, John F, Anthony Webster, and Rachael Vorberg-Rugh. *Building Co-
    operation: A Business History of the Co-operative Group, 1863–2013*. Oxford:
    Oxford University Press, 2013.

Winders, Bill. "The Vanishing Free Market: The Formation and Spread of the British and US Food Regimes." *Journal of Peasant Change* 9, 2 (2009): 315–44.

Winstanley, Michael. *The Shopkeeper's World, 1830–1914.* Manchester: Manchester University Press, 1983.

– "Concentration and Competition in the Retail Sector *c.*1800–1990." In *Business Enterprise in Modern Britain: From the Eighteenth to the Twentieth Century,* edited by Maurice W. Kirby and Mary B. Rose, 236–62. London: Routledge, 1992.

– "Retail Property Ownership in Edwardian England." In *A Nation of Shopkeepers: Five Centuries of British Retailing,* edited by John Benson and Laura Ugolini, 180–205. London: I.B. Tauris, 2003.

Wohl, Anthony S. *The Eternal Slum: Housing and Social Policy in Victorian London.* Montreal and Kingston: McGill-Queen's University Press, 1977.

Wood, Walter. *North Sea Fishers and Fighters.* London: Kegan Paul, Trench, Trübner and Co., 1911.

Woods, Robert. "The Effects of Population Redistribution on the Level of Mortality in Nineteenth-Century England and Wales." *Journal of Economic History* 45, 3 (1985): 645–51.

Woods, Robert I, Patricia A. Watterson, and John H. Woodward. "The Causes of Rapid Infant Mortality Decline in England and Wales, 1861–1921, Part 1." *Population Studies* 42, 3 (1988): 343–66.

– "The Causes of Rapid Infant Mortality Decline in England and Wales, 1861–1921, Part 2." *Population Studies* 43, 1 (1989): 113–32.

– *The Demography of Victorian England and Wales.* Cambridge: Cambridge University Press, 2000.

Wrigley, Edward A., and Roger Schofield. *The Population History of England, 1541–1871: A Reconstruction.* Cambridge: Cambridge University Press, 1981.

Wrigley, Neil, and Michelle Lowe, eds. *Retailing, Consumption and Capital: Towards a New Retail Geography.* London: Longman, 1996.

– Wrigley, Neil, and Michelle Lowe. *Reading Retail: A Geographical Perspective on Retailing and Consumption Spaces.* London: Routledge, 2002.

– "The Globalization of Trade in Retail Services." Paris: OECD, 2010.

Wrigley, Neil, Neil M. Coe, and Andrew Currah. "Globalizing Retail: Conceptualizing the Distribution-Based Transnational Corporation (TNC)." *Progress in Human Geography* 29, 4 (2005): 437–57.

Yeo, Stephen, ed. *New Views of Co-operation.* London: Routledge, 1988.

Zangwill, Israel. *Children of the Ghetto: A Study of a Peculiar People.* London: Macmillan, 1896.

Index

The letter "t" following a page number denotes a table.